D0220299

Doing Research in Cultural Studies

INTRODUCING QUALITATIVE METHODS provides a series of volumes which introduce qualitative research to the student and beginning researcher. The approach is interdisciplinary and international. A distinctive feature of these volumes is the helpful student exercises.

One stream of the series provides texts on the key methodologies used in qualitative research. The other stream contains books on qualitative research for different disciplines or occupations. Both streams cover the basic literature in a clear and accessible style, but also cover the 'cutting edge' issues in the area.

SERIES EDITOR
David Silverman (Goldsmiths College)

EDITORIAL BOARD
Michael Bloor (University of Wales, Cardiff)
Barbara Czarniawska (University of Gothenburg)
Norman Denzin (University of Illinois, Champaign)
Barry Glassner (University of Southern California)
Jaber Gubrium (University of Missouri)
Anne Murcott (South Bank University)
Jonathan Potter (Loughborough University)

TITLES IN SERIES

Doing Conversational Analysis
Paul ten Have

Using Foucault's Methods
Gavin Kendall and Gary Wickham

The Quality of Qualitative Research
Clive Seale

Qualitative Evaluation
Ian Shaw

Researching Life Stories and Family Histories
Robert L. Miller

Categories in Text and Talk
Georgia Lepper

Focus Groups in Social Research
Michael Bloor, Jane Frankland, Michelle Thomas, Kate Robson

Qualitative Research Through Case Studies
Max Travers

Methods of Critical Discourse Analysis
Ruth Wodak and Michael Meyer

Qualitative Research in Social Work
Ian Shaw and Nick Gould

Qualitative Research in Information Systems
Michael D. Myers and David Avison

Researching the Visual
Michael Emmison and Philip Smith

Qualitative Research in Education
Peter Freebody

Using Documents in Social Research
Lindsay Prior

Doing Research in Cultural Studies
Paula Saukko

Doing Research in Cultural Studies

An introduction to classical and
new methodological approaches

Paula Saukko

SAGE Publications
London • Thousand Oaks • New Delhi

SAGE Publications Ltd
6 Bonhill Street
London EC2A 4PU

SAGE Publications Inc.
2455 Teller Road
Thousand Oaks, California 91320

SAGE Publications India Pvt Ltd
B-42, Panchsheel Enclave
Post Box 4109
New Delhi 100 017

British Library Cataloguing in Publication data

A catalogue record for this book is available
from the British Library

ISBN 978-0-7619-6505-3

Library of Congress Control Number 2002115862

Typeset by C&M Digitals (P) Ltd., Chennai, India

Contents

Acknowledgements

Methodology is often a sidetrack of one's work, a means to get to an end. However, for some people, thinking through the 'means' of doing research becomes an end in and of itself, as happened to me. I would like to thank all those people, who have cultivated the methodological sidetrack of my work and, thereby, directly, or indirectly, contributed to this book.

I would like to thank my first adviser, Veikko Pietilä, who, a long time ago, first nourished my interest in the philosophy of methods or methodology. I would also thank my peers during the early days of my graduate study in Finland for good discussions and supportive friendship; thanks particularly to Heikki Heikkilä for long discussions and e-mails on Hannah Arendt and dialogue.

My interest in methodology became to occupy the centre stage during my doctoral studies at the University of Illinois, Urbana-Champaign. My greatest intellectual debt is to Norman Denzin, who first suggested the idea of this book and has supported it throughout the process. If any of this makes any sense, it is thanks to Norman, whereas all the nonsense is entirely my responsibility. I also want to thank my dissertation committee members, Clifford Christians, C.L. Cole, Lawrence Grossberg and Paula Treichler for sound advice and for introducing me to areas of scholarship, such as dialogism, science studies, and 'materialist' cultural studies, that I had not known before, and that all form a part of this book. Thanks also to John Nerone and Leslie Reagan for introducing me to the study of history, and to Sandra Braman on insights on 'chaos' and to James Hay on insights on 'space'. I greatly enjoyed, as well as benefited from, in an academic sense, the collegiality of my fellow students in Illinois. Special thanks to Lori Reed for her continuing support and witty remarks on everything from feminist politics to connections between Gilles Deleuze and Deepak Chopra.

In England I want to thank Annabelle Sreberny for several good discussions and Gillian Youngs for directing me to a couple of sources. I also want to thank James Stanyer for useful editorial comments on the first two chapters. Warm thanks to all my students, who have taught me, particular thanks to Jon Asmundsson and Lina Khatib for being inspiringly good students and for discussions on the 'real'. I am grateful for Terhi Rantanen for phonecalls that have kept me sane, and for providing me with a bed and great company during my visits to the London libraries.

In many parts of this book, I keep reminding of the importance of the 'material' aspects of social reality. In this spirit, I want to thank the various institutions and foundations that have made the research that form the basis of this book possible. I want to thank the Academy of Finland, Finland–US Educational Exchange Commission (Fulbright Commission), Finnish Cultural Foundation, Georg and

Ella Ehrnrooth Foundation. Thanks also to Scandinavia Foundation, and last, but not least, the Graduate College and Institute of Communications Research at the University of Illinois for funding my doctoral research. I also want to thank the University of Leicester for research leave, which enabled me to complete the first draft of this manuscript.

My overall greatest gratitude is to my partner in life, Jouni Paavola, who has read, edited and debated each and every one of the chapters of this book in their various incarnations. I also want to thank Jouni for not only taking care of my intellect but also my body and soul as well as our son Aksel, with whom he bravely 'adventured' every single weekend of a particularly nightmarish spring, while I was writing. I thank Aksel and my mother, Elviira Saukko, for reminding me of the infinitely rich and complicated emotional and social dimensions of life that make it worth living and that scholarship often has a hard time capturing.

Finally, I want to thank the series editor David Silverman and my editor Michael Carmichael for having faith in the book in the first place and the anonymous reviewers for their feedback and support. My sincerest thanks to Michael Carmichael and Zoë Elliot from Sage for pushing me to finally finish the book.

Paula Saukko

Part I

Thinking Methodologically

Introduction: Locating Cultural Studies and the Book

One of the arguments of this book is that research or research methodologies are never 'objective' but always located, informed by particular social positions and historical moments and their agendas. Thus, to locate this book, it has its early origins in my research on the discourses and lived experiences of eating disorders, largely women's mental dis-eases, characterized by a dangerous pursuit of thinness. I was originally driven to study these conditions, because having been anorexic myself, I was perplexed, or even angered, with the way in which these conditions were studied in two respects. First, I was annoyed with the way in which the studies rendered anorexic women 'disordered', or incapable of assessing their thoughts and actions. In many studies, anorexics' speech was treated as simply a 'symptom', from which the 'true' meaning, such as a psychological or social pathology, could be read by the expert, such as a psychiatrist or even a feminist cultural critic. Secondly, I was frustrated with the social and political projects and arguments that the anorexic – apparently unaware of the 'meaning' or roots of her condition – was made to stand for. The interpretations of anorexia have usefully drawn critical attention to the sexist nature of body ideals and family structures and the dysfunctionality of (post)modern self-control. Still, interpretations of anorexia also often confirm the inherently pathological nature of anorexics, or women in general, as vain, overly dependent on others and their opinions, and prone to buttress general social compliance and conservatism.

Thus, driven by these two concerns of mine, I embarked on a research project that aimed both to develop ways of doing justice to the lived experience of anorexia and to critically analyze the discourses that had constituted it. However, while my interviews with women who had anorexia contained many challenging and interesting insights, they were also underpinned by the problematic medical notions of anorexia, I wanted to criticize. This led me to my first methodological dilemma: How can one do justice to the lived experience of people, while, at the same time, critically analyze discourses, which form the very stuff out of which our experiences are made?

Furthermore, my analysis of discourses on eating disorders led me to unexpected places. Studying the history of the contemporary diagnostic criteria for anorexia, led me to study 1920s US immigration policy, and the postwar or Cold War American political, cultural and intellectual context. My analyses of the popular figureheads that have made eating disorders known, Karen Carpenter and Princess Diana, further directed me to the battle between 1960s radicalism and Nixon era neo-conservatism and later, closer to my new home, to the contradictory New Labour politics and ambience of Great Britain of the 1990s. However, mapping the social connections of anorexia and its definitions, led me to another methodological dilemma: How can one criticize discourses, which constitute 'reality', such as anorexia, while, at the same time, make statements about historical and political reality?

In the end, what had started as an exploration of a personal indignation, had taken me to study the major social and political processes, developments and structures of twentieth-century North America and Europe, in a way that I was not prepared for. As the research progressed, I had to come up with a framework for studying the lived, discursive, and historical and social dimensions of anorexia, and to shift between different methodological perspectives and genres of writing. While the different methodological approaches frequently complemented one another, they also mounted in practical difficulties as well as theoretical contradictions. Based on my research, and a wealth of other people's research, this book aims to provide a guide map on how to study the lived, discursive and social and political nature of contemporary reality. My intention has been to write a book that I would have liked to read before I started my research.

Crosscurrents in cultural studies

My intellectual commitments are not, however, shaped by my research alone, but they are also guided by the history of cultural studies, and the way in which this history has played out in places I have worked or studied. Cultural studies as a discipline was forged in the 1970s in the by now legendary Birmingham Centre for Contemporary Cultural Studies. I was introduced to cultural studies at a later stage, in the 1980s, when doing my first degree at the University of Tampere, Finland. This was a time when cultural studies was no longer a marginal enterprise, but it was becoming mainstream and taking over academic departments in Scandinavia. Thus, even if I studied a presumably 'objectivist' subject, such as journalism, our curriculum focused on ideology, hegemony, resistance, postmodernity, representation and narrative. My first fledgling research projects on Costa Rican alternative press and young Finnish squatters' movement, were deeply embedded in the British variant of cultural studies, and, in particular, its interest in 'resistance'. Both me and my student peers back in the 1980s, as well as my own twenty-first-century students, liked the both critical and 'upbeat' aura of resistance, which saw some 'hope' in culture, unlike some of the pessimistic critical analyses, which saw culture mainly to have a pacifying function. Resistance underlined the creative potential of popular cultural forms, such as youth cultures and movements, to challenge dominant ideologies and society, even if this potential was not necessarily interpreted to lead to radical, social change.

My research on anorexia may have, in its very early stage, been informed by some vague idea of anorexics resisting discourses on anorexia, but these notions soon dropped out of the agenda. This was partly due to the fact that the interviews I conducted with women, who had had anorexia, were complicated in a way that could not be described in terms of either being subjugated to dominant ideologies or resisting them. Furthermore, studies on resistance were increasingly being attacked for, for example, telling more about the scholar's political fantasies, such as fantasies of youthful, feminist or working-class, rebellion, than the phenomena being studied (Morris, 1990; Nightingale, 1992; Stabile, 1995). However, I think analysis of ideology continues to provide insights into empirical research on lived experiences, texts and contexts. I also think that the later methodological currents in cultural studies cannot be comprehended without knowledge of these classical approaches, which often continue to underpin studies done within the paradigm, even if they no longer use this vocabulary. For these reasons, I spend a couple of chapters in this book outlining the ideological and resistance approaches to studying lived and textual culture and discussing their shortcomings and continuing relevance.

My abandoning of the resistance-paradigm also coincided with my move, in the 1990s, from Finland to Urbana-Champaign to do my doctorate at the University of Illinois. At this time Urbana-Champaign was a Mecca of the American version of cultural studies, testified by my star-studded dissertation committee, consisting of Clifford Christians, C.L. Cole, Norman Denzin, Lawrence Grossberg and Paula Treichler. My major adviser, Denzin, was developing new modes of interpretative inquiry in response to the postcolonial and feminist attacks, which argued that social science has not understood marginal groups, such as women, working-class or non-Western people, but used them to justify the scholar's political and theoretical projects, ranging from colonialism to Marxism (see Clifford and Marcus, 1986). The new interpretative or ethnographic research programme aimed to find more collaborative ways of studying and writing about people that would be both more sensitive to different worlds and aware of the limits and commitments of our own understanding (Denzin, 1997a). At the same time, my other committee member, Grossberg, was beginning to criticize the 'cultural turn' in social research and to argue that we should begin to pay attention to increasingly exploitative material and economic developments, fallen into oblivion as a result of the interest in cultures and experiences (e.g. Grossberg, 1998). In this situation, I felt somewhat tugged and pulled between two currents in empirical research in cultural studies that were interested in either the microcosmos of individual experience or the macrocosmos of global, economic powerstructures (Saukko, 1998).

Reconciliations

However, recent developments in empirical research and methodological discussions in cultural studies have somewhat blurred these crosscurrents. The harbingers of the original new ethnographic critiques, Clifford (1997) and Marcus (1998a), together with others (Appadurai, 1997; Haraway, 1997), have begun to talk about the way in which our research spills over traditional paradigmatic as well as geographic boundaries. This spilling has blurred the distinctions between, for instance, culture and economy, as well as shattered the idea of easily definable research objects, such as a subculture or a village. Thus, the sociologists' youth subcultures or the anthropologists' villages no longer appear isolatable locales but more like nodes in networks traversed and shaped by flows of transnational media, money, people, things and images. The same way, following my research topic, anorexia, which is often thought of as a psychological problem, spilled across different spheres of life and levels of analysis. Thus, as my research continued, anorexia started to appear most intimately and intensely personal and interpersonal, and, at the same time, highly mediated by medical and popular discourses, and subtly, but firmly, interlinked with wider social, political, and even global military, regimes.

   In this scenario of blurring boundaries, sometimes described by the millennial catchword, 'globalization', the old methodological divisions between experience, culture, and 'reality' – or 'audiences', 'texts' and 'production' in media studies – have become less clear. This new situation has, in a sense, brought me to the areas of interest of my other committee members, namely, science studies (Cole, 1998; Treichler, 1999) and dialogic theory (Christians, 1988, 2000). Cultural studies of science have been at the forefront in developing a hybrid methodology that gets us beyond the debate, roughly put, whether material reality determines, or is more important than, language and culture, or whether language or culture determines, or is more important than, reality. To borrow Haraway's (1997) idea, discourses, such as the discourse on anorexia, are best seen as 'material-semiotic' forces, which emerge from a specific historical context and effectuate changes that are both symbolic and very concrete. Thus, the discourse on anorexia shapes our most fundamental sense of our self, how we define what kind of a self is 'healthy' and what kind of a self is 'disordered'. At the same time, it gives rise to specific regimes of treatment and lifestyle, becomes part and parcel of popular media imagery, and is mobilized to pathologize or buttress a variety of social and political regimes.

   The discourse on anorexia weaves these symbolic and concrete, local and global, facets together; yet, each facet also has its own specificity. A person's life-history and the history of the Cold War may be interlinked, but one needs a different approach to capture lived and general history. From a methodological point of view this poses two challenges. First, in order to comprehend a particular facet of this experience, one needs to rigorously apply a suitable methodology. For example, if one wants to capture and convey the uniqueness and nuances of a life-story of an anorexic woman, one needs to carefully consult and apply the new ethnographic body of work on ways of studying and writing about different lived worlds. Second, one needs to be aware that this uniqueness is not the only thing there is to lived experience. Experience is also shaped by social discourses, such as medical definitions, and by the historical and social context, in which it is located. However, in order to capture these other dimensions of the experience of anorexia one needs different methodological approaches and methods, such as discourse analysis or historical research.

The thought of mastering a set of diverse research approaches, and combining them, may sound daunting for any beginning researcher as well as an experienced scholar, struggling as we all are with multiple pressures on our time. The success of any research project depends on a difficult balancing act between being both ambitious and doable. Thus, I would not suggest all research projects combine several views. Rather, the aim of the different chapters of the book is to outline different ways of doing research and to promote a way of doing them in the best possible way, by highlighting their specificity, strengths, possible problems and omissions. For instance, I would like to see more of the best and most beautiful new ethnographies that convey the subtle texture of a unique or 'singular' lived experience and, at the same time, make it speak for the 'universal', that is, to pinpoint some crucial dilemma of our contemporary social world. At the same time, I want to problematize the habit of offering familiar stories of personal intrigue and bodily scandal, such as detailed descriptions of the horrors of being fat (Kiesinger, 1998), as 'authentic' experience, the way some strands of experimental research as well as daytime talk-shows do. However, in the discussion of different research approaches I not only want to highlight their specific features but also the ways in which they are related to one another. Locating points of convergence between different approaches, such as studying lived and global realities, aims to point to ways of combining them, in order to piece together maybe more complex and nuanced, even if never complete, analysis of the phenomenon we study.

This need to build dialogues between different views, brings me, finally, to my current academic home, the Centre for Mass Communication Research at the University of Leicester. In the 1970s, the Leicester centre framed itself, and was framed by the wider British academic community, as the political economic and social scientific counterpole to the culturalism of the Birmingham centre. However, those days have long been gone, and today Leicester is, perhaps, best known for its research on international communication, which has lately been reconfigured under the term globalization. The discourse on 'the global' may smack as a bit of an intellectual and popular spring fashion. However, globalization calls for an analysis of the interaction between the lived, mediated, religious, ethnic, gendered, economic and political dimensions of the contemporary world. As such, it has created an interdisciplinary space, where various theoretical as well as methodological approaches have been able to live in a semi-peaceful coexistence, fomenting dialogues, debates, borrowing and cautious interbreeding.

Throughout this book I underline the need to pay attention to how cultural or intellectual phenomena, material circumstances and political regimes are intertwined. As I am doing the final technical edit to this book, I am, once again, reminded of the importance of these interactions. I correct the pages, knowing that the original cradle of cultural studies in Birmingham has just been 'restructured', and my own conditions of work in Leicester have deteriorated beyond any recognition due to ongoing 'reorganization'. Even if it seems that the latest bout of budget cuts have hit the interdisciplinary field of British cultural and communication studies hard, ends are always just beginnings. I am on my way to the University of Exeter, becoming part of an inter-disciplinary research-team investigating the social implications of genomics. More than, perhaps, any other new social development, genomics pushes for new ways of understanding and studying the links between the material and the cultural both in personal and social life. It calls for more, not less, methodologically savvy, critical, cultural analyses of new social phenomena that challenge our fundamental sense of our self and our social arrangements.

Outline of the book

Before I move on to outline the structure of the book, I want to clarify that this book is about 'methodology', not on 'methods'. The difference made by the Greek epithet 'logos' (knowledge) is that, whereas methods refer to practical 'tools' to make sense of empirical reality, methodology refers to the wider package of both tools and a philosophical and political commitment that come with a particular research 'approach'. Methods and methodology often go together, so that a hermeneutic methodological approach, which aims to gain a 'thick' understanding of other people's experience, often goes with a method, such as participant observation, that allows for the scholar and the people being studied to develop a mutual trust with one another. However, same methods can also support different methodological commitments. So, the interview method can be used to support a realist methodological approach, which aims to gather 'factual' information, or to support a hermeneutic methodological quest to gain a thorough understanding of a person's life-story (see Alasuutari, 1995; Kvale, 1996; Silverman, 2001).

The first reason I have chosen to focus on methodology is that there are quite a few methods books around that are suitable for cultural studies (e.g. Alasuutari, 1995; Flick, 1998; Silverman, 2001). However, the main reason why

I have decided not to write on methods is that many methods books (but certainly not all of them) view methods in positivist terms as 'magnifying glasses' that are inserted between the scholar and the 'reality' being studied. It is understood that if these methods, or lenses, are used correctly, or according to instructions, they will help the scholar to get closer to an 'accurate' or objective and unbiased view of reality. One of the basic aims of this book is, however, to explore how the reality changes when we change the research approach, or lens, through which we look at it. Thus, I will not be discussing 'participant observation' as a method. Rather, I will be discussing 'new ethnographic' attempts to do justice to the lived worlds of others and 'poststructuralist' approaches that critically analyze the social and institutional discourses that interlace any lived experience or world. Both the new ethnographic and poststructuralist approaches may use participant observation, but their 'observations' may be strikingly different.

However, despite this somewhat broader focus, I would say that the book is a 'how-to book'. Even if some of my discussion may be more abstract than some of the writing on methods, it is still intended to provide ideas on 'how to' do research within each of the research paradigms discussed. However, I am not offering a book on how to 'objectively' study social reality, using a scientific method. I am offering a book that encourages reflexive social and cultural research on social reality in a fashion that is aware of its theoretical and political commitments and their repercussions, strengths and omissions. I take the recent emergence of both empirical and theoretical books focusing on cultural studies 'methodology' (McGuigan, 1997; Couldry, 2000; Lewis, 2002) to be symptomatic of an increasing acknowledgement that we need to be more reflective about the way in which our research always opens up a partial and political perspective on reality. However, even if this book does not subscribe to the idea that we should find out 'one' truth about 'one' reality, it does not want to advocate the relativist idea that different methodological approaches open up multiple, incommensurable 'realities'. On the contrary, it wants to foment conversations or dialogues between different methodological approaches to the world, in order to cultivate a type of cultural studies sensitive to the complexity and multidimensionality of the contemporary global, social and personal reality.

To proceed with the outline of the book, it is structured following the 'X-Files formula' (Lavery et al., 1996), according to which each chapter can be read independently, just as each episode of *X-Files* can be watched independently. Still, the reader, who reads the entire book, gets more out of each individual chapter than the reader, who reads a particular chapter of interest, just as the regular viewer of *X-Files* 'knows' more about each episode than the occasional viewer.

The book is divided into four parts. The first part, of which this introduction together with Chapter 1 forms a part, discusses the history of cultural studies methodology, clarifies what is meant by the term and outlines a 'dialogic' way of combining the methodological approaches that will be discussed in the subsequent chapters. The second part discusses research approaches that make sense of lived experience. It outlines ways of studying lived lives in terms of 'resistance', from the phenomenological or hermeneutic new ethnographic point of view of understanding the Other and from the poststructuralist perspective that investigates the way in which social and institutional discourses interlace our lived experiences and identities. The third part outlines ways of studying texts or discourses. It discusses modes of analysis that examine texts in terms of 'ideology' and genealogical approaches that unravel the historical nature of phenomena that we take for granted. It also outlines Derridean deconstructive analysis, which unravels the hidden dichotomous norms embedded in texts or discourses, as well as points towards ways of rendering deconstruction more constructive or capable of not merely criticizing culture but of suggesting social alternatives. The final or fourth part constitutes the conclusions of the book. The first chapter of the section, Chapter 8, discusses critical geographic works on 'space' and how they can be used to make sense of both macro-processes of globalization and some of their everyday implications. Chapter 9 introduces several ways of doing 'multi-sited' and 'multi-scape' research, which combines lived, discursive and material/spatial approaches to studying contemporary social reality, in order to capture some of its global and local, emotional and economic, and poetic and political dimensions.

While *Doing Research in Cultural Studies* introduces classical empirical approaches in cultural studies, such as analyses of resistance and ideology, it is slanted towards the new approaches, such as new ethnography, genealogy and multi-sited analysis. The reason for this focus is that while many people in the field are 'doing' these kinds of research, there are not many books that would reflect on how they are done, and hardly any books on how they can be combined in order to foment dialogues between different theoretical, methodological, empirical and political positions within cultural studies.

1

Combining Methodologies in Cultural Studies

Main questions

- Empirical research in cultural studies is structured by an interest in the interplay between lived experience, texts or discourses and the social context. How have recent historical and intellectual developments complicated these three areas of research?
- Why is the classical notion that 'valid' research is objective problematic? What alternative notions of validity are there? What are the criteria for valid or good research?
- What are the shortcomings of the notion of 'triangulation', according to which one combines different methodologies in order to get closer to a 'truth'? What are the shortcomings of the notion that different methodologies create different, possibly incommensurable 'truths'? How does a notion of combining methodologies in terms of fostering dialogues between different approaches help to get beyond positivist notion of one truth and relativist notion of multiple truths?

The trademark of the cultural studies approach to empirical research has been an interest in the interplay between lived experience, texts or discourses, and the social context. One of the classical studies, addressing these three dimensions of social reality, is David Morley's research on audience responses to the *Nationwide* current affairs programme and its coverage of the British Miners' Strike in the 1970s (Morley and Brunsdon, 1999[1980, 1987]). Combining these three views allowed Morley to come up with new insights on the 'active' nature of media audiences and the mediated, social and political dynamics of a historical turning point. The task of this book is to outline and discuss ways of thinking, doing and writing research in cultural studies, taking the three-faceted interest in lived realities, discursive mediation, and the social and political landscape as a starting point.

However, as cultural studies has matured, and as several historical developments have made our social reality quite different from the one in the 1970s, some challenging questions have been raised about the feasibility of its project. Three fundamental questions have been particularly pertinent to research methodology. The first one asks: Has our interest in cultures that are radically different from our own, such as working-class or non-Western cultures, been warranted, and can we understand and do justice to these cultures? The second, and closely related, methodological question asks: How can we critically analyze culture in a situation where we as scholars, and research as an institution, are an integral part of this culture and its struggles? The third question takes a slightly different task and asks: Is culture the most important topic to investigate in the face of gruelling global economic inequality and exploitation?

To illustrate what these three questions mean, one may ask them from Morley's study. First, one can ask, to what extent Morley attended to the nuances and contradictions of working-class life, and to what extent he read his hypothesis that working-class is bound to 'resist' conservative media coverage from his focus groups. Second, one may ask to what extent Morley's hypothesis was informed by the Marxist idea that there is a correspondence between a socioeconomic position and an ideological one, and whether this made him turn a blind eye to other issues that did not fit the theoretical framework. Third, one may ask to what extent interest in cultural struggles – such as media content and interpretation – has directed attention away from analyzing the complex, global, economic and policy processes that shape industrial disputes and industries, such as mining. These questions do not, of course, render Morley's landmark study irrelevant. They simply point out that there are alternative ways of studying lived experience, discourses and the social context, and that these alternative approaches are becoming increasingly prominent in cultural studies.

This book is structured around the three-faceted research interest of cultural studies in the lived, discursive and social/global dimensions of contemporary reality. However, besides discussing the classical ways of studying these three areas of life, it pays particular attention to new research approaches, such as new ethnography, genealogical research and analysis of globalization, that take seriously, and aim to respond to, the three questions that have been posed to cultural studies. However, before I proceed to discuss these methodological programmes, I take a detour to the history of cultural studies that helps to clarify the roots of its particular methodological approach as well as the roots of the contemporary methodological questions or challenges.

Histories of cultural study

Cultural studies emerged from the political and intellectual climate and situation of the Great Britain of the 1970s. This was a time, when the field of social research was structured by hard-nosed positivist empirical inquiry, often of a functionalist ilk, and traditional Marxist political economy (Hall, 1982). The more right-wing or 'administrative' research, doing surveys and small-group research, aimed to prove that pluralism and democracy have become a reality in postwar North America and Western Europe. On the contrary, the leftist intelligentsia, such as the Frankfurt School, did a series of piercing criticisms of popular culture and opinions to prove that the postwar consumer culture and media had killed all social criticism and dissent and created a nearly fascist 'mass society' (e.g. Adorno et al., 1950; Adorno and Horkheimer, 1979; Held, 1980).

In this somewhat polarized situation, cultural studies carved itself a space between and beyond these two positions. To do this, it welded together humanistic, structuralist and New Left Marxist philosophies (Hall, 1980). The humanist bent in cultural studies aimed to understand and capture the creative potential of people's lived worlds, such as working-class culture (Hoggart, 1992[1957]). Structuralism and structuralist methods, such as semiotics, focused attention on linguistic patterns and tropes that recur in texts, such as popular culture, and that shape our thinking. New Leftism brought an interest in examining the connection between lived experience and/or a body of texts and the larger social, political and economic environment. These three philosophical currents enabled cultural studies to articulate a mediating space between right-wing optimism and left-wing pessimism that allowed the paradigm to examine how people's everyday life was strife with creative and critical potential, while their lives and imagination were also constrained by problematic cultural ideologies as well as structures of social inequality. This 'middle stance' informed the classical Birmingham-period works on media audiences (Ang, 1985; Morley and Brunsdon, 1999[1980, 1987]), subcultures (Hall and Jefferson, 1976; Hebdige, 1976, 1988), and the cultures of working-class boys and girls (Willis, 1977; McRobbie, 2000) (for overviews see: Hall et al., 1980; Gurevitch et al., 1982).

However, as the political and philosophical roots of cultural studies indicate, the methodological project has been riddled with tensions from the start. One cannot, without running into contradictions, bring together a phenomenological or hermeneutic desire to 'understand' the creative lived world of another person or a group of people, and the distanced, critical structuralist interest in 'analyzing' linguistic tropes, which guide people's perceptions and understanding. Furthermore, neither the interest in lived realities or the cultures and languages that mediate our perception of reality bode well with the tendency to make statements about the social and political situation, which is always, to an extent, wedded to a realist quest to find out how the world or reality simply 'is'.

In the early days of cultural studies these contradictions could still be smoothed by the positivist notion of scientific objectivity. However, in the early twenty-first century the discrepancies between the three classic areas of research in cultural studies have been both magnified and blurred by developments often grouped under terms, such as postmodernity, late modernity, post-industrialism, postcolonialism, late capitalism, more recently, globalization and neo-liberalism (e.g. Harvey, 1989; Jameson, 1991; Rose, 1999; Tomlinson, 1999). Even if discussions around these phenomena have sometimes become markers of changing intellectual fashions, they point to important historical and intellectual processes or shifts that have changed social reality and research.

First, since the 1960s, women, blacks and various postcolonial people, and their movements, have accused institutions, including the state, education, media and so on, of institutionalized discrimination. They have also accused that research, which has always had a particular interest in underprivileged groups, has not depicted the realities of women, ethnic minorities or postcolonial people but used them to back up the scholar's theoretical and political projects, ranging from colonialism to Marxism and liberal humanist feminism (Clifford and Marcus, 1986; Said, 1995[1978]). Second, the increasing media saturation of our everyday life, ranging from the long hours we spend watching television to the more recent Internet surfing, has made our everyday life and experience more 'virtual' (Baudrillard, 1983). These new technologies and experiences have eroded our faith in the ability of media or science to 'objectively' describe reality for us, making us critically, or even ironically, aware of the way in which all understanding of the world is mediated by cultural images and discourses. Third, the late twentieth century witnessed a series of social, political and economic processes that undermined faith in postwar political and economic arrangements and ideologies. The collapse of state-run socialism in 1989 in Eastern Europe has been a blow and cause of reorientation for various leftist projects. Still, the Western postwar dreams of 'progress' or 'modernization', which were supposed to spread Western prosperity and democracy across the globe, were also dashed as these dreams never came true. Thus, we have awakened to the early twenty-first century, structured by a new division between an exhilarated talk about multiculturalism and the possibilities of creating and disseminating alternative, previously silenced knowledges and cultures, and steep inequalities and mistrust and feuding between different groups of people (Castells, 1996, 1997, 1998).

Cultural studies as an intellectual and political project has actively played into and out of these historical and social developments. At the same time, these developments have given rise to new research and methodological orientations within, and on the borders of, cultural studies. Scholars grouped under the banner of new ethnography have developed new collaborative or dialogic modes of research that aim to be truer to the lived worlds of others. Poststructuralism has led to self-reflexive and genealogical analytical strategies, which critically investigate the historical, social and political commitments of those discourses that direct people's, including scholars', understanding of themselves and their projects. Analyses of globalization have come up with more 'complex' ways of making sense of economic, political and so on developments, which challenge traditional simpler or linear modes of analysis and prediction.

These new lines of inquiry arise from the same current historical situation, marked by greater ambiguity. Yet, they run into tensions with one another in a similar way that the three methodological currents contradicted each other in early cultural studies. The new ethnographic quest to be truthful to the lived realities of other people runs into a contradiction with the poststructuralist aim to critically analyze discourses that form the very stuff out of which our experiences are made. The aim to understand the 'real' complex, contemporary global economic and political processes and structures is also not easily combined with the new ethnographic and poststructuralist insistence that there are multiple 'realities'. The question that these contradictions and challenges raise is whether we can still find some common ground to determine what constitutes 'good' or 'valid' research. In traditional methodological parlance, 'validity' is the beginning and end of all research, referring to a series of litmus tests that determine whether the research is 'true' or 'objectively' describes how things 'really' are. The current discussions point out that there are multiple realities, raising the question, whether research is a matter of opinion. If this was so, there would be no point in writing methodology books. I argue that there are still guidelines on what constitutes, if not true, then 'good' and valid research.

On validity

Mead and the 'truth' about Samoa

Before moving on to explain what I and others have meant by good or valid research, I will take my reader on a brief trip to a different time and place: to Margaret Mead's research on Samoa of the 1920s (Mead, 1929). The reason for doing this is that Mead's classical anthropology has become the focus of one of the major disputes over validity, as, soon after Mead's death, Freeman (1983) pronounced that her work was totally non-valid, wrong, or simply a gross lie. This debate, which has become a staple of many books on research methods (e.g. Lincoln and Guba, 1985; Seale, 1999), usefully illustrates the issues and problems associated with traditional forms of validity, and helps to pave the way for a discussion on new validities.

Mead's book, *Coming of age in Samoa: A psychological study of primitive youth for Western civilization* was published in 1929. In the book Mead sets out to study adolescence, asking: 'Are the disturbances which vex our adolescents due to the nature of adolescence itself or the civilization?' (Mead, 1929: 11). The study focused on adolescent females, with whom Mead as a young woman felt affinity, and she concluded that, unlike in the West, adolescence in Samoa was not a time of conflict and strife and that the budding sexuality of the young women was not a cause of great anxiety or repression. The opening paragraph of the book gives one a flavour of the picture of Samoan sexual life she painted:

> As the dawn begins to fall among the soft brown roofs and the slender palm trees stand out against a colourless, gleaming sea, lovers slip home from trysts beneath the palm trees or in the shadow of beached canoes, that the light may find each sleeper in his appointed place. (1929: 14)

In 1983 Derek Freeman published *Margaret Mead and Samoa: The making and unmaking of an anthropological myth* that set out to refute Mead's fieldwork. He argued that Samoa was not the harmonious and sexually permissive primitive society Mead had depicted, but that Samoans held premarital virginity in high esteem and that occurrences of violence and rape were commonplace on the islands. Freeman's notion of Samoan sexual mores is captured in the following:

> On a Sunday in June 1959, Tautalafua, aged 17, found his 18-year-old classificatory sister sitting under a breadfruit tree at about 9:00 in the evening with Vave, a 20-year-old youth from another family. He struck Vave with such violence as to fracture his jaw in two places. For this attack he was later sentenced to six weeks' imprisonment. (1983: 237)

A heated public and scholarly debate ensued the controversy. Different stakeholders debated the issue in *New York Times*, and in a special issue of the *American Anthropologist* (Brady, 1983), a series of experts on Samoa attacked Freeman. They criticized Freeman for comparing Mead's fieldwork in the small, remote island of Manu'a with his own work on the main island of Upolu. It was also pointed out that the Christian missionary influence would have had a greater impact on Samoan culture in the 1940s and 1960s when Freeman conducted his research than it did in the 1920s when Mead visited the islands (Weiner, 1983). Furthermore, it was noted that whereas Mead, as a young woman, used adolescent girls as informants, Freeman's description derived from adult men of rank (Schwartz, 1983).

However, the greatest strife between the two scholars was their paradigmatic orientation. Wedded to a culturalist paradigm, Mead set out to argue that behaviours (such as adolescence or sexuality), which have been thought to be shared by all humanity, have turned out to be the result of civilization, 'present in the inhabitants of one country, absent in another country, and this without a change of race' (Mead, 1929: 4). Mead's culturalist project, with its (sexually) liberalist undertones, was framed by, and stood in opposition to, the 1920s belligerently racist eugenic movement that explained variation in human behaviour in terms of genetic differences. Freeman, on the contrary, represents a later sociobiological stance. This is illuminated in his concluding chapter in which he, referring to certain violent events in Samoa, argues that in such circumstances conventional behaviours are dropped and people are taken over by 'highly emotional and impulsive behavior that is animal-like in its ferocity' (1983: 301). In his view this aggression is a proof of 'much older phylogenetically given structures' that define behaviour in addition to culture. Thus, where Mead finds a harmonious culture, Freeman finds 'primal' or biological aggression.

The paradigmatic differences between the two authors are also reflected in their writing. Mead's book is impressionistic in style, it reads, at times, as a romantic travelogue, aiming to capture the ethos of Samoan life. On the contrary, Freeman obeys the logic of classical scientific realistic reporting and his 'refutation' of Mead, strife with minute numerical details such as precise times of the day, reads like a police-report or a court case.

What this debate tells us, is not whether Mead or Freeman was 'right' or 'wrong' about Samoa. It rather illuminates that the 'truth' about Samoa is complicated by, at least, three issues. First, the fluidity of Samoa itself (different opinions, groups, historical change, and so on), second by the commitments that frame the research of the scholars (historical, political and theoretical investments), and third by the language (impressionistic or realist genre) used to describe Samoa. To elaborate on these three issues, first, Samoa does not hold still as a fixed object of study but ends up multifaceted, contradictory (Shore, 1983: 943) or amoeba-like, changing from one angle and instant to another. There are young girls, village elders, myths, customs, different rules, institutionalized and informal trespasses, rank-based and gendered social and political divisions, struggles and perspectives, all constantly evolving and transforming. Second, the anthropologist's vision is coloured by her and his personal gendered, raced and aged inclinations and paradigmatic and political allegiances. As Clifford (1986) notes, both Mead and Freeman render Samoa a parable or allegory for the West, and their oppositional readings end up encapsulating the classic juxtapositions harboured in the Western notion of the 'primitive': Apollonian sensual paradise and Dionysian violence and danger. Third, the language proves not to be a neutral medium of communication but part of the message. Mead's broad-brushed impressionistic style paints a dreamy, soft-shaped portrait of Samoa. Freeman's use of hard-core objectivist realism presents us a police-report on the aggressive Samoans and a court-case against Mead, ending up no less ideological and political than Mead's writing.

There are many cases similar to the Mead-controversy, some of the most famous ones have challenged W.F. Whyte's *Street corner society* (Whyte, 1955[1943]; *Journal of Contemporary Ethnography*, 1992; Whyte, 1993), and, most lately, Rigoberta Menchú's autobiography on the Guatemalan genocide (Menchú, 1984; Beverley, 1999; Stoll, 1999; Arias, 2001). These continuous debates illuminate the ways in which we continue to be infatuated with fighting whose research is 'true' and 'valid', and whose is 'false', or 'biased'.

From validity to validities

The Mead controversy is grounded in the positivist notion of science, which understands the purpose of research to be the creation of true and objective knowledge of social reality, following a scientific method. The goal of positivist research is to produce valid results, understood to be nothing less than 'the truth' (Hammersley and Atkinson, 1995). Thus, the argument became, whether Mead or Freeman were telling the 'truth', and on what grounds.

The positivist criterion of truthfulness or validity is understood to be universal. This means that the same rules of truthfulness apply, whether the research wants to capture the 'objective reality' (social facts, such as economic developments) or people's subjective or intersubjective experiences (the meanings people give to their lives and actions) (Alvesson and Sköldberg, 2000: viiii). The Mead–Freeman debate concerned both the general truth about Samoan society and its ethos as well as what Samoans thought of their life and activities, and Freeman argued that Mead got them both 'wrong'.

The general goal of truthfulness is, in positivist methodology, translated into a series of detailed procedures and checks. I am not going to delve into these checks at length (for good overviews see: Lincoln and Guba, 1985; Seale, 1999). Yet, the Mead–Freeman controversy reveals their problems. One of the central criteria for validity in research is 'reliability', which refers to the idea that if a different scholar conducted the same research, (s)he would come up with the same or similar results. However, one can imagine that if one would send both Mead and Freeman to Samoa, they would never agree or come up with an 'inter-rater' consensus. Their theoretical and political commitments are simply so different that they are practically looking at different Samoas. Another criterion for validity in research is neutrality, which refers to the need to make sure research is not being biased by the scholar's personal or political commitments. The Mead–Freeman controversy illustrates that scholarship, like any social activity, is bound to be part of a historical, social, political and theoretical environment and its commitments. Furthermore, looking at the different genres of writing of Mead and Freeman, highlights the fact that the language we use to report our findings makes neutrality impossible, as all language is social and cultural and never a transparent medium that could describe the reality 'as it is' (MacCabe, 1973).

Despite the fact that we can hardly come up with a 'truth' about Samoa, there are still better and worse ways of conducting research in settings like Samoa or anywhere else. Trying to imagine what guidelines and criteria for good research would look like after traditional validity no longer seems feasible, scholars have begun to suggest alternative notions of validity (e.g. Lincoln and Guba, 1985, 1994) and multiple validities (Lather, 1993). Talking about validities, instead of validity, has two advantages. First, it draws attention to the fact that the theories, methods and modes of writing that underpin our research open up different and always partial and political views on reality. Instead of considering this an outrage, scholarship suggesting multiple validities ask us to be more critically aware of what drives our research. Second, acknowledging that there is more than one way of making sense of social phenomena, asks one to come up with a more multidimensional, nuanced, and tentative way of understanding one's object of study. The battle over the validity of Mead's research on Samoa ended up in a shouting match over whether Samoa was or is an Apollonian Paradise or a Dionysian Hell. Multiple validities suggest that we should approach reality in less simplistically dichotomous ('true' or 'false'; 'right' or 'wrong'; 'heaven' or 'hell') and more complex terms.

The notion of multiple validities does not mean that there are no rules for conducting research. It simply means that rather than one universal rule that applies everywhere there are different rules, and we need to be aware how they make us relate to reality differently. Drawing on the Mead-controversy, the methodological focus of cultural studies as well as some other works on alternative validities (Lincoln and Guba, 1985; Lather, 1993), one can delineate three broadly different methodological approaches that each subscribe to a different notion of validity. The first, hermeneutic methodological approach obeys what I would term a 'dialogic' validity, which means that it evaluates research in terms of how well it manages to capture the lived realities of others. Thus, it would assess the value of research on Samoa in terms of how well it manages to be true to the lived reality of Samoans. The second, poststructuralist methodological approach subscribes to what I would term 'deconstructive' validity, and it assesses the value of research in terms of how well it unravels problematic social discourses that mediate the way in which we perceive reality and other people. Thus, poststructuralist research would assess the value of research on Samoa in terms of how thoroughly it unmasks the colonialist tropes that describe Samoa in terms of 'primitive' sensuality and danger. The third, realist or contextualist methodological approach inheres to a contextualist validity, which evaluates research in terms of how well it understands the social, economic and political context and connections of the phenomenon it is studying. Thus, it would assess the value of research on Samoa in terms of how thoroughly and critically it maps the internal and external structures of power and inequality, such as rank-hierarchies, forms of livelihood, colonialist politics, trade and culture, that shape the life of Samoan village elders and adolescent girls.

These three methodological approaches, and concomitant validities, roughly correspond to the 'humanistic', 'structuralist' and New Leftist of 'contextualist' bents in early cultural studies. There are also parallels between the three 'new' methodological approaches and validities and older notions of validity. However, despite these continuities the three methodologies/validities push research in cultural studies and social sciences more generally to new directions. In what follows, I will discuss how these new approaches/validities both continue and break away from older ways of doing research.

Alternative validities

Dialogic validity

To start with discussing, in more detail, the hermeneutic approach and accompanying 'dialogic' validity, it can be said that it evaluates research in terms of how truthfully it captures the lived worlds of the people being studied (Lincoln and Guba, 1985, 1994; Lincoln, 1995). This broad principle can be further broken down to three specific criteria for 'good' or valid research:

1 *Truthfulness*. Research should do justice to the perspectives of the people being studied, so that they can, in the main, agree with it. This entails collaborative forms of research, such as measures to allow the people being studied, such as Samoans, to have a say in the way in which they are studied and represented (in traditional research parlance the latter is referred to as 'member check' (e.g. Seale, 1999)).

2 *Self-reflexivity*. Researchers should be reflexive about the personal, social, and paradigmatic discourses that guide the way they perceive reality and other people. This entails that scholars need to try to become aware of the cultural baggage, such as notions of the 'primitive', that mediates their understanding of different worlds.

3 *Polyvocality*. Researchers should be conscientious that they are not studying *a* lived reality but *many*. This means that they should make sure that they include the views or voices of major 'stakeholders', such as young girls as well as village elders (Lincoln and Guba, 1985), trying to be true to their diversity as well as relations and tensions between them.

Dialogic validity is reminiscent of the old ethnographic goal of capturing the 'native's point of view'. Where it departs from the old ethnographic project is that it does not claim to have access to some privileged 'objective' position, from which to describe the lives of others. Dialogism does not view research in terms of describing other worlds from the outside, but in terms of an encounter or interaction between different worlds. The main criteria of validity of this approach then is how well the researcher fulfils the ethical imperative to be true to, and to respect, other people's lived worlds and realities.

Deconstructive validity

Poststructuralist research and the accompanying deconstructive validity evaluates research in terms of how well it manages to unravel social tropes and discourses that, over time, have come to pass for a 'truth' about the world. There are three poststructuralist strategies to unravel discourses that mediate our understanding of the world that constitute three different criteria for good research within the tradition:

1 *Postmodern excess*. The postmodern or Baudrillardian (1980; also Lather, 1993) notion of 'excess' of discourses points out that there is a potentially infinite number of 'truths' or ways of approaching the reality. Thus, research is assessed in terms of how it manages to highlight the multiple ways in which a particular phenomenon can be understood, in order to destabilize any 'fixed' understanding of it. The Freeman–Mead controversy is an illustration of postmodern

questioning, as it highlights that there are myriad, different 'truths' about Samoa.

2   *Genealogical historicity*. Genealogy, associated with the work of Foucault (1984), challenges truths by exposing their historicity. Thus, research is evaluated in terms of how well it unravels the way in which certain taken-for-granted truths are not universal or timeless but products of specific historical and political agendas. An example or genealogical research is the analysis of the historical, political and theoretical commitments of Mead's and Freeman's works, which make them render Samoa very different.

3   *Deconstructive critique*. Deconstruction, associated with the work of Derrida (1976), aims to question the binaries that organize our thought, in order to expose their hidden politics. Thus, research is evaluated in terms of how it manages to unearth the constitutive binaries that underpin our understanding of a particular phenomenon. An example would be an analysis of the constitutive binary between the sensual or aggressive nature of 'primitive' societies and the 'civilized constraint' of the Western world that interlace both Mead's and Freeman's works.

Poststructuralist critique may, occasionally, bring into mind the traditional research endeavour of uncovering 'bias' in research or, for example, in news coverage. However, poststructuralism parts from this line of inquiry in that it argues that there is no 'unbiased' way of comprehending the world. Therefore, its notion of good research is twofold. First, good or valid research is understood to expose the historicity, political investments, omissions and blind spots of social 'truths'. Second, good or valid research is also understood to be aware of its own historical, political and social investments, continuously reflecting back on its own commitments.

Contextual validity

Research on social context and concomitant contextualist validity refer to the capability of research to locate the phenomenon it is studying within the wider social, political, and even global, context. In this sense contextualism is committed to a form of realism, that is bound to make statements of how the world 'really is'. This realist underpinning contradicts the hermeneutic and poststructuralist methodologies and validities, which both underline that there are multiple 'realities' and that the world looks different when observed from a different social place or historical time. Yet, both the dialogism and poststructuralism are driven by a democratic and egalitarian impulse to listen to multiple voices and to challenge authoritative discourses. When these approaches argue that they are listening to, perhaps, silenced voices or challenging authoritative discourses, they claim that some people are more, and some are less, powerful and able to get their voices heard, and some discourses are more powerful and more authoritative than others. In order to make those claims, scholars need to resort to some notion of social and historical context and structures of inequality and need some criteria on how to analyze them. However, contextual validity not only refers to a requirement to comprehend the social context but also to a requirement to comprehend the way in which research is located within and shapes this context. The twofold nature of the task of capturing the social context in research can be encapsulated by two criteria for contextualist research:

1   *Sensitivity to social context.* This refers to the duty of scholarship to carefully analyze, for example, historical events, statistics and developments, using and comparing different resources and views. This simply means that research cannot be haphazard or based on a hunch. Studying Samoa from this perspective would mean to carefully analyze the history of the islands, their social structures and interaction with the outside world through commerce, missionaries, even anthropologists. Even if both Mead and Freeman discuss the social context of Samoa, this fades into the background against their project of capturing the 'ethos' of a relatively timeless 'primitive' society.
2   *Awareness of historicity.* This criteria refers to the ability of research to understand its own historicity. Thus, research on Samoa would need to be aware of the ways in which it is implicated in the social context of which Samoa forms a part, such as structures of colonialism or anti-colonialist struggles (see Bhaskar, 1979). This means that social science and its object, historical society, cannot be separated, and analyzing the social context also enables research to become aware, and be able to critically evaluate, its role in it.

Cultural studies has sometimes been hesitant to say much about, for example, social or economic structures, as it argues that we cannot describe those structures without the mediation of culture and language. However, cultural studies frequently makes reference to how this or that cultural practice consolidates class, race or gender inequalities and so on. What the notion of contextual validity underlines is that we need to be careful about those statements. For example, my doctoral student recently set out to investigate the historical facts about the Israeli–Palestinian conflict in order to contextualize her analysis of films on it. She soon found out that there was not 'a' history on the conflict but multiple complex and controversial histories. This underlines two things. First, we should analyze historical and social 'facts' carefully, attending to details, complicated processes, and different perspectives, and not to go with popular assumptions or maybe jingoistic basic textbooks. Second, we need to be aware that our accounts are never separate from history but always historical and political, being shaped by and shaping the landscape we are studying.

The list of validities discussed is not meant to be exhaustive. It is designed for the purposes of this book to outline some central modes of doing qualitative research in cultural studies. The different notions of validity draw attention to the unfeasibility of the notion of validity as singular 'truth'. The list of validities also illuminate the fact that, abandoning singular validity, does not entail a state of 'lawlessness' in research, but that they each set forth specific guidelines, rules and criteria for good research.

Combining methodologies

Triangulation

Looking at the list of three different types of methodological approaches and their accompanying different validities begs a question: Is there a way to bring the three approaches together in a research project? After all, combining methodologies is required if one is to continue the cultural studies tradition of studying the interplay between lived experience, discourses and texts and the historical, social and political context.

One does not, obviously, always need to combine methodologies. There are many research projects that obey only the rules of one of the validities. Some new ethnographic projects are concentrated on working to be true to the lived worlds of, often disenfranchised, people. The same way, many critical analyses of media texts mainly aim to criticize the way in which they construct authoritative truths. As has been said earlier, being true to lived realities of people may be difficult to combine with critical analysis of the discourses that form part of the people's lived realities. The same way, an analysis of global and social structures may contradict, or simply surpass, the people's local or lived sense of their environment.

However, if one wants to combine approaches, one needs a framework that helps to do this. Traditional social and cultural inquiry usually refers to techniques of combining different theories, methods, sources and material, in terms of 'triangulation' (Denzin, 1989; Flick, 1998). The classical aim of triangulation is to combine different kinds of material or methods to see whether they corroborate one another. Thus, one could, for example, complement one's participant observation on, for example, Samoa, by consulting documents and colonial archives, in order to find out whether the people 'lie' or misremember things (this is, in fact, quite close to the way in which Freeman understood and conducted his project to refute Mead). All in all, the classical aim of triangulation is to get a more accurate or truthful picture of the social world. This aim reflects the original meaning of triangulation, which comes from navigation where it refers to the use of different bearings to give the correct position of an object (Silverman, 1992: 156).

Interpreted as a pursuit of truth, triangulation is not particularly useful for combining the three methodological approaches, discussed above. This is because the basic goal of these approaches is to problematize any simple notion of 'truth'. Dialogism aims to be true to the lived worlds' of the people being studied, and rather than trying to find whether girls or village elders spoke the 'truth', would aim to capture the different worldviews of both. Genealogy would point out that one cannot find a truth from, for example, colonial archives, as they are locales that 'produce' historical and highly politically invested truths about people and places (as 'unruly' and so on) to be 'governed'. Part of Freeman's 'evidence' on the aggression of Samoans, for instance, comes from colonial administration's reports on 'troubles' on the islands. While it is quite feasible to think that there is violence on the islands, these kinds of archives are bound to focus on it, as they are logs on the 'managing' of the islands. This finally brings one to the contextualist insight that research can never be objective as it is always part of and shapes the social landscapes, such as structures of colonialism, that it studies.

To understand the specific nature of positivist triangulation, and to be able to compare it with other ways of combining methodologies, it is useful to ana-lyze how it understands ontology (the nature of reality) and epistemology (the nature of knowledge). The classical positivist understanding of reality is that it is 'fixed'. Thus, in classical physics, the physical reality is understood to be a knowable and relatively stable 'object' that can be accurately observed through the use of scientific methods (microscopes, calculations and so on). The same way, in positivist social science, the society is understood to be an observable entity that stays put and can be captured using statistics, surveys and interviews. The trouble with this ontological position is that, as we have seen in the Mead debate, reality does not hold still, but is amoeba-like, multifaceted, evolving, looking different from different angles (from the perspectives of the young girls, village elders, colonial archives etc.).

The ontological commitment to the idea that reality is a fixed object that exists separately from research informs the positivist epistemological goal of research to 'reflect' reality. According to positivism, the reason for using methods (conversation analysis, semiotics, statistical analysis) is to get closer to 'truth' about the reality. Different methods are viewed as 'magnifying glasses' that help the scholar to see the reality more clearly, or in a less biased and more system-atic manner. The aim of combining different methods is to use different lenses to calibrate an optimally clear vision. As a consequence, the positivist discussion on how to do research is often quite technical, aiming to perfect the method's ability to capture reality correctly. However, the idea of research that exists out-side, or uses methods to beam itself above, reality is not feasible, as research is a social activity. Both Mead's and Freeman's research are heavily invested in the social agendas of their time, rendering Samoa a parable for their politics (Clifford, 1986). Instead of considering this an outrage, one could ask how else could it be, and what would be the purpose of social inquiry without a social agenda. Yet, the trouble with the positivist denial of a political agenda is that it becomes coveted; pushed to the sphere of eternal truths instead of political debate and decision-making. This is evident in the way Mead and Freeman frame their research as a timeless and unbiased 'truth' on a 'primitive' society, instead of situating their commentary on Samoa as part of heated, highly politi-cal and controversial (post)colonial debates over human nature (see Table 1.1).

TABLE 1.1   *Paradigms of combining methodologies*

Paradigms	Ontology	Epistemology	Metaphor	Goal of Research	Politics
Triangulation	Fixed reality	Reflect reality	Magnifying glass	Truth	No bias
Prisms	Fluid reality	Social construction of reality	Prism refracting vision	Conveying multiple realities	Pluralist science and society
Material semiotic	Interactive reality	Material/ semiotic construction of reality	Prism diffracting light	Creating egalitarian realities	Egalitarian science and society
Dialogue	Interactive reality	Material/ semiotic construction of reality	Dialogue	Dialogues between multiple realities	Egalitarian and pluralist science and society

The positivist ontological and epistemological programme has lately been widely questioned. In physics, so called 'quantum physics' has illustrated that research into physical phenomena does not merely describe them but interferes or alters them. In social science this is all the more obvious, so that Marxism was a scientific project that not only described nineteenth-century industrial societies but also profoundly transformed them, informing both the establishment of state-socialism in Eastern Europe and Western welfare states (Bhaskar, 1979). Because of the inherently political nature of research, I underline that this book is primarily on 'methodology' and not 'methods'. The notion of methodology draws attention to the fact that the tools and approaches (methods) that we use to make sense of reality, are not mere neutral techniques but come with a knowledge or ideology ('logos') that often makes the 'reality' seem quite different. My aim is not to help the reader to get rid of this inherent 'bias' of all research but to become more aware of the worldviews and politics embedded in our research approaches, in order to advance better and more egalitarian research and better and more egalitarian realities.

Research as a prism

Richardson (2000) has suggested that, instead of talking about triangulation, we should begin to talk about combining different ways of doing and writing research in terms of 'crystallization'. Crystals, Richardson points out, are prisms. Therefore, crystals not only 'reflect externalities' but 'refract them within themselves' (2000: 934). What the metaphor of crystals brings into light is the way in which reality changes when we change the methodological angle or perspective from which we look at it.

The notion of research prisms subscribes to an ontology and epistemology that are quite different from the positivist ones. It views reality as fluid (ontology) and, rather than seeing the task of research to accurately describe this reality, it argues that research creates or socially constructs the realities it studies (epistemology). Rather than view research as describing a reality from the outside, this perspective locates research within reality, as one of the processes that 'makes' realities. Often, the prismatic vision of research is committed to projects that bring to the fore multiple perspectives on reality, or multiple realities, with the specific aim of challenging the old idea that there is one privileged way of looking at reality, or one reality. Scholars working within this paradigm have been particularly interested in creating 'alternative' realities that contradict accepted scientific truths. Part of this project has been to give voice to silenced or subordinated knowledges or realities. Academics, subscribing to the idea of research as a prism, point out that science has historically been, and still often continues to be, a closed realm of white, privileged, Western men, who make definitions and decisions with far-reaching consequences for our lives, all in the name of unbiased scientific 'objectivity' (for general critiques, see Haraway, 1997: 24–31; also Harding, 1991, 1993; Latour, 1993). Consequently, they have developed ways of doing and writing scholarship that would be truer to, for example, women's and non-Western people's ways of relating to, and communicating about, the world (see also Narayan and George, 2001). An example of what this means is a poem Richardson (1992) has written on the life-story of a woman, 'Louisa May', whom she had interviewed as part of a project on unwed mothers. Through the poem, Richardson wanted to convey Louisa May's life in her own terms and in her own Southern rhythm, without reducing her to statistical, sociological categories of class, educational level and so on. Thus, methodologies and writing strategies are not seen as means of reflecting reality, presumably 'objectively', but as devices that the scholar uses to create and convey different realities (see Table 1.1).

Coming back to the three methodological approaches and validities I outlined above, the notion of a prism would suit combining dialogic validity (conveying new/neglected realities) and deconstructive validity (dismantling old authoritative, such as male anthropological or sociological, realities). Both the dialogic and deconstructive enterprises draw attention to the way in which language and research 'create' different realities, providing tools for both critically analyzing mainstream realities as well as for creating alternative ones.

However, the idea of prisms sits uneasily with contextualist validity. If one thinks of context in terms of, for example, global, economic structures of inequality, one can say that one can view them very differently from different perspectives. Yet, there is also a stubbornly 'real' dimension to global structures that is similar everywhere; even if economic and political processes are experienced in perhaps highly different ways by different people and in different places, they still affect all of us, binding our realities and fates together. The idea of methodologies as prisms that convey different realities often views its task to be the understanding of difference or comprehending that the way in which we perceive the world is just one possible one. One can say that it aims to enhance comprehension or conversations between different realities, enabling us to, for example, feel empathetic affinity with a different world, such as Louisa May's. Fostering this kind of affinity or understanding has its undeniable merits. However, it is not well suited to analyze the way in which, for example, global economic developments affect us both similarly and differently. Thus, it is not well suited for fostering political or policy initiatives that would bring people together to transform these structures.

One could say that, if one would remove 70 years from the writing, Mead's impressionistic description of young Samoan girls is close to the prismatic effort to bring to the fore a different way of relating to the world that has previously been neglected (and here one needs to remember how rare female academics and female-oriented perspectives were in Mead's time). However, even if the story opens a window onto a fascinatingly different world, this world seems to be floating in timeless isolation. We have very little sense of how colonialism, as a cultural, political, economic and military process, shapes Samoa. Therefore, we have hardly any way of imagining how our realities and theirs might be interlinked, except by a kind of human affinity, and how it might be possible to build some collective project or politics around it.

Material-semiotic perspective

If the problem with positivist research is that it views there to be only one 'truth' about the reality, the problem with research subscribing to the notion of 'prisms' is that it understands that there are endless or multiple truths about the reality. If positivism autocratically imposes its 'truth' on other views, the notion of prisms and multiple, incommensurable truths make it difficult to envision politics that would begin to change our shared reality together. Trying to find some mediating ground between these two positions, it is useful to resort to Donna Haraway's methodological idea of 'diffraction'. The notion of diffraction is both close to Richardson's idea of prisms that refract reality, while also departing from it in a significant way. Diffraction, unlike refraction, refers not simply to a symbolic or social construction of reality – or to 'creating worlds with words' (Austin, 1965) – but it understands research as a force that alters or creates reality in both symbolic and material terms. Thus, if refraction refers to the process through which vision changes when it goes through a prism, diffraction refers to the way in which light, as both an optic and a material force, is transformed when it passes through a prism (Clough, 2000: 162).

The difference between the notion of research as a process of symbolically constructing reality and the notion of it as a process of symbolically and materially constructing reality can be illustrated by an old dispute between the two main figureheads of the poststructuralist movement: Derrida and Foucault. Derrida's argument was that nineteenth-century Enlightenment 'rationality' constituted or legitimated itself through the invention or new 'scientific' definition of madness or 'irrationality'. Against this, Foucault (1979b) pointed out that this 'act' was far from being purely a matter of linguistic definition, as it entailed locking the madmen up into asylums, of stripping them of any basic rights and of condemning them to a life-time of physical, social and emotional deprivation. What this story highlights is that research and science do not make the world 'seem' a particular way, but that research and science, such as psychiatry, bring about certain, very concrete and sometimes very problematic worlds. To return to Samoa, one can point out that anthropological research on the islands have been part and parcel of both colonialist and anti-colonialist politics, and, rather than merely describing or giving meaning to the life on the islands, they have been part of processes that have effectuated fundamental cultural, political and economic changes on Samoa.

The lessons that a material-semiotic view on research has to teach are twofold:

1   It draws attention to the limits of positivism in that it highlights that research is never objective but a reality changing material-semiotic force, which always has an agenda or is political.
2   It also draws attention to the limits of the social constructionist view in that it highlights the fact that research cannot create realities at will, or simply through telling a different story. Research is both enabled and constrained by a host of intertwined cultural/political/economic/ecological processes, and we need to understand those processes, if we are to intervene in them.

Thus, the way in which the material-semiotic perspective views the nature of reality (ontology) and the way in which we can know it (epistemology) is different from both the positivist and prismatic perspectives. It does not view reality to be either a fixed entity to be described (the positivist view) or fluid symbolic clay to be moulded into different realities (prismatic view), but understands the relationship between reality and research to be one of interaction. Thus, while the material-semiotic perspective understands research not to describe but to 'create' worlds, it underlines that reality exists beyond research and that it can 'fight back', making some types of research and conclusions more possible than others (Massumi, 1992). This means that it departs from the prismatic notion of 'writing different realities' arguing for a 'materialistically' tempered notion of 'creation'. It acknowledges that research is always facilitated and constrained by the existing social and material environment and it needs to understand, for example, structures of social inequality or the basics of ecological reality, if it is going to change them.

Similar to the 'prismatic' perspective, the goal of research in this configuration is to render research permeable to a wider variety of perspectives. However, the idea of prisms interpreted this goal in pluralistic terms to allow all voices or realities to be heard. Somewhat differently, Haraway (1997) and

Harding (1991, 1993, 2001) see the goal of incorporating different views in more egalitarian terms as a means to enhance more equal scientific, social and economic structures. Haraway, borrowing from Harding, terms this methodological approach 'strong objectivity'. Strong objectivity refers to a commitment to take into account different perspectives – particularly those of the subjugated groups, such as Samoan girls, as they are likely to be critical of existing forms of knowledge – in order to produce more inclusive or encompassing, and thereby more 'accurate', accounts of the world. Haraway (1988) acknowledges that research is never objective but always partial or 'situated', however, this does not constitute a licence to be parochial or narrow-minded. On the contrary, the fact that research is always political, underlines our ethical responsibility to be aware of 'what kinds of realities and beings we are creating, out of whom, and for whom' (Haraway, 1997: 58). This means that we should be conscientious of how our particular research, for its small or big part, produces the reality it looks at, such as the notions of sensual or dangerous 'primitives', which have given rise to a host of discourses and practices, providing support for sexual liberalization, tourism, countless films and media images as well as sterilization campaigns. In order not to produce narrow-minded, racist research that perpetuates inequality, research needs, according to Haraway and Harding, to be rigorous and use a 'systematic method' that facilitates taking into account and critically evaluating different views on the phenomenon it is studying. This systematic collecting and assessing of perspectives, particularly subjugated ones, helps to produce research that is both more encompassing or scientifically rigorous and more aware of its political and ethical implications.

Within the material-semiotic perspective, the goal of combining different methodologies, and their respective validities, is to produce these 'better' or more inclusive accounts of the world, or more inclusive worlds. The dialogic principle enables scholarly practice to tune into the perspectives of different groups, particularly those of disenfranchised groups, such as young Samoan girls or the 'mad'. Deconstruction helps to critically analyze the long-sedimented discourses on 'primitives' or 'mentally disordered' that masquerade as truth but express the politics of a select few, thereby opening up space for new and a more egalitarian range of views. Contextualism enables one to make sense of the way in which both notions of primitive sexuality and mental disorders are intertwined with complex social, political and economic structures, such as colonialism, eugenics or liberal humanist interest in and fascination with difference. As a whole, combining methodologies helps to bring forth 'strong objectivity' that produces knowledge that is both more 'accurate' and more egalitarian.

Methodological dialogues

Despite its many merits, the material-semiotic perspective makes me uncomfortable in one respect. The notion of diffraction (as well as the notions of reflection and refraction) is optical, and vision, as a sense, is one of the most linear, and least interactive, ones. The visual logic of the material-semiotic position shines through from, for example, the writings of Haraway and Harding that take a relatively traditional view on the practicalities of empirical research and writing. Thus, they understand 'strong objectivity' to refer to research that systematically combines different, including subjugated, views and then synthesizes them into a more inclusive and accurate scientific statement politically committed to fighting social inequality and exclusion. This position differs from traditional research principles in that it takes a political position, but its 'revised' commitment to being 'scientific' adheres to traditional synthetizing research style that translates other perspectives into a scientific view, in a way that obeys the visual logic of detachment, constancy and control.

In my view, this optical framework does not quite do justice to the ideal of inclusiveness or to the notion of research as interaction with reality. It reveals that the idea of material-semiotic nature of research is weak, where the notion of prisms is strong, namely, the dialogic principle of listening to the texture and nuance of different worlds. Therefore, I would like to return to Richardson's (1997, 2000; also Denzin, 1997a) idea that methodologies and modes of writing may be better or worse in tune with the pattern of communication of certain groups or the operating mode of certain spheres of life. Thus, in order to do justice to the lived realities of, for example, Samoan girls, one may need a collaborative or dialogic research strategy and a more poetic style of writing. The same way, a contextual analysis and realist writing may suit an investigation of colonialist cultural, political and economic structures. This does not mean that we should delegate women and life-stories into the emotional/fictive/ private and politics and economy into contextual/realist/public, as this may consolidate structures of inequality and confinement (caring for women, and control for men). It rather underlines the fact that modes of reading and writing or inscribing reality are always political and that unless we do justice to their specificity we risk not being sensitive to all the social and subjugated views, values and interests that we want to inform a more inclusive, egalitarian and pluralist research.

The ideal of an 'encompassing' view, embedded in the notion of strong objectivity, draws attention to the general, whereas the notion of prisms underlines the importance of capturing the particular. If one is to imagine a methodological position between the general and the particular, however, it is best to switch sense from vision to sound or conversation. Vision segments reality into one true view (positivism), several different views (prisms), or a particular but encompassing view (material-semiotic view). The metaphor of sound or conversation views different realities in more porous or interactive terms. Instead of arguing for fusing different realities into one view, or capturing separate realities, the notion of sound imagines different realities and methodologies in terms of soundscapes that each have their distinctive chords, but that also resonate and interact with one another. An example would be a jazz trumpetist's solo, which gets translated into the audience's tapping of their feet and plays into and out of other multicultural sounds and politics of contemporary urban neighbourhoods (see Deleuze and Guattari (1987: 530–50) on rhythm for inspiration). In each of the milieus, the sound of jazz strikes a different chord; yet, the artistic/performative, embodied, and urban/political incarnations of jazz also bleed into one another. The same way the different lived experiences of sexuality, the cultural, political and medical discourses that mediate it, as well as the scientific, socioeconomic and global political regimes that it forms a part speak in different tone and about different sexualities; yet, they also resonate and interact with one another. Thus, a sound-based approach to combining methodologies, and their respective validities, enables a multidimensional research strategy, which both respects the specifity of different modes of inquiry/reality and points to unities and intersections that bind different methodologies and realities together.

To illustrate what a sound-based or dialogic approach to combining methodologies would look like, I will sketch a possible way of analyzing the sexuality of Samoan girls from different perspectives. My intention is not to say what Mead or Freeman should have done. One cannot judge a piece of research done 70 or 20 years ago by contemporary standards or social agendas, even if some of the questions that they raise are still pertinent today. Rather, I simply draw on the Mead–Freeman debate in order to provide some heuristic ideas for doing multidimensional research, in somewhat similar spirit as Frow and Morris (1992) sketch a way of studying a shopping mall without actually ever studying it.

Thus, if one was to start with analyzing the lived reality of the Samoan adolescent girls, one could use the principles of hermeneutic or dialogic approach and aim to – in collaboration with the girls and being critically aware of one's cultural baggage that might hamper one's understanding of them – capture the issue from their perspective. In a similar fashion, and in the spirit of poly-vocality, one could aim to understand the issue of sexuality from the perspectives of boys, and of older villagers, men as well as women. If one was to study the discourses that mediate the way in which we, and they, understand the girls' sexuality one could start with critically examining the Western social-psychological discourse, which Mead wanted to problematize, that has constituted adolescent female sexuality as a 'problem' and a source of agony. One could discuss the origins and politics of this discourse that governs female sexuality by constituting it as a 'problem' and then aiming to 'solve' it by either protectively suggesting abstinence or arguing for a freedom from repression or in favour of 'natural' sexuality. One could then continue to study how this discourse, first, intersects with notions of 'primitive' sexuality, which is used to back up either prurient or 'free' sexual behaviour as the 'natural' one. Second, one could investigate how the discourse on 'primitive' sexuality forms part of colonialist, eugenistic and touristic discourses that define people from the South as more 'sex' or 'body' than 'mind', thereby, defining them as more 'animal-like' than 'human'. One could then continue to examine how these racist discourses on sexuality form part and parcel of colonialist and postcolonialist regimes of military, political and economic rule that have affected life and society in places like Samoa in fundamental ways. However, one could also investigate how notions of natural, buoyant sexuality form part of regimes of social thought and actions, such as Mead's culturalist liberalism, that, in all their contradictions, have fought against racist policies. Finally, one could come back full circle and study how global discourses and practices related to sexuality, from Western missionary and other 'civilizing' missions to contemporary global media today, guide normative notions of sexuality in Samoa, so that it is conceivable that when interviewing Samoan girls, one can hear echoes of local culture, social-psychological notions of adolescent sexuality and Western interpretations of 'primitive' sexuality.

A study like this would not answer the positivist question of: What is female sexuality in Samoa like? On the contrary, it would study the politics embedded in various discourses that produce, in both symbolic and very material terms, the sexuality of Samoan girls and a range of other practices and agendas to which it is attached. However, capturing the 'politics' embedded in young girls' intimate experience of sexuality and the politics underpinning eugenic and exoticizing discourses on sexuality and their relationships to colonialist and counter-colonialist policies will require different methodologies and genres of writing, to the point that the 'results' of these three perspectives may seem to speak of a different reality. Capturing the particularity of these perspectives is pivotal, if one is going to be true to the project of enhancing research and politics that takes into account, and does justice to, different perspectives on the world.

Bringing the different methodological and political perspectives into dialogue with one another cultivates multidimensional research and politics that is capable of attending to the complexity of social phenomena, such as Samoan sexuality. This research strategy does not try to come up with one enlightened view (triangulation) or to acknowledge that there are multiple views (prisms). Rather, multiperspectival research aims to hold different perspectives in creative tension with one another. For example, if, as part of studying Samoan sexuality, one was to examine the social implications of Mead's work from a dialogic or multiperspectival standpoint, it would appear as neither 'good' nor 'bad' but complicated. On one hand, she defends the Samoans and their life against Western universalizing moral codes and notions of intrinsically superior and inferior forms of human nature. On the other hand, Mead exoticizes the Samoans, ending up affirming the Western trope of universal sensual and natural 'primitiveness'. From a dialogic point of view, Mead's liberal humanism is not epistemologically or politically *either* 'correct' *or* 'incorrect' but has *both* its rights *and* its wrongs. This kind of dialogism cultivates research and politics that can appreciate the multidimensionality of social problematics and not to resort to one-dimensional judgements.

Exploring different perspectives and using different methodologies the way I have just outlined is doable, but it is a large undertaking. My intention is not to suggest that every research project should collect a multitude of perspectives. What I do want to underline, however, is that even if one studies a single aspect of something like Samoan adolescent female sexuality, it is useful to bear in mind that it can be approached from several angles and is part of a larger puzzle. One may want to capture the lived sexuality of a Samoan woman through a life-story interview. Yet, one needs to bear in mind that her account may be interlaced with all the local and global discourses on female and primitive sexuality and both fiercely critique and support these discourses and the political agendas that speak through them. Thus, a life-story is: (1) an expression of lived reality, to be understood dialogically; (2) shot through with social discourses that can be unravelled through deconstruction; and (3) articulates wide local, national and transnational politics, to be analyzed contextually. Therefore, even if one studies a particular area, such as a lived reality, it is useful to be aware that it encompasses multiple dimensions. This is what I discovered when interviewing anorexic women, whose stories were shot through with discourses that define anorexia and all their contradictory national, transnational and highly gendered political and social agendas. The more I study the Mead–Freeman controversy, the more I realize the commonalities between the discourses on anorexia and on adolescent sexuality on Samoa. In both cases the 'true' nature of the female body and self becomes a battleground and a battle cry for a host of complex personal and political struggles. Thus, combining methodologies to study how our intimate experience of our body and self are connected with global regimes of power that bind us with distant people, might foster translocal politics that would question those forces, discourses and practices that subjugate us, while being prepared to consider fundamental differences of opinion and interest and be prepared to negotiate them. In short, it would be committed to egalitarian politics that would acknowledge that part of the egalitarian project is to come to terms with the fact that 'equality' may seem different from different perspectives.

Conclusions

The methodological project of cultural studies is structured around a three-dimensional interest in lived experiences, discourses or texts and the social context. The challenge of this project is that the three areas of focus refer to different methodological approaches. Understanding lived experience demands a hermeneutic or phenomenological approach that aims to understand lived realities. The interest in discourses calls for a (post)structuralist analysis of the tropes and patterns that shape our understanding of our social, cultural and research environment. Analyzing the social and political context, however, is always wedded to some form of realism that wants to make sense of how the society and its structures 'really' operate. These three methodological approaches may complement and enrich one another, but they also run into contradictions. One cannot easily combine a hermeneutic quest to understand lived realities and a (post)structuralist interest in critically analyzing the discourses that mediate those realities. At the same time, the hermeneutic and (post)structuralist approaches' interest in either multiple realities or the political nature of all realities does not bode well with the realist project of making sense of social reality. Furthermore, the new philosophical and practical challenges brought about by new ethnography, poststructuralism and globalization – which demand research to become, at the same time, truer to different realities and capable of making sense of the increasingly important global reality – have both further pulled research apart as well as underlined the need for dialogues between scholarly as well as political positions.

In this situation, the old notion of 'validity' as truthfulness seems no longer feasible. On the contrary, it has been suggested that instead of validity, we start talking about validities. Against the background of cultural studies interest in the lived, discursive and social/global dimensions of reality, as well as recent methodological discussions, one can suggest three different validities. First, dialogic validity assesses research in terms of how well it remains true to the lifeworlds of the people being studied. Second, deconstructive validity evaluates the value of research in terms of how thoroughly it is aware of the social discourses and tropes that mediate our understanding of reality and frame our research. Third, contextualist validity measures the validity of research in terms of how well it manages to locate the phenomena, as well as research itself, in the wider social, political and global context.

Together, these validities highlight different criteria for good or valid research. At the same time, they raise the question of whether, and how, these different validities, and their concomitant methodological approaches, could be brought together. The traditional way of combining methodologies in social and cultural research is triangulation, which refers to the use of different methods in order to get a more accurate idea of social reality. However, the trouble with using the heuristic of triangulation to bring together the three validities and methodologies is that they do not necessarily cohere to an accurate vision of reality as they explore different facets of reality or different realities. Richardson (2000) has suggested that instead of talking about triangulation we should begin to talk about prisms, which highlights the fact that reality changes when we change the methodological perspective from which we look at it. The notion of prisms does justice to the potentially profound differences between different ways of approaching the reality, but the problem with it is that it bypasses the fact that, even if we may approach the global, social world differently, it also binds our fates together. Thus, drawing on both Richardson's idea of prisms and Donna Haraway's notion of material-semiotic construction of reality, I will argue for a mode of combining methodological approaches in terms of creating dialogues between them. The dialogic mode of doing research would be attentive to the lived, cultural as well as social and material aspects of our realities, and acknowledge that there may be disjunctures between them. It would aim to cultivate modes of social and cultural analysis that would be both sensitive to different realities and capable of building bridges between them. This mode of research would, hopefully, also encourage a politics that would bring different groups, with their different concerns and views, together to begin to build a common, more egalitarian and pluralist world.

Exercise 1

- Design a research strategy for studying a topic of your choice. Think how you would study your topic, using as a guideline: (1) the dialogic validity; (2) deconstructive validity; and (3) contextual validity?
- Discuss how the three approaches might contradict or complement one another.
- Do you think that one of the research approaches is more pertinent to making sense of your topic? Why?
- Would it be best if you focused on one perspective, such as lived experience? What kind of research strategies or methods would you use to explore your topic from the chosen perspective? How could you enrich your preferred methodological perspective by analyzing how other approaches bleed into it (by, for example, analyzing how discourses interlace experiences)?
- Or would it be feasible to study the lived, discursive and social/global dimensions of the phenomenon that you are studying? How could you study these three dimensions in a way that would be manageable? How could you bring the different analysis together without coming up with (1) strict causalities ('social context determines lived lives') or (2) a situation where different perspectives talk past one another ('lived experiences tell about little people and social context tells about big history, and they speak about different realities')?

Part II

Studying Lived Experience

2

Studying Lived Resistance

Main questions

- A classical approach to studying lived experience in cultural studies is informed by the notion of 'resistance'. How do the critical and textualist approaches define 'resistance'? How are the two approaches to the study of resistance different? How are they similar? What are the strengths and shortcomings of each?
- How does a 'contingent' notion of resistance help to bring together the strengths of the two other approaches? Why is it more feasible to speak of, and study, resistances, in the plural?

The classical approach to studying lived experience in cultural studies is informed by the notion of 'resistance'. Against the backdrop of pessimistic Marxist analysis of culture as mainly 'opium for the masses', resistance, as a concept, provided early cultural studies with a way to argue that people have some creative and critical abilities to 'resist' domination. Thus, to begin to discuss ways of studying lived realities in the paradigm it is legitimate to begin with research on resistance.

However, studies on resistance can be, methodologically and philosophically speaking, rather different. Thus, in order to highlight certain key methodological issues and differences, I have distinguished three analytically different approaches to resistance (real studies on resistance often combine elements of the three). The first, 'critical contextualist' approach to studying resistance, such as consumption of subversive media images, is particularly interested in its effects on 'real' structures of dominance, such as patriarchal or class structures.

Studies done within this approach often end up rather pessimistic about the powers of resistance to transform social structures. The second, 'optimistic textualist' approach to resistance focuses on symbolic resistance, such as Madonna fans' interest in her overt sexuality, arguing its effects are, in and of themselves, 'real'. Studies done within this approach often end up rather optimistic about resistance and its ability to challenge structures of power.

Even if the above mentioned two approaches to resistance seem rather different, and arrive at nearly opposite conclusions about it, they also share a similarity. This similarity is their tendency to analyze resistance in terms of its alleged effects on a 'system', such as 'patriarchy'. The third, contingent approach to resistance, studies it in more contingent terms. It analyzes a particular resistant activity from several perspectives and from the points of view of different spheres of life, evaluating what types of power this activity resists and what types of power it buttresses. One could say that, rather than studying power vertically in terms of whether or not local activities change the system, the contingent approach to resistance studies power in more lateral terms, assessing its usually moderate effects on other activities, acknowledging that the large-scale or cumulative effects of resistance are often hard to assess.

Studies on resistance may currently be considered passé. However, I argue that many of the research dilemmas scholars studying resistance have tried to solve continue to haunt research on lived experience in cultural studies. Thus, research continues to struggle with the dilemma of how to capture the creative aspects of lived realities, while analyzing the discourses that interlace those experiences, and, in a sense, keep people under 'bad' or 'false' consciousness. The same way the issue, of whether 'real' power is material or symbolic, and how one can separate and study the two aspects of it, remains a pressing concern in cultural and social research. Thus, I would argue that the legacy of resistance studies continues to underpin contemporary research on lived experience in the paradigm, and the lessons these studies have to teach are of continuing relevance.

Critical contextualism

On labour and love

To start discussing resistance-analysis one can go back 25 years to Willis's (1978) landmark book, *Learning to labour*, that explored British working-class boys' – or 'lads', as he calls them – ritualistic resistance of school. Willis' project was to investigate why 'working-class kids get working class jobs' (1), and to find this out he did a school-based ethnography on a dozen 'non-academic' working-class boys. His study explores the ways in which the lads create a counter-culture that gives them a sense of superiority in relation to the conformist boys – or 'ear'oles', as the lads called them – who were their justified target of ridicule and violence (14). Thus, doing every sort of misdemeanor and getting away with doing as little work as possible became a source of pride for the lads particularly in relation to the ear'oles, who were seen to embody the school values, as testified by the following conversation:

PW: (...) why not be like the ear'oles, why not try and get CSE's? They don't get any fun, do they?

Derek: Cos they'm prats like, one kid he's got on his report now, he's got five As and one B.
            – Who's that?

Derek: Birchall.

Spanksy: I mean, what will they remember of their school life? What will they have to look back on? Sitting in a classroom, sweating their bollocks off, you know, while we've been ... I mean look at the things we can look back on, fighting on the Jas [i.e. Jamaicans]. Some of the things we've done on teachers, it'll be a laff when we look back on it. (14)

According to Willis, the lads' counterculture, challenging and rebuking the middle-class behavioural code, not only perpetuated their underachievement at school. It also resonated with working-class shopfloor culture, marked by male camaraderie and macho-bravado and valorization of practicality and suspicion of superiors and abstract thought. In the end, Willis argues, this rich and creative, even if also sexist and racist, counterculture, which may be seen as contesting the alienation of school and work, pushes the lads into working-class jobs and eventually reproduces the labour-structure (175).

This short description of Willis's study illustrates both how Willis studies and conceptualizes resistance. Through ethnography, he unravels the colourful, rambuntious counterculture that challenges middle-class conventions. However, Willis concludes that, eventually, this resistance does not challenge the 'real' structures of domination but, on the contrary, socializes the lads to become blue-collar workers.

Before I discuss the philosophical and methodological underpinnings of Willis's separation between resistance and 'real' dominance, I want to, however, shortly discuss Janice Radway's (1984) methodologically similar study on why women like to read romances. Radway's study is more multidimensional than Willis's, and she contextualized the reading through studying the ways in which the emergence of the romance novels was related to the industrial formula of 'category literature' and the spread of suburban bookstore-chains. As an English literature scholar, she also studied the narrative structure of the novels. The main focus of her study was, however, on readers of romances, whom she studied using surveys and a more focused interview study on a group of women from a town she termed 'Smithton'. Talking to the Smithton women, Radway discovered that, from the perspective of managing everyday life and time, reading romances created a time or a space within which a woman could be entirely on her own, in contrast to being expected to be available for the service of others (61, 211).

What most intrigued Radway, however, was the way in which the women defined a good romance. The good romance was characterized by a formulaic plot in which the hero initially seems fiercely masculine, harsh and distant and, after a series of misunderstandings are cleared, is revealed to be an affectionate and tender, almost feminine, soul, characterized by his love and devotion for the heroine. The ideal heroine was interesting, such as intelligent and possibly slightly deviant, such as a tomboy. Nevertheless, these qualities were secondary to the attraction provided by the novels' detailed description of how the heroine, eventually, succumbed to the doting lover, as described by Radway:

> In the midst of recounting the rest of the tale, they proudly exclaimed that Nanny 'spoke six languages,' was 'a really good artist,' and 'did not want to marry him even though she was pregnant' because she believed he was an 'elegant tomcat' and would not be faithful to her. These untraditional skills and unconventional attitudes are obviously not seen as fulfilling ... because they are legitimated and rendered acceptable by the novel's conclusion when the hero convinces Nanny of his love ... Here's the group recitation of this moment:

> *Dot*: He starts stalking her and this is virtually ...
> *Kit*: It's hysterical.
>   ...
> *Dot*: No, I don't need you!
> *Ann*: And he says I'll camp on your doorstep; I'll picket; unfair to; you know ... (80)

According to Radway, there are many elements in the practice of reading romance that resist patriarchy, such as the frequently featured 'tomboyish' heroine. The doting hero can also be conceived as resisting, as it embodies a more perfect masculinity that would respond to the women's needs, in an almost motherly fashion (212). However, Radway asserts that even if the fantasizing about the sensitive man addresses a real problem, namely that patriarchy does not allow for a more feminine or nurturing masculinity, it leaves this structural issue largely intact. According to Radway, romances may even consolidate existing gender relations, as they suggest to the reader that the spouse, like the hero, loves her deeply though this may not always be apparent (215).

Thus, in a fashion very similar to Willis, Radway unearths how a rich, resistant female subculture challenges patriarchal practices through an innocuous practice, such as reading romance novelettes. However, just like Willis, Radway concludes that, in the end, this resistance does not challenge the real patriarchal structures that interlace family and human relations and may even end up consolidating them.

Resistance and context

The early studies on resistance (in addition to Willis and Radway see e.g. Hall and Jefferson, 1976; Hebdige, 1976; Morley and Brunsdon, 1999[1980, 1987]; McRobbie, 2000) do not necessarily form a unified tradition. For instance, whereas Willis's study has a decidedly sociological pull, Radway's approach is influenced by literary approaches and methods, such as narrative analysis. Yet, they do share common features that are worth discussing, if one is to understand the classic cultural studies approach to lived resistance, which is still echoed in many studies done in the paradigm.

I will call the early resistance school, represented by Willis and Radway, 'critical contextualist' for two reasons. First, it takes a decidedly 'critical' view on resistance, looking carefully at both its creative as well as futile aspects. Second, it is underpinned by a focus on 'context', so that resistance is evaluated against its effect on 'reality', such as labour and educational structures or gender roles. The philosophical roots of this position can be traced to cultural studies' turn to Antonio Gramsci's theory on 'hegemony' to analyze the contradictions of culture (Gramsci, 1971; also Grossberg, 1997). According to Gramsci, 'hegemony' or cultural leadership, which legitimates existing social order, is produced by cultural institutions, such as media, school, the church and so on. However, unlike some of the more pessimistic analyses of popular culture, which saw it largely as an opium to keep the masses at bay (e.g. Adorno and Horkheimer, 1979), Gramsci argued that hegemony is riddled with contradictions. He argues that, in order to be effective, hegemony has to win the consent of the people. Thus, in order to 'woo' the masses, cultural institutions need to, on some level, incorporate elements that go against the grain or 'resist' the values and interests of the powerful. At the same time, Gramsci argued that people were simply not 'duped' by the hegemonic institutions but were also capable of critically resisting their logic.

In order to understand the philosophical basis of Willis's and Radway's understanding of resistance, it is useful to look at what Gramsci sees to be the origin of people's potential to resist. The origin of people's critical attitude towards power structures are located in what Gramsci calls 'good sense', which stands in opposition to 'common sense'. The difference between the two senses is encapsulated in this often cited passage from his prison notebooks:

> ... 'the active man-in-the-mass' has two theoretical consciousnesses: one which is implicit in his activity and which in reality unites him with his fellow-workers in the practical transformation of the real world; and one, superficially explicit or verbal, which he has inherited from the past and uncritically absorbed. (Gramsci, 1971: 333)

This Gramscian distinction between the good practical sense and the confused and contradictory common sense of the masses fleshes out the 'doubly-articulated' nature of experience, which is: (1) determined by social position, and (2) lived through ideological mediation (Grossberg, 1997: 217). What this means, is that, first, there are 'real' social structures. Second, that, on a level, people 'know' them via their practical experience of the world, which accounts for their resistance. Third, this practical knowledge of those structures gets obfuscated by ideology or hegemonic culture – which has its contradictions but mainly legitimates existing institutions – that mediates the relationship between people and the world. Thus, Radway argues that the grounds of Smithton women's resistance are located in their immediate or practical lived experience of dissatisfaction with non-nurturing relations with men, structured by patriarchy. Therefore, the women are not 'dupes' of reading romances, because of the escapism they provide. On the contrary, they read them because the reading addresses a 'real' problem. However, the reading does not provide a solution to patriarchal relationships but rather holds the women in a tension-riddled or 'imaginary' promise of true or nurturing romance. The same way, Willis argues that the lads' counter-school culture is not sheer maladjustment but lives against and reacts to the 'real' alienating aspects of school and commoditization of labour. However, this resistance, which is experienced as a kind of 'freedom' by the lads, in the end turns into a means of maintaining the labour structure (Willis, 1977: 137).

The methodological programme of critical, contextualist studies is, thus, driven by an interest in seriously studying the practices of the subjugated groups, such as misbehaviour at school or reading romances, which may appear trivial or foolish. Studying them seriously means studying them from the point of view of how they resist real structures of oppression, such as alienation of school or patriarchal interpersonal relations. However, the value of this resistance is also evaluated against an assessment of, whether this resistance changes those structures of oppression or not. The frequent answer to this question is that resistance ends up imaginary and not changing the structures, which it opposes. This approach has its undeniable insights in that it recognizes the meaningfulness of people's actions; yet, it also critically analyzes the way in which these actions may be rendered relatively futile.

However, the problem with this approach to resistance is that it presumes the scholar to be able to know what 'real' structures people are resisting. Thus, even if the scholars studying resistance posit that people's actions are meaningful, they also presume that the people themselves do not really know the meaning of their actions but that this needs to be discovered by the scholar. The trouble with this position is that it presumes that, whereas the 'people' are under the spell of cultural hegemony or ideology (such as sexism), the scholar is able to 'see' this reality clearly and correctly. This attitude does not cultivate critical self-reflexivity in the scholar, that is, it makes research blind to the ways in which the scholar's notion of 'real' structures of oppression are often heavily ideologically mediated, having their roots in the theoretical and political commitments driving the research.

Difficult distinctions

The question, whether scholars' interpretation of 'real' structures of oppression tells more about their theoretical and political commitments than about the structures, has been raised by Marcus (1986) and Ang (1996) in relation to the works of Willis and Radway. As these critical discussions of these specific works are of general methodological relevance, I will discuss them at some length.

Marcus praises Willis for his unusual and ambitious aim to bridge the micro and the macro. He argues that the strength of Willis is the way in which he does a careful, situated ethnography on the 'local' (the school) and, then, makes a creative leap to look at this local from another perspective (the workplace or the factory), which enables him to make the local or the 'lifeworld' to say something about the operation of the 'system' or structures of labour (Marcus, 1986: 171). Yet, Marcus argues that Willis's study also illustrates the problems in this kind of attempt to study the link between the particular and the general. His main criticism of Willis is that the study tends to use the ethnography on the 'lads' to authenticate the Marxist framework, driving the study.

Marcus argues that Willis's tendency to read his theory into, or from, the lads' behaviour is manifested, for example, by the structure of the book. The book is split into two parts. The first part focuses on the ethnography, being strife with vivid descriptions of the lads' parlance and pranks; the second part, 'analysis', is a theoretical discussion of the lads' behaviour from a general theoretical perspective. This structuring produces two orders of meaning. First there is the 'material' and, then, there is the interpretation what this material 'really' means. The fact that there may be a disjuncture between the material and the interpretation of its 'real' meaning is illustrated by the fact that, when Willis presented his study to the lads, they enjoyed listening to his description of the pranks but did not recognize themselves in his theoretical discussion on labour structures.

A further problem Marcus finds in Willis's work is the way in which Willis ends up choosing the 'lads' for further study. Willis's interest in the dozen rowdy lads – and particularly the outspoken and rambunctious Spanksey – can be argued to be driven by a classical notion of the white, working-class, rebellious subject that underpins much leftist social scientific thinking. The force of this frame is illustrated by the fact that Willis ignores any in-depth study of the middle-class or working-class conformist boys – the 'ear'oles' – who tend to become reified as representing the 'system'.

In a similar vein, Ang (1996) has criticized Radway for reading her rationalist feminist framework into the Smithton women's behaviour, or rendering them 'embryonic feminists' (Ang, 1996: 103). According to Ang, Radway sees romance reading to serve a 'therapeutic' function; it provides a literal escape from the demands of housewife and mother and also symbolically gratifies women's psychological need for nurturance (98). Ang attacks these distinctions between 'real' oppression and 'imaginary' or therapeutic and consoling satisfaction. She argues that this distinction makes Radway bypass the main force that drives women to read romances: the titillating luxuriating in the moments of seducing and being seduced (105). Radway belittles this titillating pleasure, which ends up seeming a poor substitute for the 'real' thing, which is feminist challenging of patriarchal structures. Ang notes that the problem with this posture is that Radway ends up reading the Smithton women from the point of view of her rational feminist framework, instead of opening up a dialogue for mutual learning that would admit that Radway may also have something to learn from non-feminist women who 'may have more expertise and experience in the meanings, pleasures and dangers of romanticism' (107).

The methodological lessons learnt from these studies and their critiques are threefold. First, Willis's lads and the Smithton women may be guided in their actions by ideologies or social frames, such as working-class 'hands-on' machismo and romances. These ideologies may have their subversive and pleasurable aspects as well as counterproductive effects to the people's everyday lives and in terms of consolidating structures of labour and patriarchy. Yet, Willis's and Radway's research are also guided by ideologies, namely Marxist labour-theory and rationalist feminism, respectively. These frameworks direct the scholar's focus, so that (s)he is likely to discover things that fit her/his framework (such as the reproduction of labour or patriarchy) and omit those that do not. This points to the fact that there is no scientific 'objective' position beyond ideology, and relinquishing that positivist fantasy may make us more prone to critically reflect on those frames that mediate our interpretation of our objects of study.

Second, and related to the first point, Willis and Radway both, to some extent, jam the experience of the schoolboys and suburban women to their political and theoretical frames. As a consequence, they may not be open to some of the texture and nuance of the lived worlds of the boys and women, particularly not to those aspects that would challenge their frames, such as the experience of the conformist boys or the titillating pleasures of romancing. This 'missing' or losing of lived experience in translation is the criticism new ethnography has raised against traditional forms of research. The main criticism of new ethnography has been that the traditional research posture, which claims that the scholar 'knows' the people better than they do, may end up producing scholarship that tells more about the theoretical and political agendas driving the research than the people being studied.

Third, there is an interesting dimension to Willis's and Radway's studies, which point towards the more recent research approaches to study experience in a way that situates it as part of a wider social landscape of other locales and activities. Both Willis and Radway contextualize the specific topic they investigate, namely school behaviour and reading romances, by resorting to another perspective, which in Willis's case is the factory and in Radway's case the gendered interpersonal relations. This broadens the study in that, looked at from this other perspective, the phenomenon under investigation seems rather different. Looked at from the perspective of the boys ending up in factory-work, their school-pranks no longer seem so 'resistant'. Even if Radway does not study the women's relationships with their partners, she alludes to it, which raises questions about the 'resistant' nature of reading about the ideal nurturing hero.

This practice of looking at a phenomenon from several perspectives resembles recent multiperspectival, such as multi-sited and polyvocal, research approaches, which will be touched upon later in this chapter and discussed in more detail in the subsequent chapters of this book, particularly in Chapter 9. However, the difference between the multi-sited studies and Willis's and Radway's research is that Willis and Radway tend to frame the other location (the factory and the human relations of the women) as being more 'real', or more important from a structural point of view, than the other one (school, reading romances). Constructing hierarchies between different sites is problematic as it denies the significance of certain activities or spheres of life. One should not declare that the subversive pleasures derived from consuming media, such as romances, is void of meaning unless it produces changes in heterosexual intimate relations (which Radway cannot really say, as she does not study the Smithton women's relationships, but see Radway, 1988 for a suggestion). It would be more fruitful to study how a phenomenon looks from different perspectives, locating it within the wider social context and illuminating its different, possibly resistant, subjugated and subjugating, dimensions. This call for examining of resistance within the larger context of different social forces and locations is the legacy and contribution of this critical approach to contemporary cultural and social research.

Textualist optimism

However, there is another way of studying resistance, which I have termed the optimist, textual approach. The studies by Willis and Radway paint a somewhat gloomy picture of social reality, where working-class boys and suburban homemakers both engage in 'resistant' activities which, nevertheless, get absorbed into supporting the structures that subjugate them in the first place. On the contrary, the studies done from the optimist, textual perspective have a rather upbeat aura, having faith in the efficacy of resistance to the point that they have been branded to embody a 'populist' version of cultural studies (McGuigan, 1992; Stabile, 1995).

John Fiske is one of the scholars who has given resistance a poignantly optimistic reading. His proliferate studies on resistance range from analyzing Madonna fans' interest in her overt sexuality (Fiske, 1989), college students' pleasures derived from watching the mocking depiction of family in *Married with Children* (Fiske, 1994a) to the interplay between the controversial TV-sitcom

Murphy Brown, the Anita Hill–Clarence Thomas hearings, LA riots and 1992 US elections won by Bill Clinton (Fiske, 1994b).

Unlike Willis and Radway, who temper their findings of resistance with a kind of 'reality check', Fiske emphasizes the importance of symbolic struggles. What this means is that he underlines that symbolic struggles are 'real'. For example, if a lower middle-class 'mod' dresses up in mock high-fashion gear, he should be interpreted as resisting symbolic structures that work through fashion. This challenge to a symbolic structure, such as fashion, should be acknowledged to be 'real' and significant, even if it does not challenge class structures (see Hebdige, 1977). Furthermore, Fiske has argued that symbolic struggles have wide political – or quite 'real', if you like – impacts (1994b: 2). To prove this point, Fiske has analyzed how the debates over the depiction of single motherhood in the TV-sitcom *Murphy Brown*, attacked by the Republican vice-president Dan Quayle, the hiatuses produced by the Hill–Thomas hearings and Rodney King beatings, accounted for Bill Clinton's victory in 1992.

In one of his classic studies, Fiske (1989) analyzes the resistant nature of Madonna and young girls' interpretations of her. In it he discusses an interview with a young fan, Lucy:

> She's tarty and seductive ... but it looks alright when she does it, you know, what I mean ... it's acceptable ... with anyone else it would be absolutely outrageous ...

> We can note a number of points here. Lucy can only find patriarchal words to describe Madonna's sexuality – 'tarty' and 'seductive' – but she struggles against the patriarchy inscribed in her own subjectivity. The opposition between 'acceptable' and 'absolutely outrageous' not only refers to representations of female sexuality, but is an externalisation of the tension felt by adolescent girls when trying to come to terms with the contradictions between a positive feminine view of their sexuality and the alien patriarchal one. (98)

In this discussion, Fiske defines Lucy's liking of Madonna as providing a space for her to explore an independent form of female sexuality that is neither just an object of male desire (whore) or of male discipline (madonna). This instance, where Lucy 'struggles' with why she likes Madonna's tartiness is, for Fiske, resistance. He does not see any reason to resort to some outside 'check' to establish the effects of this resistance, such as studying how Lucy behaves in her sexual relations. It is the symbolic work that Lucy performs, liking and trying to articulate why she likes Madonna's challenging sexuality better than some others, that counts as resistance.

Fiske's Madonna-study, and his research on resistance over all, has provoked much criticism, to the point that he has become a bête noire in cultural studies, argued to epitomize the 'banality' of a certain line of inquiry on resistance (Morris, 1990). The criticisms of Fiske can broadly be understood to be targeted at three dimensions in his work, namely, his decontextualist method, his politics, and his tendency to render 'Lucy' as ventriloquist of his agenda.

The claim that Fiske's studies lack analysis of wider context boils down to the difference between someone like Fiske and Willis. Commentators (e.g. Nightingale, 1992) have argued that Fiske's study is spurious, based on a fleeting interview with a young woman, from which he draws grand conclusions. Thus, the both broader and deeper attention that Willis and Radway pay to the people they are studying makes their research better grounded in the complexities of their everyday lives, which then reveals contradictions that emerge when one pierces through the surface appearance of some resistant activity, such as pranks.

It is true that contextualizing the phenomenon one is studying, may give a richer or more multidimensional understanding of it. However, as discussed above, arguing that the fact that a resistant activity, like media-consumption, is 'ineffective', because it does not change other structures of dominance, denies the activity in question its significance. One could say that Fiske may extrapolate too much – in terms challenging structures of patriarchy – from Lucy's fleeting comment about tarts. Still, one could also say that stating that Lucy's resistance is futile unless it changes structures of patriarchy or her life, is also reading too much into her words. The methodological truth might lie somewhere between these two positions, acknowledging that Lucy may indeed really resist stale notions of female sexuality through her interest in Madonna, while admitting that this is only a small part of Lucy's life and an even smaller part of the much larger puzzle of gender inequality.

However, one may need to qualify this methodological conclusion about Lucy by saying that the methodological and political appropriateness of any statement on resistance needs to be sensitive to individual contexts. Fiske's unfailing faith in the power of texts and his populist commitment to celebrate resistance tends to render his work annoyingly enthused, making it sound as if we have arrived at an era of buoyantly democratic media and society. Fiske's celebration of how homeless men 'resist' when watching the film *Die Hard* (Fiske, 1989), feels eerie against the background of the dire social and material situation of homeless people. This type of research may also direct attention away from pressing problems of social welfare. In this light, one can see the merits of Willis's and Radway's sobering analyses of the ways in which the structures of labour and patriarchy work against the resistance embedded in the school boys' pranks and women's romancing.

Still, in a different context, cultural analysis à la Fiske may be quite illuminative. My students find Fiske's work quite useful for explaining, for example, why rap music and style, with its baggy and glaring clothes and loud music, is so popular among Korean and Japanese youth, feeling constrained by the extremely competitive educational system and strict codes for dress and behaviour, with their militaristic undertones (also Yasuda, 2002). This behaviour may not transform the educational or military systems, but it does challenge the strictly assimilationist, and sometimes militaristic, cultural rules in everyday life, which may, or may not, indicate wider cultural and social transformations.

These kinds of subversions and pleasures should not be uncritically and spuriously celebrated, the way Fiske sometimes does. Yet, they do 'matter' in a way that is not captured by the idea of them as mere symbolic ripples on the surface of 'real' structures.

However, there is also a methodological trait that unites Fiske, Willis and Radway. This is a trait that Morris (1990), in relation to Fiske, has called 'ventriloquism'. Ventriloquism refers to Fiske's interpretative strategy, which presumes that while people may be doing interesting things, it is the scholar who is capable of deciphering the true meaning of these words and deeds, whereas the people themselves can never really comprehend what they are doing. Morris has in fact pointed out that even if Fiske claims that he is proving Madonna fans are not 'bimbos', he himself renders them bimbos, who are unaware of their doings. To some extent, ideologies always work 'behind our backs'. Yet, the dichotomous notion that people are 'outside of the true' and scholars 'within the true' makes research more likely to project its own agendas on people, that is, render them ventriloquists for their political agendas, whether it is populist feminism (Fiske), rationalist feminism (Radway) or Marxism (Willis). This problem is shared by all the different resistance studies, but it is not a problem specific to cultural studies but interlaces any positivist social scientific research. The challenge of trying to be true to other people's lived realities has never been adequately addressed within resistance-studies, but it has been the specific focus of new ethnographic modes of studying lived experience, which will be discussed in Chapter 3.

Contingent resistances

Based on the discussion of the critical, contextualist approach to resistance and the optimistic, textual one, one can conclude that they both are caught up in an imaginary, where resistance is claimed to either affect, or not to affect, the 'system'. Therefore, they both obey the logic of a vertical notion of power, where the 'bottom' or the local either is, or is not, understood to change the 'top' or the global/systemic. However, this type of notion of power tends to attribute too much to the activity in question. Therefore, to overcome this polarized and vertical mode of analysis, it may be fruitful to shift towards a more contingent or lateral notion of power and resistance. Instead of thinking whether a particular local resistance has systemic effects, it might be a better idea to explore what kind of specific effects it has, or how it relates to other issues, events and processes in different places and spheres of life.

One of the ways in which scholars in cultural studies have tried to come up with a more complex notion of resistance is through so-called theory of articulation. In rough terms, articulation refers to the process, where ideologies are produced out of possibly contradictory elements, which accounts for their complexity (see Laclau and Mouffe, 1985). This notion of ideology or discourse as an articulated amalgam has two theoretical and methodological insights that advance studying resistance.

First, by underlining the constructed and contingent nature of discourses, it shatters the essentialist tendency in some cultural studies to search for resistance in some particular and predictable places, such as white, male, working-class culture. Laclau and Mouffe argue that resistance does not emanate from a particular position (such as class position) but that this position has to be made to 'mean'. Furthermore, they argue that the idea that resistance is lodged in particular socioeconomic positions does not do justice to the multiplicity of power relations. Starting from Foucault's famous sentence, that 'where there is power, there is resistance' (Foucault, 1978: 95), articulation-theory pays attention to diverse forms of resistance – against sexism, racism, environmental destruction and so on. These different forms of resistances may also be more pertinent to particular areas of life, so that some forms of resistance may react to economic arrangements, others to emotional structures, and still others to cultural discourses, and sometimes a form of resistance intertwines many elements. What theory of articulation underlines is that there is no reason to determine, a priori, that one particular type of resistance is more important than others (more 'real' so to say) but that the importance of resistance needs to be evaluated in each context.

The second, and closely related, methodological lesson that articulation theory has to teach is that it draws attention to multiple forms of resistance and their contradictions. This encourages a more nuanced scholarship, which looks at lived experience and social discourses from multiple angles that illuminate different resistances and dominations. This more complex notion of discourse and identity might also push for more self-reflexive scholarship that acknowledges that, for instance, the Smithton women, may not only be resisting non-nurturing patriarchal relations with men, but their non-rational pleasures derived from romances may also be seen to resist or to antagonize rationalist feminism, represented by Radway.

The contingent notion of resistance is embodied, for instance, in some popular cultural studies collections that contain articles that present a panoply of contradicting views on phenomena, such as Madonna or pornography (Schwichtenberg, 1993; Dines and Humes, 1995). These collections illuminate, for example, the complex ways in which fans, haters, blacks, whites, men and women interpret Madonna. These analyses point at ways in which Madonna's image and its interpretations may acquire different meanings and get articulated to different politics in different places, getting intertwined with a host of political agendas that go beyond gender and sexuality, such as black religion, slavery and hyper-individualism. These collections paint a complex picture of the various politics, something like those Madonna articulates, pointing beyond the rather limited discussions of whether she is a sex object or subverts that position.

Contradictory local(es)

To give an example of a recent ethnography that, in a sense, applies or embodies the contingent notion of resistance one can look at Andy Bennett's (1999, 2000) study on rappers in Newcastle upon Tyne, a racially homogeneous (White) working-class town in the northeast of England. Bennett does not use the vocabulary of resistance-studies, but echoes of this tradition can be heard throughout his discussion. What makes Bennett's study interesting is the way in which he weaves or juxtaposes discussions of different aspects of Newcastle rap, and their resistant and dominant or interesting and problematic features. Bennett is clearly sympathetic towards the rappers, while also critically analyzing them, but he does not draw too clear-cut conclusions on, whether rap is resistant or dominant but rather lets the different views collide against one another.

His analysis focuses on two types of rappers in Newcastle: the black-identified and the white-identified. The black-identified rappers, congregating around a small local recordstore 'Groove', believe that black American rap is the only 'real' one. On the contrary, the white-identified ones work to come up with their own or 'Geordie' rap true to the local culture. The black-identified rappers, in a counterintuitive twist, argue that black music is truer to their identity as white working-class British, as Bennett illustrates:

> *Jeff*:   All the time before, white people were into black music, hip hop's just the same. There's a message in black music which translates for white working-class people.
>
> *A.B.*:   What's that?
>
> *Dave*:   It's about being proud of where you come from ...
>
> *Jim*:   The trend at the moment is to be real ... to rap in your own accent and talk about things close to you ... don't try to be American like. But that's why British hip hop will always be shite ... I went to New York ... It was brilliant, it changed my life. You can't talk about white hip hop, it doesn't exist. (Bennett, 1999: 11)

Starting from this counterintuitive posture, Bennett analyzes how this group relates to, and articulates, a series of social contradictions in Newcastle. On one level, preferring a black, American 'authentic' form of music, becomes a badge of cultural distinction for the group, defining them as aficionados or superior in relation to amateurs, who have an occasional or 'trendy' interest in rap. However, at the same time the association with blackness in a white town also becomes a stigma for the group, which, in the club and pub life of Newcastle, has to deal with deflected racist harassment, and name-calling, exemplified by the way in which the group is branded 'wiggers' (Bennett, 1999: 12). This further complicates the original meaning of 'wiggers', which usually refers to 'inauthentic' white people who appropriate black styles. This supposed 'inauthenticity' gets complicated in a nearly all-white town, such as Newcastle, where the group has to deal with very authentic racism that is projected upon them because of their stylistic affinity. To make matters even more complicated, this stigma of 'wiggers' is worn by the group as a kind of pride, an act of defiance, which sets them apart from other local youth, who are defined as racist, small-minded, small-town people, who are into 'crap commercial music and fashion stuff' (Bennett, 1999: 14).

As the discussion hopefully illustrates, instead of defining the Groove-rappers as necessarily resistant or dominant or dominated, Bennett evaluates how they attach themselves to diverse local and global agendas, appearing differently in different lights. Thus, affinity with black music may be a bid for distinction that separates the 'true' aficionados from 'trendy' consumers. However, this affinity may also provoke local townspeople to harass the group, in a decidedly racist fashion, which complicates the idea that these people are simply 'using' black culture to construct their own identities. Still, the identification with blacks can also serve to construct the group as worldly or superior in relation to the presumably parochial and small-minded people, in a sense denying the group members' association with the provincial working-class town of Newcastle, the cultural and social status of which in the English hierarchy of towns is decidedly low.

In a similar fashion, Bennett also discusses the contradictions of white-identified rappers and also rappers in Frankfurt am Main, where rap originates from the local US bases and gets articulated to the experiences of Turkish immigrants. All in all, Bennett's study illustrates a mode of studying resistance in a way that is sensitive to its contradictions and avoids too clear celebratory or lamenting stances.

Bennett's study is also an example of a context-sensitive study, in that it illustrates how rap forms part and parcel of local and global issues and struggles, which, in a sense, melts away the division between real and symbolic resistance. Thus, when black-identified rappers in Newcastle get harassed by racists, when the rappers themselves rebuke locals as parochial White trash, and when Turkish immigrant rappers attack neo-fascism in Germany, it becomes obvious that rap, as a cultural form, gets intertwined with politics that articulate concerns that spill over into different areas of life, such as racism, regional and class differences, and new right politics and violence. Still, the point is not to argue that resistance challenges everything (or nothing). Rather, the task is to analyze what issues or structures of inequality, specifically, a particular type of resistance in a particular place and time challenges. Resistance may, or may not, challenge cultural, racial, sexual or economic inequalities, or all four of them. Resistance in a particular time and place is often intertwined with events and processes in other places, and a good way of assessing the social networks in which a particular activity happens is to study its connections with other places and events. It is difficult to assess the impact of a particular form of resistance on wider social structures of inequality. Thus, instead of celebrating the efficacy of resistance or lamenting its futility, a contingent notion of resistance asks research to investigate what exactly does it do.

Conclusions

The analysis of lived resistance in cultural studies tends to fall into two camps. The first, critical contextualist approach tends to evaluate resistance, such as deriving subversive pleasures from media products, in terms of, whether it changes 'real' social structures. This approach often ends up on a sobering note about the ineffectiveness of resistance. The second, textualist, optimist approach argues that symbolic resistance, such as the consumption of, for example, subversive images of gender or sexuality, is 'real', as it transforms culture and can have further spill-over effects. This line of inquiry often ends up being quite optimistic about the possibilities of resistance and social change. The third, contingent approach to resistance mediates between and beyond these two approaches. It acknowledges that symbolic resistance may, or may not, have wider effects, but that symbolic effects are 'real' also. It calls for an analysis of resistances, in the plural, that is sensitive to different forms of resistance and subordination, which evaluates their implications against the local and social contexts. Thus, instead of studying whether a particular resistance transforms a particular 'system' of social inequality, which may be difficult to assess, a more contingent notion of resistance asks, in a more down-to-earth manner, scholarship to investigate what a particular form of resistance does.

Exercise 2

- Choose a lived experience that you think of as 'resistant' (this could be anything from liking certain popular cultural forms to school or consumer behaviours). Do a mini-research on this experience, conduct an interview or observe an event or a situation. Based on your research, what elements of this experience would you identify as 'resistant' and 'dominant'?
- Think of different forms of resistance. Is the activity you are investigating resisting in terms of, for example: (1) lifestyles and behaviours; (2) cultural ideologies; (3) social institutions; (4) political or economic structures? Evaluate whether the kind of resistant behaviour you are studying has an impact or not.
- Bear in mind that what is seen as 'resistance' often tells about the researcher's own political fantasies. Think carefully what makes you deem certain ideas or actions as 'resistant'. Outline a way of further studying the experience from the points of view of different people or in several locations, in order to be sensitive to alternative, multiple, and possible contradictory, forms of resistance. Think how you could be sensitive to complexity and avoid producing simplistic dichotomies between resistance and dominance.

3

New Ethnography and Understanding the Other

Main questions

- **What different strategies new ethnography uses, in order to be 'truer' to the lived realities of other people?**
- **How can self-reflexivity enhance our understanding of other people? What are its pitfalls?**
- **Why is it important to be attentive to the plurality of lived realities or voices (polyvocality)?**
- **How does an examination of social inequality complement new ethnography? How does it help to make particular lived realities speak for wider social issues? How does it help to illuminate their partial and political nature? How can new ethnography help to add nuance to analysis of social inequality?**

'New ethnography', as a term, refers to forms of social and cultural inquiry that have taken seriously the charge that social sciences have depicted the people being studied, particularly disenfranchised groups, such as working-class youth or non-Western people, in ways that do not do justice to their sense of reality (e.g. Clifford and Marcus, 1986). Even if the name implies so, new ethnography is not necessarily defined by its use of the ethnographic method, and people working within the paradigm may use a variety of research tools, including ethnography, life-story interviews and autobiography. Rather, the defining feature of new ethnography is its commitment to be 'truer' to lived realities of other people. As such, new ethnography usually challenges concepts – such as 'resistance' – that social research uses to categorize or label individuals. It argues that these labels do not reflect the lived realities of the people being studied but often render them supporting evidence for the scholar's theoretical or political frameworks or projects.

The two-faced project of new ethnography – of being true to different lived experiences and to critically interrogate concepts that we have used to categorize those experiences – translates to two research orientations within the approach. The first is a hermeneutic or phenomenological quest to understand different lived worlds. The second is a poststructuralist aim to unravel discourses that mediate our understanding of both the internal lived and the external social worlds. Referring to Chapter 1, the 'understanding' strand of new ethnography corresponds to 'dialogic validity', which evaluates research in terms of how well it manages to capture different realities. The poststructuralist endeavour corresponds to deconstructive validity, which evaluates research in terms of how well it challenges, or is aware of, social and political discourses that underpin the way in which we view lived and social realities. The two approaches, underpinning new ethnographic research, create a tension within new ethnography between being close or true to a different lived reality, and being aware of its always partial and political nature. Throughout this chapter I will address the difficult balancing act of being true to the lived and being aware of the commitments and limits of its 'truth'. However, this chapter tilts more towards the understanding or 'dialogic' side of the new ethnographic project. The following Chapter 4 focuses on ways of studying how social discourses permeate lived experiences and the ways in which we can study them.

In what follows, I will first briefly discuss the phenomenological idea that one can only understand the Other through reflecting on its similarity to, and difference from, the Self, which underpins the 'understanding' aspect of new ethnography and accounts for its characteristic personable and reflective nature. In the subsequent three sections I will discuss, in detail, the central tenets of new ethnography, which roughly parallel my earlier discussion on dialogic validity and its three central features: truthfulness to different lived realities, critical self-reflection on one's own commitments, and attentiveness to multiple lived realities or voices (polyvocality). However, taken literally, the aim to be truthful to different lived realities leads us to relativism or the idea that any perspective is as good or laudable as any other. Therefore, in the fourth section – and through a discussion on the controversy over the supposed 'bias' or 'inaccuracy' of Rigoberta Menchú's testimony on Guatemalan genocide – I suggest that any lived reality needs to be evaluated against the wider social context and its structures of inequality. Complementing the quest to capture lived realities with a more traditional attention to social analysis, makes the lived speak for wider social issues as well as illuminates its partial and political nature as well as its relative importance. In the last section I will illustrate how to both take social structures of inequality seriously and to complicate the way in which we have become accustomed to understanding those structures, drawing on my research on anorexic women, whose stories tease out the contradictory politics embedded in the notion of the anorexic as a relatively privileged middle-class 'goody girl'.

Between Self and Other

Traditionally, social and cultural research has considered 'objectivity' to be a virtue in research, whether one studies social structures or lived experiences of people. This positivist approach to researching experience was apparent, for example, in the way in which the scholars, informed by the notion of 'resistance', sorted people's experiences into either 'resistance' or subjugation to dominant ideologies. Particularly since the 1980s, however, the positivist research enterprise has come under attack, and, for example, postcolonial and feminist critics have questioned ethnographers' ability to 'truthfully' describe other people's experiences. These criticisms have pointed out that social research often ends up using the lived lives of other people to justify and prove some of the grand narratives of our times, ranging from colonialism to Marxism and liberal humanist feminism (see Clifford and Marcus, 1986).

Starting from these criticisms, new ethnography has sought ways of studying people's lived lives in a way that would do better justice to the way in which the people see themselves and their worlds. The idea of getting the 'emic' or native's point of view right has traditionally been the goal of social and particularly ethnographic research. However, new ethnography does not claim to capture the people's view 'right' from the outside, but aims to be faithful to people's lived perspectives. The quest to be truer to different lived realities, and the acknowledgement that we can never grasp them 'objectively, has led new ethnographic research to appropriate the phenomenological 'method' of analyzing other people's experiences by reflecting on how they are similar to, and different from, our own (e.g. Maso, 2001). Thus, one of the characteristic features of new ethnographic pieces of work is a dialogic shifting between the scholar's Self and the perspective of the Other people being studied. The first aim of this shifting of perspectives is to become aware of the personal and social baggage that hinders our comprehension of different experiences. Second, becoming critically aware of the limits of our own understanding fosters a sensitivity or openness towards possibly radically different lived worlds.

Another characteristic feature of new ethnography, as well as phenomenology, is that it is particularly interested in modes of experiencing the world, such as emotions (Douglas, 1977; Ellis, 1991), embodiment (Merleau-Ponty, 1962) or the sacred (Buber, 1970; Levinas, 1985), which have often been neglected by rationalistically orientated modes of social scientific inquiry. One of the arguments of the paradigm is that these non-rational ways of relating to the world often correspond to the realities of disenfranchised groups, such as women or non-Western people, and have been silenced by the Western, white male focus on rationality. Subsequently new ethnography has developed modes of study and writing that aim to be truer to the emotional and embodied forms of knowledge. Together with the emphasis on non-objective or dialogic modes of understanding, the focus on non-rational aspects of experience has translated into personable, reflective and prose-like modes of writing, to the extent that a different form of writing has become a trademark of new ethnography.

However, sometimes new ethnography's focus on the intense and intimate particularity of lived experiences may make the social world fade into the background. This produces two methodological problems. First, unless we pay attention to social structures of inequality, we have no basis for arguing, why a particular lived reality may be considered 'silenced', or why certain experiences are more worthy of attention than others. This myopia may lead to positions that do not have a sense of proportion, so that 'having English as a second language' is seen as equally 'oppressive' as institutionalized racism and poverty (see Freire and Macedo, 1996 on Ellsworth, 1989). Keeping an eye on the social context, in making sense of neglected lived realities, puts them in perspective. It illuminates the partiality and relative importance of lived views but also makes them speak for, and against, the wider social context that has rendered them silenced or marginalized in the first place.

The second methodological problem that can accrue, if one does not pay attention to the social nature of lived realities, is that one treats them as if an unique way of relating to the world. If one does not acknowledge that lived experiences are always thoroughly mediated by social, institutional and popular discourses, one may end up rehashing familiar stories on bodily scandal or personal intrigue as 'authentic' or previously silenced views, the way day-time talk-shows do (e.g. Denzin, 1992; Shelton, 1995; Clough, 1997, 2000; Atkinson and Silverman, 1997; Gubrium and Holstein, 1997). The way in which individual lived experience is always interlaced with social discourses will be explored in more detail in Chapter 4, however, keeping in mind the always social and political, and never innocent or universal, nature of experience is important in any kind of research on lived realities.

Being truer to lived realities

To begin to unpack how new ethnography goes about being truer to lived experiences I will turn to two works that illustrate somewhat different research strategies. The first one is Lather and Smithies' book on women with HIV/AIDS (Lather and Smithies, 1997), which radiates a sense of affinity and closeness with the women. The second one, Ginsburg's study on pro-life and pro-choice women (Ginsburg, 1998 [1989]), on the contrary, is predicated on a sense of difference or 'alterity' both between the two groups of women as well as the author and the women. As both works are similarly committed to being true to the experience of the women they are studying, their differences gives one an idea of two different ways of doing justice to the lived worlds of others.

Lather has written extensively on critical, poststructuralist and feminist new ethnography (Lather, 1991, 1993, 2001). Despite her poststructuralist bent, her work on women with HIV/AIDS, has a strong dialogic emphasis on conducting the research on the women's terms. Involving the people being studied in the research process is relatively common in new ethnography, forming part of the quest to do justice to different realities. Some scholars have gone as far as suggesting that scholars should share the authorship, or at least royalties, with the people they study (Lincoln, 1995). More typically, involving people in the study refers to consulting with the research participants during or after the research process, in order to ensure that what is being written, more or less, corresponds to people's view of the world (in traditional qualitative research this is referred to as 'member check' (Denzin, 1989).

In Lather and Smithies' case, being true to the people they studied meant that they honoured the women's wish that the research would produce an accessible book that would break the silence on women with HIV/AIDS and offer support and information to people with the condition. The final book, *Troubling angels*, fulfils the women's wishes in that it is relatively accessible, and its main focus is on the dense personal stories of the women that tackle issues of importance to them, from healthcare to people's attitudes, partners, children, sex and fear of dying.

However, below the women's stories, there runs a parallel story on Lather and Smithies' reflections on their study. Some of the pages also contain 'factoid-boxes' with information on HIV/AIDS, its transmission, treatment, statistics and so on, and interspersed between the main text there are art work and poems on angels. The aim of the unconventional, multivocal textual strategy is to break away from the traditional research reporting style, where the people's words are followed by the scholar's 'scientific' interpretation of them. Putting the scholars' reflections to the bottom accomplishes two things. First, it aims to let the women's stories speak for themselves. Second, it makes it visible that the stories are not timeless truths but makes it explicit that they are told from a particular point of view as well as connect them to other issues and information (Lather, 2001). The different strands of the text also allow one to read women and HIV/AIDS from the point of view of personal stories, scholarly reflections, medical and policy facts and analysis as well as from a contemplative perspective through the angel-artwork.

To illustrate what the stories are like I will turn to the story of Lisa, who transmitted HIV to her son Alex, when pregnant:

Chris: So he started having some deterioration around eighteen months.
Lisa: Yes, that's when his counts really fell. That's when I quit work. Four or five months later I quit school because he was doing all

> right. He had gone in for a surgery for a feeding tube while he was
> still pretty healthy and that enabled us to do homecare.
>
> *Chris*: And you were providing this care?
>
> *Lisa*: Yes. He would have bad days, but he would still have good days
> when we would go to McDonald's and it wouldn't hurt him to
> move. We did a lot of travelling. When he felt good, nothing got in
> the way. And when he felt bad, we sat on the couch and did what-
> ever he wanted to do for one day or two days or for five days if
> that's what it took. (Lather and Smithies, 1997: 91)

Below this personal story the authors' reflections at the bottom connect the issue of pregnancy to wider concerns. Chris Smithies discusses – in great medical detail and with statistics – the various treatments available to HIV positive women, who become pregnant, and also points out the fact that these treatments are too expensive for most HIV positive women, who live in the Third World. It also critically discusses the general view that HIV positive women, who become pregnant, are irresponsible as well as the therapeutic services available for children, whose parents or themselves are infected.

The unusual text of Lather and Smithies teaches three methodological lessons. First, Lisa's story on Alex illustrates the fact that it would be impossible to convey the intensely moving and sad feelings that are being evoked by this narrative, using traditional scientific reporting. This underlines the fact that modes of study and writing are always political, as the supposedly 'objective' genre of scientific reporting leaves entire areas and dimensions of life outside of its ambit. Second, the underlying text by Smithies works to connect Lisa's story to wider medical, social and global dimensions of pregnancy and HIV. As such it expands the personal towards the wider political. At the same time, Smithies' personal reflections on exchanges she has had with people on HIV and pregnancy, render the narrator and the context of narration visible, so that Lisa's story emerges as written from the specific point of view. Third, despite the multiple splits of the text, Lisa's narrative shines through the text as an evocative truth about having a child with HIV. This accounts for the power of the story. However, the strong reality-effect that the text creates, makes the reader take it for a 'truth' on HIV-mothers. None of the surrounding texts destabilize Lisa's testimony, thereby, not raising the possibility that this might be a very particular account and there may be radically different stories on HIV and children.

Faye Ginsburg's study on pro-life and pro-choice women underline the importance of this third point, raising the question of how to be true to lived realities, when those realities set forth irreconcilable truths. Whereas Lather and Smithies' work is characterized by a commitment to take the women's opinions into account at all stages of research, from planning to getting feedback on the final product, Ginsburg does not involve the women in her research in a way that could be termed 'participatory'. Working in a situation marked by political tension between the two groups she is studying, Ginsburg could not really turn into an advocate of either of the groups. Rather, her goal was to gain the trust and respect of the women by presenting a 'balanced' view of them, which was also in line with her aim to make sense of the issue of abortion from both sides of the fence (also Gille, 2001).

Most critical/cultural ethnographies focus on subordinated groups, which may be considered 'nice' or worthy of political support. The extraordinary aspect of Ginsburg's work is that she takes the challenge of studying a group of women, pro-lifers, who are considered anti-feminist. In this antagonistic situation, Ginsburg tries to understand the world from the point of view of these women and to communicate the 'counter-intuitive' fact that these women, perceived as foes of feminism, saw themselves defending female values of care, nurturance and selflessness against violent masculine competitiveness and materialism. This is exemplified by her account of Karen's story:

> ... [Karen's right to life activism] articulates a critique of materialism and sexual inequality in American society. For her abortion signifies a social denial of nurturance, defined as a quality acquired through the activities of caretaking.

> I think we've accepted abortion because we're a very materialist society and there is less time for caring. To me it's all related. Housewives don't mean much because we do the caring and the mothering kinds of things which are not as important as a nice house or a new car. I think it's a basic attitude we've had for some time now. (Ginsburg, 1998[1989]: 185)

Ginsburg (1997) tells how she initially tried to 'translate' these experiences into language that would make them plausible for mostly left-liberal anthropologists, by emphasizing their pro-feminine and anti-materialist aspects. She notes that this was also what pro-life women hoped she would do, seeing her as a vehicle for getting their agenda to otherwise inaccessible audiences. However, Ginsburg decided to counter this 'mistaken identification' between her and pro-life women, not only because she did not want to be seen as having turned into their 'advocate', but also because she did not want to expropriate them into her own agenda but to respect the integrity of their stance (296).

In the final book, the stories of the pro-life and pro-choice women are each allowed their own, parallel speaking power in consecutive chapters. Thus the caring of the pro-life women is contrasted with the caring of the pro-choice women, who see their reward being when women, who have come to the clinic, thank them for making a difference in their life and being 'so warm, and so caring and so non-judgemental' (Ginsburg, 1998[1989]: 155). The women's stories are complemented with analyses of populist movements in America and the historical developments that have brought about the separate and unequal spheres of public freedom and private nurturance that structure the women's stories. Much like in Lather and Smithies' work, the life-stories of the women occupy centre-stage. The contextualizing narratives help to connect these stories to wider social issues, such as the fact that, in their own different ways, both groups of women want to ameliorate the inequality of women in a society still structured by stark division between the public and the private.

The way in which Lather and Smithies and Ginsburg have conducted and written their studies is rather different. However, both works do a remarkable job in being true to the lived experience of the women they have studied. One could say that Lather and Smithies stay even closer to the women's embodied experience than Ginsburg, but, as a consequence, their stories end up also being too close to coming across as the sole truth on an experience, which neglects other points of view. Ginsburg's style of doing and writing research is more detached and contextualizing or historicizing, but she does an enviable job in both doing justice to the women's worlds as well as exposing their partiality. As such, the two works illustrate two different modes of being true to lived lives that have slightly different styles, strengths and weaknesses, but which both more than reach the new ethnographic goal of doing justice to the texture of lived lives from the people's point of view.

Self-reflexivity

The counterpart to being true to Other realities in new ethnography is to be critically aware of the way in which one's Self and its commitments shape the research. Self-reflexivity is not a new invention, and in the 'older' forms of ethnography it was seen as a means to undo the scholar's bias (Hammersley and Atkinson, 1995). However, the new ethnographic project argues against the possibility of 'unbiased' scholarship, and views reflexivity as a tool to enhance awareness of our situatedness and, subsequently, to be more receptive to perspectives that approach the world from a different position.

Lather and Smithies as well as Ginsburg critically reflect on their self and their social and political commitments and preconceptions, in order to do better justice to the women they are studying. I will not, however, continue discussing their research. Rather, I move on to discuss the works of two famous anthropologists, with a new ethnographic orientation, namely Michael Jackson and Marjorie Shostak. The reason why I have chosen to focus on these two authors is that they both reflect on a rarely discussed issue, which is located at the heart of any anthropological field experience in the South: the interested nature of the relationship between the scholar and her/his informants and the enormous disparity in wealth and privilege that interlace this relationship. Jackson (1998) reflects on this issue in relation to his Sierra Leonian informant Noah, and Shostak's discusses it in a sequel to her landmark book on the life of a !Kung woman Nisa (Shostak, 1983, 2000).

Starting to think back to his relationship, several decades ago, with his Sierra Leonian informant and translator Noah, Jackson (1998) notes that despite his own initial near total dependence on him, Noah tended to look up to Jackson with a mixture of respect and expectation:

> Noah saw me as a 'mentor' (*yugi*) – someone in whom he had 'placed his hope', who could teach him to drive a vehicle, pay his way, rescue him from hardship, and ultimately help him travel abroad. (100)

Jackson notes that he often felt uncomfortable with Noah's demands and his assigned role as a protector and, thinking further back, admitted that he often also felt irritated by what he considered Noah's 'vagary'. However, trying to make sense of these feelings, Jackson critically reflects on his own motivations and expectations:

> With my first year of fieldwork passing all too quickly, I often became irritated by [Noah's] lassitude and distractedness – my way of construing the fact that he was not constantly at my beck and call. (105)

Jackson's story on the tension-riddled relationship between him and Noah, which eventually broke their friendship, covers a lot of terrain, discussing their family-histories and cultural differences. However, in a pivotal sentence, which is both critically self-reflexive and utterly political, Jackson encapsulates what went wrong with him and Noah:

> These were our failings. They reflected our idiosyncratic personalities as well as our different cultural backgrounds. And they reflected the structures of colonialism, the long shadows of which still fell across West Africa in the late 1960s. (103)

This sentence dislodges the interpersonal relationships between Jackson and Noah from the familiar realm of personal strife, locating it within the wider context of colonialist relations. Jackson's discussion of his irritation with Noah's insidious expectations and general 'lassitude' brings into mind common Western conceptions of people from the South, familiar from countless novels, travelogues and, perhaps, from our personal experiences of contact with people from less privileged circumstances. However, Jackson turns the tables on these conceptions by exposing the way in which they are lodged in colonial expectations of services and dutifulness from the 'natives' and concomitant asking for special favours from the white man. Thus, the story uses self-reflection in an exemplary manner to pierce through historical and power-laden social tropes and arrangements that impinge on our understanding of other people. It allows us not only to become aware of the limited nature of our own understanding and to get a glimpse of a radically different reality but it also unravels the heinous power structures that mediate between the two.

However, self-reflection is no panacea for wrestling out of our preconceptions, but it may, sometimes, turn into a vehicle of validating one's worldview. This happens for instance, in Marjorie Shostak's sequel to her acclaimed book on the life of a !Kung woman Nisa (Shostak, 1983, 2000). Shostak's return to

Botswana is, in part, informed by her desire to heal from breast cancer, but it also makes her revisit the publication of *Nisa* (1983), after which she had fulfilled her promise to send cows for Nisa. One of the threads that run through the book is very similar to the topic tackled by Jackson, that is, Shostak's unease with Nisa's demands for more gifts. As illustrated by a quote from her journal:

> But Nisa just seems to have so little compassion, at least for me. He's smart, and self-promoting, and able to ask for what she needs. But we never get beyond that. When she 'sweet-talks' me, it's about how much I've done for her. She likes me because I have rewarded her for our work. She has no idea of what I feel. I don't even think she likes me in any real sense. (2000: 181)

Shostak's story telling, characterized by personable reflection on her attempts to understand Nisa and on the friendship between two women from poignantly different worlds, captures some of Nisa's uniqueness instead of reducing her into an anthropological exemplar. Yet, despite her self-reflection, Shostak remains lodged in an understanding of female friendship in rather white, middle-class Western terms of sisterly sharing, rapport, and 'giving for free' (also McConnell, 2000). Shostak's investment in a second wave feminist trust in a shared female humanity or sisterhood has been pointed out by Clifford (1986), in relation to her previous work on Nisa. It reveals the problematic aspect of the presumption, partly deriving from a particular reading of the phenomenological tradition, that there are certain states of mind or emotions, such as 'friendship', that are universal or shared by all of humankind. It neglects the idea that the way we experience intense and intimate feelings, such as being friends or in love, may be profoundly different in different cultures, contexts and between individuals from different backgrounds.

Donna Haraway has, indeed, argued that self-reflexivity is a 'bad trope', because it gives the impression that it gives us access to a 'truer' knowledge of the world (Haraway, 1997: 16). If self-reflexivity becomes an occasion for the scholar to dwell on her/his sentiments, without critically interrogating them, it may end up lending emotional or existential credibility to her/his preconceptions, as happens in Shostak's case. However, interpreted critically, it enables the scholar to become acutely aware of the always situated and limited nature of her/his worldview, thereby, opening up space for different interpretations of other people's as well as our own realities.

Polyvocality

However, any attempt to be truer to a lived experience needs to bear in mind that lived experiences and realities are many. Studying lived experience or voices in plural, rather than in singular enriches new ethnography in two main ways. First, it gives a 'fairer' account of the phenomenon under study, illuminating it from the perspectives of different 'stakeholders' (Lincoln and Guba, 1985). Second, contrasting several, potentially contradicting, lived realities, helps to overcome the temptation to think of a particular lived experience as the 'truth' on a matter and to do justice to the specificity of each experience, while bearing in mind their particularities.

While attentiveness to multiple perspectives or voices, or 'polyvocality', can enrich many kinds of research projects, it can be particularly illuminative when investigating topics, interlaced with deep controversy or polarized opinions. I have already discussed Ginsburg's study on pro-choice and pro-life women, which effectively interrupts the common-sense notion of pro-lifers as 'foes of feminism'. Another example is Kathleen Jones' book (2000) on the killing of her white, female student, Andrea, by her black boyfriend, Andrés, which, through looking at the event from multiple perspectives, aims to go beyond the familiar story on Martyrs and Monsters, plaguing media coverage, and even feminist politics, on domestic violence.

Jones is drawn to study the life and death of Andrea through her role as the head of the women's studies department, where she studied, and having to organize the political and personal aftermath of her killing, including press conferences, student counselling, and memorial events. Serving as a connection point for different people and institutions that had crossed paths with Andrea allowed Jones to get a glimpse of her multiple lives or multiple Andreas, as captured in the description of her funeral:

> Now, other sides of Andrea came into focus. They were boldly reflected in a display of memorabilia her mother had brought from home, and heightened by the words of speaker after speaker from parts of Andrea's life not ordinarily conversant with one another. ... Together they provided cacophonous evidence of the personae of Andrea: the pictures of her as a girl with many pets; ... fashion photos of Andrea dressed in any number of haute couture outfits; Andrea standing by the Santa Cruz coast, her normally flowing red curly hair twisted into 'dreds'; Andrea proudly displaying her crafts – her silver mermaid pins and multicoloured beaded bracelets; Andrea in camping gear and Andrea in vamping gear; Andrea posed before the Women's Resource Center sign; and baseball-capped, T-shirted Andrea, tired smile on her face, birds-eye camera-angle framing her one more time in the room of the student center where she had hidden her backpack of belongings and slept away from her boyfriend on nights when it got too difficult at home. (2000: 27)

What this quote exemplifies, is that polyvocality does not only have to mean resorting to different individual or group perspectives, but can also be applied to make sense of the multiple voices that speak through any individual's lived experience. In this respect one can refer to Bakhtin's notion of dialogic characters, which are complex personas that invite the reader into their experience and to listen to the multiple social accents that speak through them (Bakhtin, 1981; also Volosinov, 1973). Bakhtin contrasts dialogic characters to monologic ones, which are flat or one-dimensional figures that fulfil one social function

in the text, such as 'the hero' in the chivalric story. One can say that many
positivist works produce monologic characters, as they tend to reduce experience
to a 'cause', such as 'victim personality' in the case of domestic abuse. What new
ethnography tries to do is to get and give a more nuanced and multifaceted
picture of individual experience so that Andrea cannot be pigeonholed as a
victim or a die-hard feminist, a girl with dreds, pets, or in fashion outfits.
Rather, as Jones concludes, she is 'a nineties' girl' who can be all those things
and more.

However, studying Andrea's life, leads Jones also to investigate Andrés in
complex terms. As she notes on the opening pages of her book, Jones felt she
would not be doing justice to Andrea and her feelings, unless she admitted that
Andrea loved Andrés, and that Andrés was not a monster, even if he choked
Andrea to death with his bare hands while she was telling him he hurt her
(2000: 6). In trying to comprehend the internal universe of Andrés, who in
remorse, committed suicide the night before his conviction, Jones listens to a
tape Andrés made for Andrea on his thirtieth birthday. On the tape Andrés,
after a fight, tried to make sense of his life, as illustrated by an excerpt:

> You know as fucked up as my whole childhood was it was pretty cool but I'm trying to
> figure out what is my problem with my – I mean I've got my own thing with relation-
> ships. ... My relationships with women – my relationships throughout my entire life were
> mostly with women. Those have been the only positive relationships I ever had. ... And
> I don't know, babe. And I wanna, I wanna be able to open up, I wanna be able to fuckin'
> cry out, I want to be able to be everything. I just fuckin' can't. (116)

Describing this internal reality of Andrés, who was addicted to crack cocaine
and could not finish his studies, Jones gives us a sense of his reality as well.
Overall, in shifting between the complex personas and lives of both Andrea and
Andrés – who, just like Andrea, wanted to love and be loved – Jones shatters
the narrative of Martyrs and Monsters that plague discussions on domestic violence. What this jagged discussion accomplishes, according to Jones, is that it
pushes the issue into the realm of sensational exceptions. The polarized card-
board characters of this discussion on domestic violence do not allow women
and men to recognize themselves in the narrative and are not capable of
fomenting dialogues about the complex interpersonal dynamics of this difficult
issue (177).

However, Jones' story on Andrea and Andrés also reaches beyond the interpersonal dyad. Interspersed with the story on Andrea and Andrés are notes on
Jones' own autobiography as a feminist of a previous generation, and her observations on the O.J. Simpson trial, which, eerily enough, was going on around
the time of Andrea's death. Thus, Jones' polyvocal research strategy does not
simply refer to the juxtaposing of different lived experiences or voices. Rather, her
narrative reads as a pastiche that pieces together life-stories, interviews, reminiscences, tapes, media coverage, family photographs and historical events. Pulling
together these different voices from different realms of life, allows Jones to

construct a story that speaks about the complexity of the issue at internal personal, interpersonal and political levels and locates the Andrea/Andrés story in the wider context of history of feminism and race relations in the United States.

What this research strategy accomplishes is that it overcomes the tendency of traditional social inquiry, and its drive to 'categorize', to often produce black and white stories, where people, issues and their social dimensions fall too neatly into simple taxonomies and causalities. On the contrary, a polyvocal research strategy of listening to the many, possible contradictory, accents of each experience and weaving them together with equally complex and con-tradictory social issues paints lived and social worlds in more subtle shades of grey. This kind of more nuanced picture may be better suited to make sense of the contemporary social reality, shot through with myriad differences and intersecting and juxtaposed inequalities, and more conducive of dialogues between these differences at both personal and political levels.

Testimony

However, if we take the principle of understanding different realities and listening to multiple voices to its logical extreme, we end up embracing the relativist idea that any perspective is as good as any other. None of the new ethnographic works discussed in this chapter are relativist, as they all have a straightforward political and ethical agenda. However, if, and when, we decide which voices to listen to, and how to adjudicate between different voices, we need some criteria. In order to think what those criteria might be, we can look at the controversy over the veracity of Rigoberta Menchú's testimonio on the Guatemalan genocide, which focuses on the claim that she presents Guatemalan civil war in one-eyed terms that does not do justice to the different views held by the indigenous people (Menchú, 1984; Stoll, 1999).

Testimonio, as a genre of writing and as a political strategy, is not necessar-ily 'new ethnography', but it is part of the same historical sensibility and is predicated on a similar commitment to bring forth a silenced experience. Often associated with the bloody recent history of Latin America, the method of testimonio is more 'direct' than new ethnography. Testimonio is seen to pro-vide a first-hand witness account of atrocities and oppression, and the intellec-tual or ethnographer, who writes up the account and distributes it, is seen as a messenger or 'editor', rather than 'author'. Testimonio is also a border genre. In a sense, it is a personal account from an indigenous or local point of view; yet, it speaks for a collective experience and is thoroughly transcultural, aiming to communicate and translate peripheral experiences to a metropolitan audience (Yúdice, 1991; Beverley, 1999; Pratt, 2001). The following, often quoted, pas-sage from Menchú's testimonio on the massacre in the town plaza of Chajul, gives a sense of the nature of the genre and helps to illustrate the controversy around the book (see Menchú, 1984; Beverley, 1999; Stoll, 1999; Arias, 2001):

Anyway, they [the soldiers] lined up the tortured and poured petrol on them; and then the soldiers set fire on each of them. Many of them begged for mercy. ... Some of them screamed, many of them leapt but uttered no sound – of course, that was because their breathing was cut off. But – and to me this was incredible – many of the people had weapons with them, the ones who'd been on their way to work had machetes, others had nothing in their hands, but when they saw the army setting fire to the victims, everyone wanted to strike back, to risk their lives doing it, despite all the soldiers' arms. ... Faced with its own cowardice, the army itself realized that the whole people were prepared to fight. You could see that even the children were enraged, but they didn't know how to express their rage. (Menchú, 1984: 179)

In a trademark new ethnographic fashion, this paragraph invites the reader into a reality that may seem radically different or distant to us. Moreover, it evokes an almost embodied identification with the people, or, as Beverley notes, 'reading this passage, we also experience this [the children's] rage – and possibility of defiance even in the face of the threat of death' (1999: 71). While much new ethnographic work invites the reader into understanding a different reality, and to question one's own reality, the effect of testimonio is more immediately political: it provokes an outrage and calls for action or solidarity-work.

Yet, besides its evocative potential, the passage on the massacre in Chajul has become the locus of the debate on the veracity of Menchú's entire testimonio, as Stoll (1999) in his widely publicized book claims the massacre never happened. Stoll argues that while similar events did take place in the Guatemalan highlands, no public execution took place in Chajul, where the army simply dumped dead bodies, possibly including the body of Menchú's little brother, Petrocinio, and set them on fire as a 'warning' for the villagers. What Stoll aims to say, by combing through the events of Menchú's testimonio for errors or exaggerations, is that Menchú's testimonio is melodramatic and one-eyed and covers up the fact that some indigenous people were reluctant towards insurgency and forced to take sides in the conflict between the army and the guerrillas, which led to the destruction of their villages.

Speaking methodologically: What are we to make of this? Should Menchú's testimonio have been constructed in a more polyvocal manner, giving space also to the voices doubting the political and military organizing of indigenous people? As Beverley (1999) notes, this kind of argument misses the point of Menchú's testimonio, which rather than simply speaking the collective voice, is intended as a strategic act to construct this collective voice and to bring into existence, both internally and internationally, a movement to counter the genocide (also Spivak, 1993). This underlines the fact that, interpreted vaguely, the quest to capture different realities and multiple voices leaves us no ground on which to argue that, when talking about genocide, we may want to talk in one non-ambivalent voice against it.

The exigencies of agreement, which often accompany revolutions, have, on several historical occasions, led these movements to eat their children. However, to argue that Menchú's testimony on genocide is as 'legitimate a

Mayan voice' as the voice of any 'young Mayas who want to move to Los Angeles or Houston' (Stoll, 1999: 192–3, quoted in Beverley, 1999) is absurd. As Pratt has pointed out, the 'ethical scale' it is using is seriously flawed. It ends up conflating the incongruencies of Menchú's story and internal disagreements within the indigenous communities with the murderous atrocities committed by the army and the cruelly steep social and economic inequalities and injustices of Guatemalan society (Pratt, 2001: 45).

New ethnography as a movement emerged out of a desire to bring to the fore the silenced worldviews of disenfranchised people. This has led to the acknowledgement that there are multiple forms of disempowerment and silencing, from fat-oppression to racism (Ellsworth, 1989). However, even if the project of drawing attention to different forms of subjugation and silencing is a laudable project *per se*, one has to acknowledge that not all forms of oppression are equal and that some, such as ethnic cleansing, are far graver than others (Freire and Macedo, 1996). This is important for two reasons. First, the inability to adjudicate between different forms of oppression leads to relativist or pointless pluralism that effectively perpetuates disenfranchisement, discrediting a testimony on state-run genocide as just 'one voice among many'. Second, assessing lived realities against the wider background of social structures of inequality does them better justice as it makes them speak for wider social issues and structures of power, which have rendered the lived realities we want to bring to the fore marginalized or subjugated in the first place.

However, when we begin to talk about structures of inequality, we unavoidably end up making claims about 'real' differences in power and privilege. Thus, we should acknowledge that there is a touch of realism, or truth-claim, in any genuinely social analysis and that this has methodological repercussions. It means that, when studying lived realities, we should be committed to a careful, critical analysis of the social, historical and political context, in which it is located, so as not to resort to making easy-handed comments about its 'oppressed' nature. It also means that we should aim to be 'honest', in the sense of not lying and to let the reader know when stories are part fictions of composites of different stories (as in Menchú's case) (Denzin, 1997a).

Yet, a commitment to studying lived realities within the social context should not mean a return to the traditional notion of the scientist as the arbiter of truth. On the contrary, contextualization should always be aware of the fundamental new ethnographic observation that the context and form of what accounts as truth is mediated by those same social structures of domination, which we are trying to describe in the first place. For example, Stoll accuses Menchú for not living up to the Western positivist ideal of 'accurate' historical record, with all its nationalist and colonialist underpinnings. However, Menchú's border-genre testimonio does not obey the logic of positivist historiography or. Western literature (with their notorious omissions) but is partly an oral collective memory, a tactical act of the subaltern, as well as a literary autobiography, following different truth-criteria and sense of reality. There is no escaping the schizophrenia between wanting to make sense of social reality and examining the inevitably political nature of the way in which we approach the reality. Thus, any new ethnographic quest to give voice to subordinated and silenced experiences necessarily takes place in the always political, but also ethical, space between scientific objectivity and pointless pluralism.

Between the particular and the social

To conclude the discussion on new ethnography, I will use my own research on women with eating disorders to outline how to bring together an attention to social structures of inequality and a new ethnographic sensitivity to how those structures may be understood or lived very differently. Anorexia provides a rich ground to explore the different facets of both 'real' and 'lived' structures, as it is located at the intersection of two key variables of social inequality: gender and class. Anorexia is often argued to epitomize gender-subordination, embodying the destructive nature of the ideal, objectified femininity. Still, it is also viewed as a disorder of the privileged, as it affects mostly white, Western, middle-class women. Together these two culturally mediated 'facts' have given rise to a contradictory discourse on anorexia as an emblem of the pathological and effeminate nature of middle-class 'mass' culture.

To start on a self-reflexive note, the association of being anorectic and being middle-class is of particular personal importance to me, as I had anorexia as an 11-year-old working-class Finnish girl in the 1970s. My starving was partly informed by fantasies of being so 'ill' that I would be taken away from my alcoholic working-class family to a nice middle-class foster-home. I also recall abhorring the fatty foods my family consumed as a sign of their lack of 'culture', which I associated with the yoghurts, spacious homes and educated and cultivated parents that marked the lives of my peers in the upper-middle-class private school I attended. Still, I was bewildered by the notion of anorexic as a middle-class girl, who obsessively tries to be pretty and good. I thought this notion did not fit me, or was 'wrong'. Still, I was also deeply offended by it, because the notion of the 'goody' middle-class girl forms an integral part of working-class lore – embodied, for instance, by the then popular punk-song *Rikas isä ja koira* [Rich daddy and a dog] – that repudiates the effeminate nature of middle-class culture.

When interviewing other women who had had anorexia, and came from professional middle-class families, I was intrigued by the way in which they tackled the class-basis of anorexia. An American graduate student, Jeanne in her thirties, who was anorexic as an undergraduate, brought up the notion of the anorexic as a white middle-class girl in relation to a therapist, whom she perceived as 'cold': she went on to say:

> She acted as if she didn't want to be bothered talking about this stuff. Yet, in retrospect, I can see her attitude, it's such a middle-class white girl problem. She was the head of the

mental facility there, and I'm sure she's seen it all; there are people dying out there, with problems worse than anorexia, so this was probably just nothing to her.

Jeanne's passing remark on the disdain and even scorn buried in the notion of anorexia as a middle-class disease hit a personal nerve, and I asked her what she thought of the notion of anorexia as a problem of people, who don't have any real problems. After a pause, Jeanne responded that she did not really 'have much sympathy for herself' for having had it. 'But I think that was part of the problem then also, I didn't have much sympathy for whining and crying about it. And it was only at the behest of other people that I took a turn away from that' – she both took a stern stance towards herself and critically reflected on her sternness towards herself. Our conversation veered to other topics and came back to the issue of white middle-class privilege, when discussing what people think of anorexia. 'It's life-threatening and everything, but it still seems so self-indulgent, I still wrestle with that', Jeanne said. Feeling the urge to maybe somehow justify anorexia I told her that anorexia was said to be affecting also poor and African-American women. 'Oh really, I didn't know that, that's interesting', she responded. In an associative leap, she told about her father, who came from a very poor family with ten children:

> He would tell us how meal times were just this huge battle of who could get the most food, because there was so little to go around. And he says, and he said that to me also when I wasn't eating, that he could never understand people, who didn't want to eat. That he would always want to eat. It was this sort of a left-over feeling for him, from when he was growing up, that eating was survival, whereas to me it was a way of becoming undesirable.

In order to fully appreciate the insight of Jeanne's story, as well as to illuminate its partiality, it may be contrasted to the story of Taru. Taru was a Finnish undergraduate student, who had anorexia in her teens when dancing ballet. Taru also raised the issue of middle-class background of anorexics, when I asked her about people's perceptions of anorexics.

> I think there are several ways that people think of anorexia. There is this stance, typical of young men, that, oh shit, that's sick; and that don't you tell me that you're one of them too. This is an aggressive stance, whereas there is also this kind of understanding attitude, typical of older women, who have sympathy or pity toward the anorexic and are, for example, careful not to offer her any food. … And then there are those, who view anorexics as women, who think they are too precious to eat, or that anorexia is a consequence of too high standards of living, that this is something these women have simply come up with, and that in reality everyone is free to eat good and healthy food. Whatever the attitude, however, the anorexic comes across as a pitiable creature. I think that's awfully negative, and it makes one feel ashamed to admit, particularly to men, that one has been anorexic.

What these three stories illuminate is that the idea of anorexia as a middle-class condition has three dimensions. First, it is a socioeconomic 'fact'. Second, this fact is highly politically mediated as illustrated by the notion of the pathological 'goody' girl. Third, this fact and the discourses that mediate it can be articulated differently by different people, and listening to these different voices may illuminate the complexity of the politics embedded in this fact and legend.

Referring back to my own story as well as the stories of Jeanne and Taru, one can identify (at least) five different personal and political dimensions of the anorexic, middle-class good girl. First, it exposes the problematic underside of the dominant middle-class healthyist and genteel lifestyle both for the middle-class people themselves as well as to people, like myself, that aspire to that class (dis)position. Second, it may articulate a legitimate, working-class critique of the dominant middle-class attitude, which tends to universalize and prioritize its modes of living and problems and to discredit other grievances. This stance is articulated by my childhood working-class culture's rejection and disdain towards middle-class culture. Third, the discourse on anorexia as the dis-ease of the wealthy may form part of the critical self-conscious of middle-class women, such as Jeanne, who is critically aware of her privilege and feels affinity with people that have less, such as her father's childhood family. Fourth, the notion of the sissy middle-class girl may also, however, tell about the deep-seated sexism of working-class culture, as exemplified by the punk machismo of my childhood friends. Fifth, the idea of middle-class women's 'whining' about nothing also tells about a general sexist tendency to belittle women's problems or label them non-progressive or unimportant, which contribute to women's sense of shame of themselves and their problems, as illustrated by Taru's critique.

What I hope to illustrate with my analysis is that an analysis of a social issue or a 'fact', such as the middle-class nature of anorexia, can be studied in a way that both acknowledges its 'factuality' and exposes how this factuality can be perceived in multiple, possibly deeply different, ways. New ethnography has sometimes been criticized for drawing attention to the personal at the expense of social and structural issues, grievances and inequalities. My intention has been to demonstrate that new ethnography can deal with utterly social and structural topics. What is most important, is that new ethnography can 'democratize' discussions on social structures, as it can combine acknowledgement of structural facts (the privileged class-background of anorexics) and bring to the fore that there is no one 'true' way of describing those facts but that those descriptions are always political. As such, new ethnography may foster political dialogues between different groups in that it is capable of tapping into different perspectives and forms of subjugation that may increase understanding between different groups beyond the stalemate between working-class disdain towards the 'goody' middle-class girls and their sense of anger and hurt.

Conclusions

The goal of new ethnographic research is to develop modes of study and writing that enable the scholar to be truer to the lived realities of other people. Thus, new ethnographic practice is often characterized by various strategies, such as collaboration, that aim to increase the participant's say on the way in which the study is conducted and their lives reported. Another characteristic feature of new ethnography is self-reflexivity, which aims to enhance the scholar's awareness of the social and cultural tropes that mediate her/his understanding of worlds that may be radically different from hers/his. Furthermore, polyvocality draws attention to the fact that lived realities are many, and in order to do them justice one may need to listen to multiple voices or perspectives. However, taken to its logical conclusion, the new ethnographic quest to be truthful to different lived realities makes one unable to adjudicate between them. This is graphically illustrated by the dispute over the veracity of Rigoberta Menchú's testimony on the genocide of Guatemalan indigenous people, which Stoll argues leaves out discordant opinions of some of the indigenous people. Thus, in order to avoid a kind of pointless pluralism, which would argue that any voice is as good as any other, one needs to evaluate any lived reality against the social context. However, when analyzing the social context or structures one needs to bear in mind that, even if they may have a 'factual' element to them, they can be perceived radically differently from different perspectives as illustrated by my discussion on the contradictions embedded in the notion of the middle-class goody girl. Thus, a socially sensitive new ethnography points towards ways of doing research that critically analyze social structures of inequality and is capable of attending to the fact that those structures seem different from different perspectives. One could close by noting, that ignoring the fact that structures of inequality may be perceived differently from different directions consolidates inequality.

Exercise 3

- Write a short, one to two page description of a pivotal lived experience you have had (this could be anything from your first date to a particularly illuminating class-situation). Try communicating the emotional and embodied as well as social and political nature of your experience.
- Interview one or two people with a similar experience. Compare the differences and similarities between your experience and theirs in terms of both political perspective and emotional texture.
- Incorporate the other story/stories into your own account in a way that allows each individual experience its own speaking power as well as points towards commonalities between the different views.
- Discuss in the paper how your own experience influenced your interpretation of the other stories and how the interviews changed your perception of your own experience.
- Discuss what social and political issues or contradictions the personal stories illuminate.

4

Between Experience and Discourse

Main questions

- **What different research strategies can one use to study discourses that interlace the lived experience of people, from the 'outside in' or 'objectively'?**
- **How can one study the discursive constitution of lived experience 'inside out' or self-reflexively from a subjective point of view?**
- **How can one study the discourses that form part of our lived experiences through a dialogic exchange between the scholar and the people being studied?**
- **What are the differences between critical and rhizomatic dialogic analysis? What are their advantages and disadvantages?**

The previous chapter outlined different ways in which scholars have tried to do better justice to the texture and specifity of lived experience, while locating it in the polyvocal, social and historical context. The quest to be true to lived experience, however, is complicated by the fact that it is always mediated by social discourses that define for us who we are.

Analyzing the ways in which discourses or ideologies shape how people see themselves and act in the world, has been a central part of the cultural studies project from the start. As discussed in Chapter 2, Radway (1984) argued that women consumed romances, because the ubiquitous formulaic trope or discourse of romance – with its sensitive hero, who took care of the woman – provided food for their fantasies. Poststructuralism has, however, complicated any easy faith in being able to see through discourses that direct people's thoughts and actions, by pointing out that the scholar's understanding is also mired in the social, historical and paradigmatic discourses of its time. Thus, Ang (1996) reminds us that Radway's analysis of the romancers is driven by a rationalist feminist discourse, which distinguishes between 'real' feminist actions and revelling in romances as 'fantasy'.

This chapter discusses three basic ways of studying how social discourses shape lived experience. First, I will discuss objectivist modes of studying the discursive constitution of experience, in which the scholar investigates, from the 'outside' (much like Radway), the discursive forces that shape people's identities and behaviours. These analyses can take many forms from attempts to foster 'enabling' discourses that would help in HIV-counselling (Silverman, 1997) to ironic writings on the 'disciplining' impact of proliferating discourses on 'addictions', such as Internet addiction (Umiker-Sebeok, 2001). What all these analyses share, however, is the presumption that the scholar is capable of analyzing these discourses, guiding people's actions and identities, while they remain largely unaware of them.

Second, I will discuss a self-reflexive or subjectivist mode of analyzing experiences and discourses from the 'inside'. This form of analysis acknowledges that the scholar does not have any privileged access to a space 'above' discourses but is also formed by them. Thus, the subjectivist approach is characterized by a self-reflexive, critical autobiographical or introspective analysis of the discourses that have constituted the scholar. Third, I will discuss dialogic research strategies, in which the scholar and the people being studied engage in a mutual, critical self-reflexive analysis of discourses that have constituted them.

The empirical works discussed in this chapter mostly focus on mental or physical illness. This is partly because my own research falls within this area. However, what are perceived as grave illnesses often provoke a life-crisis and a process of self-questioning and can, therefore, be seen as particularly dense moments of experience and self-reflection. Illnesses are also heavily mediated experiences, produced by medical institutions, which first 'discover' and describe them and then canonize them in diagnostic manuals. People, perceived as 'ill', may find their diagnosis and treatment helpful, or may question it, but they are likely to internalize some of the medical notions of their condition that saturate the media, treatment environments and everyday culture. Thus, illnesses can be seen as particularly discursively saturated moments that highlight some of the problems and possibilities embedded in trying to unearth social discourses that interlace our sense of ourselves.

In what follows, I will first outline Foucault's notion of discourse, which has guided many studies on lived experience. I will also discuss how Foucault's moving from studies on discipline towards studies on human behaviour as 'technology', provides a model for self-reflexive modes of analysis. Second, I will discuss 'objectivist' ways of analyzing how social frames shape lived experiences. Third, I will review some self-reflexive autobiographic studies, which illuminate how one analyzes discourses that shape one's self-understanding. The final part of the chapter discusses dialogic research strategies, such as action research and 'rhizomatic' inquiry, which are based on a critical self-reflexive encounter between the scholar and the people being studied.

From discipline to technology

Michel Foucault's theories on the discursive constitution of the self (1978, 1979a, 1985a, 1985b) have exerted an immense influence on cultural studies as a discipline, and have also provided the conceptual underpinnings for diverse kinds of studies on lived experience. Foucault's 'middle' works (1978, 1979a) focus on the ways in which institutions, such as medicine, psychiatry, criminology and so on, produce subjects through 'confession'. Thus, for instance, counselling and medicine instigate their clients to confess their 'problems' or symptoms and, by translating them into clinical terms, have historically produced 'homosexuals' and 'hysteric' women, as well as, more recently, for example, children with 'attention deficit hyperactivity disorder' (Lowe, 2002) or 'Internet-addicts' (Reed, 2000; Umiker-Sebeok, 2001).

The fact that social discourses constitute our most fundamental sense of our self troubles the basic premise of, for example, the new ethnographic quest to unearth different lived realities. This is because these apparently 'authentic' lived realities may turn out to be the product of institutional discourses. Take, for example, gay-autobiographies, which often recount how the person felt 'different' as a child. Even if this may appear to be a 'true' story of a difficult childhood, it can also be argued to reiterate the medical discourse on 'normal' gender identities, according to which boys who do not play with trucks and girls that do not play with dolls are different or abnormal (Probyn, 1996).

Yet, Foucault does not see the power of discourses as monolithic, but points out that 'where there is power, there is resistance' (Foucault, 1978: 95). So, studies may analyze how people both succumb to, and resist, discourses. For example, Terry (1999) has investigated the ways in which gay men and lesbian women, who participated in the large 'Sex Variants' study in the 1920s, were both being informed by the medical discourse on their behaviour and resisted the medical inscriptions. Thus, their flamboyant descriptions of their sexual activities, preferences, and subculture shine through the historical medical notes, even if stamped 'pathological' behaviour by the author.

Despite their revelatory insights, analysis of experiences that draw on middle Foucault run into a problem. The problem with these studies is that in their quest to critically analyze the discourses that interlace experiences they reproduce the confessional logic. What this means, in terms of qualitative research, is that researchers that study how discourses shape people's experiences end up playing the role of the expert, who interprets the truth of the person's experience back to her and prescribes 'diagnosis' (Alcoff and Grey, 1993: 273). Thus, we could imagine a situation where a gay person tells an expert that he felt different as a child. The medical expert, who diagnoses this statement as an indication that he is 'abnormal', and the cultural expert, who diagnoses this statement as an indication that he is under the influence of homophobic medicine, are not methodologically different. They both presume they know the 'truth' about the person and pass judgement on it.

In order to formulate a research strategy, which would provide a half-way house between new ethnographic interest in subordinated experiences and the poststructuralist focus on discourses, it is useful to turn to Foucault's late works. In his later works, Foucault shifts his notion of discourses from discipline to technology. Instead of seeing discourses as imposing themselves upon people from the institutional above, he pays closer attention to the ways in which people can 'fold' power against itself (Deleuze, 1988). According to Foucault, people may do 'a critical ontology of the self', which takes stock of the discourses that have constituted one's subjectivity and then aim to reimagine oneself differently (Foucault, 1988). This practice of a 'technology of the self' does not refer to any kind of 'freedom' from discourses but refers to a practice whereby people can become critically aware of the discourses that underpin their self via a careful and informed technique.

In research on lived experience, the idea of a critical ontology of the self has been translated, for example, into self-reflexive autoethnography. In this genre of analysis, the author not only aims to introspectively 'tap' into her/his experience (the way new or emotional autoethnography does; see Ellis and Bochner, 2000) but also critically interrogates those discourses that have constituted the experience for the author (e.g. Spence, 1986; Minh-Ha, 1989; Probyn, 1993; Bordowitz, 1994; Frank, 1995). Thus, for example, Minh-Ha presents certain concerns and issues that are of importance to a 'third world intellectual woman', while troubling the problematic, such as empathetically colonialist, underpinnings of her self-identity as a 'third world intellectual woman'.

However, the notion of a technology of the self also enables research to imagine a mode of researching the lived experiences of other people that is less disciplinary or diagnostic. It invites research to frame the relationship between the scholar and people being studied more in terms of a self-reflexive encounter, into which both bring critical understandings of themselves and the world in which we live. The idea of a mutual self-reflexive analysis of discourses that have constituted our experiences informs several approaches to qualitative research on lived lives. One of them is critical or action research (e.g. Lather, 1991; Kincheloe and McLaren, 1994) in which the scholar and the, usually subordinated, people being studied engage in a critical dialogue, in which they both aim to question their preconceptions about one another and the situation, in order to fetch a course of action for empowerment. In my own work (Saukko, 2000, 2002b), I have developed more 'rhizomatically' dialogic ways of bringing together my own and other anorexic women's critical self-analyses. I borrow the concept of a 'rhizome' from Deleuze and Guattari (1987) that distinguish between 'root-like' causal analysis ('images of thin models "cause" eating disorders') and complex or rhizomatic analysis that envisions social phenomena as 'crabgrass', tangled with multiple other phenomena and processes, pointing to different and possibly contradictory directions. The aim of dialogue in action research is to reach a consensus and action-plan for empowerment. Slightly differently, rhizomatic understanding of dialogue helps to flesh out both commonalities and contradictions between different views, paving the way towards a nuanced research practice and action plan that can, for example, acknowledge that critiques of beauty ideals can be both empowering and disempowering (condemning women as vain or 'bimbos', condemning attention paid to the body).

Objectivist analyses of discourses

To begin to chart different ways of studying how discourses shape experience, I will first discuss what I would term the 'objectivist' approach. The studies I will be discussing all focus on various physical and mental illnesses. The common sense and mainstream social scientific approach to 'illnesses' (HIV, anorexia, alcoholism and so on) is that they are 'real' problems, which need solutions. Poststructuralism, however, understands that the way we experience our selves, as, for instance, 'alcoholic', is a product of subjectifying institutional, social and historical discourses, which make us perceive and live our selves and our lives in particular ways. Consequently, for instance, the individual's life-history, which forms such a crucial part of the popular and medical theories of mental disorders, is not necessarily seen as a 'true' account of one's life. It is rather seen as a 'product' of certain techniques of memorizing, embedded in 'memory-dossiers', such as family-albums and collections of school-reports, and medical and popular notions of traumatic or deviant childhood (Hacking, 1995; Rose, 1996: 180–1).

Thus, instead of analyzing how people can be 'cured' from illness, analyses interested in discourses aim to untangle the discourses that constitute the experience of 'illness'. However, there is no one unified way of analyzing the discursive constitution of illness, and, in what follows, I will discuss three different modes of analysis in order to illustrate some different research attitudes and strategies. The, first, 'institutional' approach I will be discussing takes a therapeutic stance towards illness-discourses, aiming to come up with better or more 'enabling' discourses that help people to cope with or prevent illness. The second, 'social' approach separates wheat from chaff by deciphering the empowering and disempowering aspects of discourses on illness both from personal as well as social points of view. The last, 'ironic' approach takes a mocking stance towards discourses on illnesses, in particular 'addictions', arguing that they simply increase self-monitoring and discipline, even if their continuing proliferation, ironically, tends to undermine their credibility.

The institutional approach

Much Foucauldian discourse-analysis, just like Foucault himself, is critical of 'therapeutic' solutions. However, the Foucauldian framework of analyzing discourses can also be used in a bid to try to create 'better' or more enabling discourses that would help people to cope with certain life problems. An example of a study that uses the Foucauldian framework to improve counselling practice is Silverman's (1997) work on HIV counselling.

In his study on HIV counselling sessions, Silverman, using conversation analysis (CA) found out two different strategies or discourses. First, counsellors, who simply delivered information, without allowing the client to speak much, made the counselling both less pertinent and more imposing for the person being counselled. Silverman calls this the 'information delivery format'. However, the second type of strategy of asking many questions and keeping quiet enabled the counsellor to relate their information to the client's specific situation and attitudes. Silverman calls this the 'personalized advice'. An example of an interview that asks detailed and specific questions from the client and is, eventually, able to 'tailor' the advice to the client's situation is the following:

C: mm hm.hhh What sort of <u>sexual</u> relationship are you having at the moment with him.
    (0.6)
P: With X.
C: Mm hm
P: er:: (1.7) We:ll (0.6) hhh God how to go into this on camera: I don't know ... hhhh er:: ... There was a period at the very beginni:ng (0.5) er:: (0.5) where a condom was not- ((Clears throat)) excuse me was not used. (0.6)
Er: [::
C: [Are you using condoms now? = Or er-
P: [uh We::lll(0.4)
    Yeah. Mm (1.0) er::: (.) still some oral se:x (0.6) er::not passing any fluids alo:ng but they say (04.) that yes you do pass fluid along. (0.4) So I'm still kind of nervous about that. = However, .hhhh (0.2) er:uh::hhh (0.8) I:-I don't know:: (0.5) what I don't.hh is er:: (0.2) how:I would have contracted it to him.
C: Mm: =
P: = er::: (0.7) I have not (1.1) er:: (1.0) had anal intercourse with hi:m.
C: Okay.
    (Silverman, 1997: 115).

This excerpt illustrates a 'customer orientated' communicative or discursive pattern that can be unravelled through conversation analysis. Detecting this pattern is useful in terms of drawing counsellors' attention to communication patterns that either help them to give effective advice on safe sex practices or make their advice less effective or insinuate a negative or 'resisting' approach from the client.

Silverman's analysis is relatively typical in that it uses a scientific method, such as conversation analysis, to identify a discursive pattern. Uncovering an unconscious pattern may be useful in that it highlights patterns of interaction that may help or hinder communication and end up either effectively relaying information or disrespectfully and in a patronizing fashion 'dictating' advice. However, this manner of doing research also has its own patronizing elements as it largely presumes that the counsellor and the client are unaware of the goings on in their conversation and need a scientist to sort this out. Furthermore, a mode of inquiry that is wedded to improving an institutional practice, such as advising people on safe sex, is also blind to the possibly problematic underside of these institutional discourses and practices (such as the guilt-invoking confessional mode embedded in safe-sex discussions – as will be seen later in this chapter).

The social approach

Another approach to studying discourses and experiences of illness is to widen the focus on the institutional/medical towards the societal and explore the historical and social roots and implications of the discourses that interlace people's lived realities. This often leads to separating wheat from chaff, or evaluation of whether these discourses buttress or challenge power structures. One can hear echoes of the resistance-paradigm, discussed in Chapter 2, in this mode of analysis, and it is possibly the most common way of studying discourses and lived experience in cultural studies.

An example of a study that analyzes the social nature of discourses that constitute our lived sense of ourselves is Alasuutari's (1992) study on Finnish blue-collar discourses on drinking and alcoholism. His ethnographic study on a working-class tavern concludes that the regulars saw their drinking and darts playing as expressing a desire for 'personal freedom' and as a protest towards 'Puritan work and consumer ethics', which drives people to strive for new commodities, so that one does not have time to 'live one's life, to enjoy' (158). Alasuutari found a 'homology' between this drinking culture and the culture of a blue-collar self-help group for alcoholics, the A-Guild, which framed drinking as just another form of the rat race and prescribed being 'lazy' and taking time off work and living on the dole for a while, in order to get out of the cycle of working hard and then spending the money on a binge.

Thus, there is a clear resonance between members' of the darts club rejection of the habit of 'collecting the pennies':

Pekka: I mean what's the point with stacking your money up under your bed?

Ale: It's stupid (laughter). Then you have to buy a new house so that there's more room for the money. (142)

And the philosophy of 'laziness' in the A-Guild:

> Then I finally realized that I always start from the wrong end and I began another practice. I stayed out of work for a half a year and didn't even apply for a job. (141)

As these excerpts illustrate, Alasuutari traces a kind of 'indigenous' or sub-cultural working-class discourse or theory on drinking and alcoholism, which emphasizes a culture of being carefree. As such, it challenges universal theories or treatment of alcoholism, as, for instance, the success of A-Guild's method of providing the ex-alcoholics a space to just hang about and do nothing but drink coffee, is based on its resonance with the working-class culture. On a more general note, Alasuutari points that A-Guild's discourse challenges some central tenets of contemporary culture, such as work-ethic and consumption. However, it also embraces other signs of the times, such as the notion of individual 'freedom' and a hedonistic desire to 'enjoy' life.

If Alasuutari takes a basically sympathetic, attitude towards his working-class 'subjects', studies on the 'new' discourse of codependency (Steedman-Rice, 1996; Irvine, 1999) take a more critical view. Codependency, a kind of addiction to people or relationships, can be seen as an offshoot of alcoholism, as its roots are in the self-help groups for wives as well as adult children of alcoholics (ACOA) (Haaken, 1993). Recent studies on the phenomenon acknowledge its gendered roots and the way in which it addresses the demands of women to sacrifice their lives for others, as when every Christmas the woman fills up her husband's stocking, only to always find hers empty in the morning (see Denzin, 1997b). They also point out that the movement provides a sense of community for people, many of whom are recently separated. Yet, Irvine (1999) also observes that the identity of people self-defined as codependent is lodged in a formulaic life-history of victimization and 'abuse' in the hands of others. This leads to what Steedman-Rice (1996: 195–96) calls an 'ethic of self-actualization', in which self and its prerogatives become a moral a priori, justifying any actions. So, Irvine (1999) recounts the story of 'Richard', who arrived at a CoDA meeting with a brand-new four-wheel-drive sport utility vehicle, after going on a shopping binge to spend the money he had received from a sale of his former family-house, before his estranged wife, who was living on welfare with the children, got hold of it. As Richard explains:

> I've always put everybody else first, you know, their feelings first, and it's just today, putting myself first. I don't want to walk around with holes in my sneakers anymore. The kids used to have nice clothes, nice shoes, nice sneakers, and everything else, and I used to walk around with holes, I don't do that anymore, It's like being true to myself, you know, not being in an abusive situation, not allowing anybody to abuse me, and stuff like that. I'm an important person. (141)

Thus, according to Irvine codependency has its contradictions. It provides people with a sense of community and challenges the gendered demands for self-sacrifice, while it also buttresses a decidedly American character trait of hyperindividualism that has its historical roots in the national experiences of migration, Puritanism, capitalism, democracy and mobility (Irvine, 1999: 158; Bellah *et al.*, 1985).

Overall, unlike the institutional approach the social one does not focus its attention on 'curing' or 'giving advice' on illness, but it rather seeks to understand what types of social politics the illness-discourse advances. This approach is good at teasing out the personal and political contradictions of discourses, which may be politically both progressive and retrograde, such as ending up both critiquing individualist competitiveness and embracing individualist hedonism. However, this approach still obeys the traditional social scientific logic that views the scholar to be able to decipher the good and the bad of the discourses that direct people's actions, imagining the people being studied as, in the main, unconscious of the social implications of their thinking and doings.

Ironic approach

The last approach to studying discourses, which define lived experiences of illness, views them as simple mechanisms of self-discipline. An example of such a stance is Umiker-Sebeok's analysis of the discourses on Internet addiction (IA) as well as discourses that parody IA. Umiker-Sebeok argues that IA is not a condition as such but a mechanism that increases self-surveillance and normalizing through proliferating definitions of 'normal' activities, such as household duties, lovemaking, work and so on. Umiker-Sebeok's analysis is based on analysis of various online support groups for addicts and informal and quasi-medical websites on IA, replete with self-tests and surveys on the level and spread of I-addiction. However, Umiker-Sebeok notes that the IA-discourse is far from unquestioned in the Net, and groups and pages lampooning the I-addicts mushroom, as indicated by the following mock 12-step program:

The Twelve Keys of Interholics
We ...
F1: ... admit that we have no life.
F2: ... believe that a Power greater than ourselves can either restore us to sanity or provide us with unlimited, no-cost Internet dial-up.
F3: ... made a decision to turn our lives over to that Great Webmaster In The Sky ("GWITS").
F4: ... performed a searching moral inventory with the Web search engine of our choice.
F5: ... admitted to GWITS, ourselves and another human being (even if only by eMail) the exact nature of our obsession.
F6: ... were entirely ready to have GWITS remove our shortcomings and remedy our lack of knowledge about the latest IRC chat technology.
F7: ... humbly asked GWITS to allow us to FTP the file updates.
F8: ... made a list of all persons we had neglected, and posted it on our personal home page.
...

Still, Umiker-Sebeok argues that this parody does not entail any kind of freedom, but simply subjugates its participants to another form of self-discipline that affirms a different code, namely, that of new lifestyle of 'digital excess'. Umiker-Sebeok concludes that the proliferation of these discourses on addiction and anti-addiction underline the Internet's potential to increase the monitoring of self and others on an unprecedented global scale. Yet, at the same time it also illustrates the potential of Internet to undermine any single-handed discipline. In a Baudrillardian (1980) move, the explosion of expert opinions and addictions leads to an implosion, where they lose their meaning, becoming just another (language) game.

If the institutional approach aimed to ameliorate illness and the social one sought to analyze the social implications of illness-narratives, the ironic stance makes a mockery of the existence of illness as such, seeing it mainly as a governing apparatus. Umiker-Sebeok does not embrace institutional logics, the way Silverman does, but she also completely disregards the lived experiences of either Internet-addicts or anti-addicts as mere tweaks of a discourse. As such it ends up rather unhelpfully nihilistic, denying the value of everything.

Analysis of narrative

The different works discussed in the preceding section have different takes on 'addictions'. Yet, what they have in common is that – unlike the new ethnographic projects of, lets say, Lather and Smithies (1997), Jones (2000) and Ginsburg (1998[1988]) – their first and foremost aim is not to tell people's stories. Rather, they trace a discursive pattern that emerges from the individual stories, articulating a particular institutional and political programme with its personal and social implications. Polkinghorne (1995) has distinguished between these two modes of analyses as 'narrative analysis', which puts research material into a powerful story, and 'analysis of narrative', which traces patterns that recur across individual stories. While these 'understanding' and 'analytical' modes of analysis contradict one another, they are also complementary in that they refer to the two facets of experience. Lived experience can be understood as an individual's quest to make sense of and act in the world, while this quest is never transparent but always informed by social frames, which, more or less, operate 'behind our backs'.

Still, the three modes of analyzing discourses and experiences are also decidedly different. One can say that Silverman's and Umiker-Sebeok's stances mark the opposite ends of the continuum in studies on discourses on illness. Silverman's study is guided by an institutional commitment to improve the efficacy of HIV-counselling. As a consequence, he neglects to interrogate its basic institutional premises, such as 'safer sex', and the hefty sexually normalizing bent of the counselling, where the client is eventually cajoled into confessing he had not had anal intercourse with his partner. On the contrary,

Umiker-Sebeok rallies against discourses on self-discipline, whether they would draw their power from discourses on addiction or on discourses on anti-addiction. However, since she does not suggest any alternatives to these discourses, she implicitly ends up embracing a similar 'anti-disciplinary' stance, underpinned by a naïve notion of 'freedom', as the one taken by the 'netheads' that she examines (or the 'pro-anorexia' websites that defend the right to starve as an individual lifestyle choice; Brain, 2002). According to Foucault, one always needs to govern oneself. Thus, instead of proclaiming freedom from governance, which simply leads one blindly to another form of governance, the question is to develop an 'ethos' that allows these games of power to be played with a minimum of domination (Foucault, 1988: 18).

One could say that Alasuutari, Irvine and Steedman-Rice try to do precisely what Foucault suggests: they analyze discourses of self-governance with a view of evaluating, whether they perpetuate domination in the interpersonal and/or social realms. This locates them between Silverman's search for ideally effective governing of the self through illness, which easily leads to domination via an explicit alliance with institutional logics, and Umiker-Sebeok's rallying against all governing, which easily leads to domination via negating any stance, which implicitly affirms a sense of anarchistic freedom. So, both Alasuutari and Irvine examine how elements of the working-class discourse on alcoholism and the middle-class discourse on codependency challenge structures of domination, such as the bourgeoisie work-ethic and competitiveness or female self-sacrifice. However, they also evaluate how elements of these discourses, such as individualist hedonism and egotism, perpetuate domination or dominant structures of power.

Still, even if the 'content' of Alasuutari's and Irvine's works are reflexive about implications of power, their form is not. What this means is that both works adopt a traditional mode of analyzing, how discourses interlace experiences, in that they presume the scholar is capable of seeing through the discourses that direct other people in their actions. Thus, if one works to unravel domination embedded in discourses that underpin our experiences, one should also work against domination in the research process itself. This means that one should develop modes of analyzing discourses, which, instead of merely investigating discourses that guide other people's understanding of themselves, would also critically reflect on the political underpinnings of one's own knowledge.

Self-reflexive autoethnography

To begin to chart methodologies that incorporate scholars' critical self-analysis, one can start with self-reflexive autoethnographies. Self-reflexive autoethnographies can be conceptualized in terms of Foucault's technology of the self, which refers to a practice of doing an inventory of discourses that have constituted one's self. Thus, the goal of self-reflexive autoethnography is twofold. First, to relate an experience and, second, to critically investigate the discourses that have constituted that experience. To illustrate this method, one can look at Bordowitz's (1994) description of his first anal intercourse, which, from the outset, is just as intensely personal, intimate and embodied, as the accounts provided by the phenomenologically oriented forms of new ethnography:

> It was the first time I asked a guy to fuck me. 1985. I wanted it bad and I was very scared. We were both very drunk. His cock was immense. I thought it would tear me apart and I wanted that. 'Fuck me,' I demanded, 'just fuck me.' He was having trouble getting it up because of the liquor. ... He crammed his half-hard cock into my tense hole. I was near dead drunk, but not relaxed. I was in pain as I felt his cock, finally filled with a credible amount of blood, slowly take up space, filling my ass. He went in and out, progressively going deeper as I tried to stretch my shrinking anus. He suddenly stopped, quietly gasped the word 'shit' as I felt his cock go limp. (29–30)

This story of an intercourse, which Bordowitz wonders could have been the instance of his HIV-infection, is vivid and evocative. However, Bordowitz challenges his 'exhibitionism', arguing it is an attempt to try 'to exorcise the discourse of blame that would judgementally bring sentence down upon me for getting fucked up the ass, liking it, and getting a fatal disease from it'. He continues by asking: 'where did this discourse exist? Among the homophobes. Among the right-wing. In my own mind' (32–3).

Bordowitz's analysis illuminates the split project of critical autoethnography, which acknowledges the need to speak of lived, subordinate and silenced experiences (being gay, living with HIV, the need for safe sex), and the need to critically analyze those social discourses, such as murderously reactionary and homophobic popular and medical tropes, which have defined those experiences for us.

Thus, one can say that Bordowitz shares the new ethnographic interest in the emotional and embodied nature of subordinate experience of, for example, sex, illness and dying. It also shares Silverman's interest, deriving from the counselling discourse, in managing 'troubles', such as unsafe sex. However, where it differs from both these traditions is that instead of taking these experiences and problems at face value, it challenges the way they are always underpinned by historically sedimented discourses. Thus, unlike new ethnography, it does not primarily try to capture the 'raw' guilt and fear that the author feels but wants to problematize these feelings as products of historical discourses, which associate anal intercourse with sin, sickness and death. Bordowitz's autoethnography also casts a decidedly critical light on Silverman's work on counselling, as it reveals the underside of practices that force people to confess their sexual practices, as these confessions are always interlaced with intense feelings of guilt associated with 'wrong' kinds of sexual practices (as exemplified by the long pauses and difficulty people had talking about their sexual practices).

Bordowitz's work aims to disentangle problematic or even heinous social discourses from more positive perspectives, just like research projects that evaluate the social pros and cons of, for example, discourses, which constitute alcoholism and codependency. Yet, it is also different from them in that it does not diagnose, from the outside, what drives people in their institutional and informal self-projects. It rather aims to analyze, from the inside out, the process of being (self-)diagnosed. This strategy frames the constitution of the self from the other side of the fence, so that the individual is seen as engaged with, rather than interpellated by, the discourses, which constitute her/his self. Yet, this does mean any simple celebration of 'active' audience, as Bordowitz's main point is the ambiguous nature of his self-analysis. This means that, while aiming to provide a critical political testimony on HIV, self-stories on it are always also bound to confess and consolidate the guilt-infested and homophobic discourses that saturate this social terrain. What this self-reflexive ambiguity accomplishes is that it undermines the diagnostic logic, which interlaces both medical analysis of people's 'troubles' as well as critical cultural analysis of medical interpellation, in that they both make pronouncements, from the outside, about the 'true' nature of people's behaviour.

Yet, even if Bordowitz acknowledges that his critical self-reflection can never escape disciplinary discourses, it does not take Umiker-Sebeok's position, verging on the ironic, that all definitions and redefinitions of the self are but another form of self-discipline. Foucault acknowledges that one can never liberate oneself from discourses or reach a state of not governing or disciplining one's behaviour in some fashion. Yet, Foucault's technology of the self reminds us that one can work towards a technique of governing oneself in a fashion that aims to be more ethical both towards the self and others. Thus, besides an ironic or dystopian trope, Bordowitz's analysis also has a utopian dimension that aims to rethink or redeem some positive ways of fetching a self amidst the epidemic.

Self-reflexive autoethnography has been used relatively widely in cultural studies. Among that classics in this area is Trinh Minh-Ha's (1989) highly poetic and avant-garde work, which addresses the need to speak from the position of the 'third world woman', in order to raise certain concerns, while deconstructing the colonial and patronizing underpinnings of that category. The same way Jo Spence's (1986) photographic autobiography critically analyzes how she has been constructed and has constructed herself through the photographic and medical apparatus as a woman (with breast cancer), trying to come up with different images. The strength of these analyses is that, working from the inside out, they provide powerful critiques of how discourses constitute us. However, this acute critical insight into the self is also the greatest shortcoming of this line of inquiry, as it may end up so focused on challenging the self that the social panorama of which the self forms a part, recedes to the background. What this means, becomes clear when looking at another line of self-reflexive inquiry: action research.

Action research

Often traced back to the work of the Brazilian critical pedagogue Paulo Freire, action research sees research and education in terms of a self-reflexive dialogue between the researcher and the researched or the educator and her/his students (see Freire, 1970). The Freirean philosophy or method originates from adult literacy teaching. Freire argued that instead of teaching literacy from textbooks, littered with symbols and ideologies derived from middle-class culture, the educators should discover the words and ideas that derive from the students' life context. This would not only enable them to read mechanically but to 'name' their world ('ghetto', 'oppression') as a first step towards changing it (Freire, 1970; Shor, 1993). Translated into methodological terms, this education refers to a mode of inquiry, in which the scholar critically reflects on her/his notions of 'proper' research/education or 'critical' analysis and allows herself to be challenged by students' worlds, which are then, in a dialogic fashion, critically investigated and contextualized.

Critical research of the Freirean vein has been used in particular cultural studies of education (e.g. Kincheloe and McLaren, 1994; Giroux, 1994a; Lather, 1991). It has two methodological cornerstones, which both join it with and differentiate it from other discourse-analytic approaches. First, it argues against critiques of ideology or discourse that replicate the 'diagnostic' or normalizing agenda they aim to challenge, by positing the scholar as 'knowing' and the people being studied or taught as if under false consciousness. This formula repeats in cultural studies analyses of discourses and lived experience from the 'outside in'. It also recurs in simplistic forms of feminist pedagogy, which makes students, for instance, parrot formulaic politically correct statements about the 'exploitative' nature of beauty images, which cannot come to terms with the complex pleasures we derive from them (Lather, 1991). Second, action research eschews individualist strategies of challenging self-constitution and stresses that self-transformation needs always to be understood as part of social and collective change (Aronowitz, 1993: 9). Thus, action research assails education and research projects focused on 'emotional breach of convention and received social realities' rather than 'changing structural events' (Giroux, 1994a: 47). This critical collectivist attitude points a finger at forms of reflexive self-analysis, which are heavily focused on refetching or folding the self, and where the structural ramifications and implications of this process fade into the background.

How these principles translate into practice is exemplified, for instance, by Butler's (1997) self-reflexive research on her critical pedagogy with African-American second graders from the housing projects of south-side Chicago. Even if the topic of black children's education does not have to do with 'illness', it overlaps with it, because these children are often framed as 'pathological', coming from a stigmatized culture of poverty, drug-dealing, crime and single-motherhood (e.g. Campbell and Reeves, 1994). Butler notes that she was initially disturbed by what she perceived as the 'fictitious' or 'inconsistent' nature of the children's stories. Critically interrogating her own investments in facts and consistency (1997: 96), she used her discomfort with these stories as a way to enter into the realities of the children.

Butler concluded that the children's frequent and often fictitious accounts of 'moving out' (of the projects), birthday parties in the pizza-parlour 'Chuckie Cheese' or visits of fathers, rather than be treated as lies or truths, provided the children in the class spaces to dream, laugh and cope with disappointment (97–9). The same way children's inconsistent accounts of drugs, gangs and guns pinpointed some crucial dilemmas in their realities. The children showed off their 'cool' by speaking about funerals and shootings and told stories about police violence, while, at the same time pronouncing that gang bangers are 'bad', that guns are 'hurtin' us all the time and that police provide them with 'safety' (102). In conversation with the students, Butler interpreted these inconsistencies as deriving from the contradictions embedded in their everyday realities, dominant media images and their parents' dichotomous admonitions about 'bad' behaviour, which aimed to protect the children, all of which led the children to endless conundrums:

> Why were the police violent and unreasonable when the messages from TV kept saying the police are there for protection and safety? How come people who sell and use drugs are 'bad' when some of the people they love most in the world sell and use drugs? How come guns are 'bad' when police give guns to people in the community? How come selling drugs is 'bad' when the money from them is what provides food and clothes? (103)

According to Butler, critically discussing these inconsistencies and the individualistic discourse of escape ('moving out') and discipline about 'staying clean' allowed the children to refocus blame away from themselves and the people they loved and to focus attention on broader, more complex explanations of oppression (104).

This mode of analysis not only analyzes or diagnoses how discursive power operates to define our lived experiences, the way the analysis of narrative does, but it also aims to challenge power-structures, which define who has the power to define whom, both at social level and in the research/educational act itself. Thus, the children are not simply 'diagnosed' to be driven by certain discourse but become, in part, analysts of themselves and their realities and communities and catalysts for the scholar's/educator's self-analysis. Furthermore, the analysis does not stop at the self but bends outward from it, in order to redirect attention from individuals and their guilt and self-transformation and towards social injustice and transformation. This reveals an individualist bias in those, mostly middle-class, self-reflexive autoethnographies, which are heavily focused on fetching or folding alternative, for instance, gendered or sexual selves (see Ebert, 1993; Morton, 1996; Fraser, 1999).

Yet, despite its commitment to openness and challenging the scholar's preconceptions, action research's community-oriented praxis has a tendency to translate critical self-reflection to quite a straightforward and uncomplicated agenda. For example, while Giroux (1994a) provides an insightful analysis of the film *Dead Poets Society*, he barely acknowledges its 'affective appeal' to his teacher students, and then swiftly proceeds to deconstruct and condemn it as middle-class individualism without paying any attention to any possible contradictions or any 'value' her students' initial reaction might have.

Rhizomatic analysis

Beyond subjects and objects

My interest in studying how discourses interlace experiences originates from my personal experience of anorexia and dissatisfaction, or even anger, with the way in which the condition is talked about in the scholarly and popular realms. I have always felt perplexed and humiliated by the way in which both popular and scientific media objectify women with eating disorders. Their words and behaviour are read as 'symptoms', from which a psychological or social pathology can be read by the expert, such as medical scientist or even a feminist cultural critic. Yet, I have also been intrigued by the fact that even if there are myriad studies on discourses, such as beauty ideals, that 'inform' anorexia, there are very few critical analyses of the normative or disciplinary nature of the discourses on eating disorders themselves (for exceptions, see e.g. Probyn, 1987; Bray, 1996; Hepworth, 1999; Gremillion, 2002).

However, even if my interest in the lived experience of women with eating disorders and the discourses that I think define them/us in problematic terms are interrelated, they also run into a contradiction, posing the question: How can one do justice to the experience of anorexic women, often silenced as 'disordered', and, at the same time, critically analyze discourses on eating disorders, which form the very stuff out of which the experiences of anorexics are made? Trying to answer this question puts me squarely at the heart of the dilemma haunting research on lived experiences and discourses, namely: Can we find ways of being truer to people's lived experiences (new ethnography) and critically analyze problematic social discourses that seep into those experiences (poststructuralism)? This methodological dilemma is particularly acute and complicated, when studying eating disorders, as the dichotomy between 'knowing' what one is doing (or being a 'subject') and 'not knowing' what one is doing (being an 'object') lies at the foundation of both the experience and research on the conditions. Thus, anorexic women often starve in order to underline being in control of their life and their body, or being a subject (Bordo, 1993). However, when they are diagnosed as anorexic they are defined as being out of control, subjugated or victimized by media images of thin models or parental expectations of being good. Thus, after diagnosis anorexic women are defined as total objects, again falling short of the ideal, elusive active and in-control subjectivity, which they tried so hard to achieve.

The way in which the methodological and 'topical' dimensions of studying anorexia are intertwined was recently brought home to me by a woman ('Eleanora'), who e-mailed me a year after I had originally sent her my article, partly based on her interview, for comments (Saukko, 2000). She wrote to me that she did not recognize herself in my description of a lonely and pained child, fallen victim of forces beyond her control. She noted that it played into the general victimizing of anorexics, which does not account for the fact that anorexic women can also be strong. Still, she observed that the notion that women always have to be strong may also be counterproductive and that her own life-course, which has sidetracked her adamant goal and career orientation, has made her more aloof and more happy, even if insecure about her future. The mini-life-story embedded in Eleanora's e-mail brings forth an ambivalence, which is left little space between the polarized discussions on anorexia between being a victim or a 'dope', and being emancipated or 'taking one's life into one's own hands'. Her critique of my work underscores the fact that this ambivalence, between knowing and not knowing, between being in control and out of control, cannot be stated in principle only but needs to underpin the way in which we relate to and write about the people we study.

Dialogues

In order to think of a way that would acknowledge the double-faced nature of our experience of ourselves – always located between knowing and not knowing ourselves – I adopted three research and writing strategies that aimed to embody this idea in the research process itself.

First, in accordance with the phenomenological, dialogic principle, I wanted to bring to the fore, both in my interviews and in the final reports, that the women's story is the product of the author's quest to understand the interviewee or Other. Thus, I wanted to understand and present the women as 'dialogic' characters. Bakhtin (1981) distinguishes dialogic characters from monologic ones that reduce the individual to a function in a formulaic trope ('the hero' in chivalric story) or a prop for a ready-made theory ('the anorexic' in much social research). Thus, instead of rendering the women tokens for theory, I wanted to construct their stories in a way that would have their own integrity, honouring the women's knowledge about themselves. I also wanted to acknowledge the particularity and partiality of my own self, both in the interview and in the research text, such as my history as an ex-anorexic and a feminist scholar, which aimed to ease the division between a knowing subject and known object and to open the scholar's position for debate.

Second, as my goal was to explore how social discourses interlace experience, I could not stop at being true to the women's stories. Still, again following the dialogic principle, I decided not to examine the discourses underpinning the women's stories 'from the outside', but I posed them as a question to the women. Thus, when I interviewed the women, I not only asked them about their experience of anorexia and bulimia (which inevitably led to discussions on body and beauty ideals), but I also asked them what they thought of the discourses that define and treat the conditions and them. The intention with this approach was to invite the women to reflect on their experience, and thereby occupy the role of the 'knower' and not only that of 'the known'.

Third, and in keeping with the principle of polyvocality, I wanted to acknowledge that I was interviewing anorexic women in the plural and not in the singular. Thus, in order to do justice to the specificity of the women's discussions, I decided that I would aim for an analytical and writing strategy that would contrast their stories to one another. Unlike much traditional interview-research on discourses, I did not want to trace a discursive 'pattern' that unites the stories. My goal was also different from action research's notion of dialogue, in that I did not aim to necessarily bring the different views together into one consensus that would facilitate a plan for empowerment. Rather I wanted to conceive the relationships between the women's self-analysis in more 'rhizomatic' or 'crabgrass' like terms (Deleuze and Guattari, 1987), as pointing to different directions, both to commonalities and discrepancies between the different perspectives. My intention was to highlight that a discourse that one woman may experience as empowering may seem disempowering from another one's perspective. Rather than brush these discrepancies under the carpet, my goal was to flesh them out and pave the way for multidimensional politics and analysis of anorexia that recognizes the contradictions of the discourses.

To illustrate how this strategy works, I will return to my interview with Jeanne, who analyzed her undergraduate years, when she was anorexic, as symptomatic of 'the Reagan years'. 'This was when women were supposed to have it all, be extremely successful in all realms and be extremely thin and good-looking', she said. So, Jeanne found herself more and more obsessed with eating less and less, and she exercised a lot too. 'I would make myself run and run and run and run. And even though I had no energy and felt like shit, you know, I'd force myself to do this', Jeanne counts. She also worked in popular campus bars, where her body was exposed to public display a lot, and she used the money she made to buy fashionable clothes, such as short tops to show off her thin body. She was also a good student and, in general, derived pleasure from pushing herself as far as she could. According to her own analysis:

> And so I would go to the undergraduate student lounge, where people could smoke. And I'd smoke, smoke and smoke and drink diet sodas and just study into the night. It was just this form of personal hell, but I enjoyed knowing I was getting all my homework done and wasn't slacking off.

Methodologically speaking, Jeanne's story can be interpreted in two basic ways. First, it can be seen as a self-reflexive critique of the way in which the hyperindividualist and competitive neo-conservative discourse of the 1980s constructed femininity (this is the 'true story' approach, with a self-reflective spin). Second, as I had read an extraordinary amount of literature on anorexia, and was relatively critical of it, I also read the story in terms of how the notion of anorexia as an obsession with modern self-control permeates Jeanne's self-understanding (this is 'the self' as constituted through social discourses approach). One could, obviously, split the argument and say that both of these views are 'true' *per se* and illuminate different facets (subject *and* object) of the experience of the self. However, this strategy reproduces the subject *or* object dichotomy, in that I would be positioning myself as 'the knower' and Jeanne as, at best, half-knower. This view would produce two sharply distinguished orders of knowledge, effectively discrediting Jeanne's powerful personal and political critique. In the spirit of dialogic understanding, the best one can do is to flesh out the ambiguity of my own interpretation and the problems embedded in each position. However, in order to render Jeanne's story as part of a conversation, it needs to be seen in relation to other stories, such as that of Taru.

Taru associated her anorexia to having danced ballet in her teens. However, she was also particularly critical of the discussions and definitions on anorexia, pointing out that they were very similar to notions she encountered when dancing ballet. Taru observed that the discourses on anorexia were not unlike the stories in sports and fitness magazines, which define women as always 'weaker' than men, with less strength, more fat and so on. Taru says stories on anorexia are similar, defining women as weak, because they can 'not take the ideological pressure', or defining their mothers as weak. Taru recounts how for 15 years, since the age of 5, she did everything she could to become a professional dancer. She put herself through an excruciating regime of endless exercises, pain, long stays abroad, crossing half of Finland to go to lessons, and nibbling on boiled rice and Tabasco-sauce. All this to make her enduring, strong, light and flawless. And finally, she was defined as a weak, flawed poor girl who could not make it. Taru told me she does not want to analyze the cause of her anorexia too much: 'I'm afraid it just reveals more weaknesses and abnormalities'.

As I was interested in critically analyzing discourses that define anorexia, I was academically and personally drawn to Taru's analysis. However, when discussing her interview at an academic conference, a member of the audience pointed out that she was still hell bent to 'be strong'. Thus, Taru's story can also be interpreted in two ways. First, it can be seen as a powerful self-reflexive critique of the way in which discourses that inform anorexia, as well as discourses that define and treat the condition move in a circle, perpetually defining women as lacking, too weak, or as always inferior in relation to a gendered ideal. Second, it can also be interpreted as continuing to subscribe to the anorexic desire to 'be strong' and 'not weak', therefore, articulating submission to the modernist discourse that idealizes strength. However, the latter interpretation undermines Taru's critical perspective, reading it as an indicator that she is still, perhaps, caught in the anorexic mentality, or, in therapeutic terms, 'in denial'. While the notion of being in denial may have its undisputable therapeutic insights and effects, it still violently disinvests one's words of any speaking power, brushing off Taru's poignant criticism as merely a 'symptom' of an underlying problem.

The methodological advantage of contrasting these two stories, and the contradictory interpretations of them is that it sets all the different views in motion. Together, neither the stories, nor my interpretations come across as totally 'right' or 'wrong', but they each seem to speak a partial truth. Even if Jeanne is relatively positive about discourses on anorexia, and Taru is highly critical of them, neither of them 'know' themselves better than the other; they simply highlight different facets of the discourse on anorexia. On a level, the stories of Jeanne and Taru clash with one another. Jeanne criticizes those discourses, which made her pursue 'strength' to the point of destructive anorexic obsession, whereas Taru challenges the discourse, which frames anorexic women's ambitions and desire to be strong as merely pathological, arguing it simply frames women as perpetually lacking in strength. Still, the perspectives of the two women also coalesce in that they both illuminate the stubborn violence embedded in the distinction between being in control or strong and its negative, being victimized, marked by an elusive, and profoundly gendered demand of being in full and independent command of one's life.

In the end, my study of anorexia underlines the need to imagine ways of studying lived experience that mediate between honouring people's experience and critically interrogating them. Much research on how discourses interlace experiences is critical of the power that those discourses exert on people by imposing a diagnosis on them. Yet, many of them are underpinned by the same diagnostic logic that argues that experts know people better than they themselves do. If we are to criticize the normative diagnostic logic that perpetuates social life – and our personal life, as discourses become internalized in the form of self-diagnosis – we need to make this criticism also inform the way in which we do research. This means that we need to fetch modes of doing research that approach experience in ambivalent terms, that take experience truly seriously while acknowledging that they are always partial and compromised by social discourses. This way we may do justice to the lived as well as criticize the problematic features of its social underpinnings (as well as, of course, acknowledge the benevolent or empowering features of its social commitments) in a way that criticizes structures of domination not only through the content or message of research but also through the way in which it is conducted.

Conclusions

Foucault's work on how social and institutional discourses interlace our most intimate experiences of ourselves has laid the foundation for an entire paradigm and practice in qualitative research on studying discourses and experiences.

Many of the studies done within this approach study discourses from the 'outside', or objectively, in the sense that they investigate how social discourses guide people's identities and behaviour. Some of the analyses have a therapeutic goal of ameliorating the institutional discourses so that they better benefit 'clients', such as ill people. Others take a radically negative stance towards discourses that define, for example, 'addictions', arguing they simply foster increasing self-surveillance and discipline. Often the problem with the institutional analyses is that they neglect to question the problematic underpinnings of the therapeutic goal itself, such as certain notions of 'safe' sex. The trouble with the radically critical approaches is that they end up implicitly embracing a state of 'freedom' from discipline, the naïvety of which can be illustrated by the pro-anorexia websites that resist medical discourses on anorexia and advocate starving as a lifestyle choice.

The most interesting studies on discourses, such as discourses on alcoholism or codependency, explore the way in which they have both dominating and empowering aspects both in personal and social senses. However, the shortcoming of these studies is that while they criticize dominating aspects of discourses, the 'diagnostic' logic embedded in their own research practice – which claims to know better what drives people in their actions than they themselves do – ends up perpetuating similar domination as the institutional discourses they study. Self-reflexive modes of study have tried to overcome this problem by acknowledging that also scholars are guided by discourses in their personal and professional lives. Self-reflexive modes of study can sometimes take the shape of critical autoethnography, which refers to a practice where the scholar, through a self-reflexive introspection, interrogates how social discourses have defined her/his experience. However, self-reflexivity can also be translated to dialogic modes of research that create a critical dialogue between the scholar and the people (s)he studies on the discourses that have defined their experiences for them. One form of dialogic study is action research, which aims to enable the scholar and the people to arrive at a critical consensus about discourses that have defined them in problematic ways in order to reach a programme of action. In my own work I have imagined the self-reflexive dialogue in more 'rhizomatic' terms that does not aim to establish a consensus but allows the different experiences to illuminate the empowering and disempowering elements of discourses and to highlight their complexity. This mode of analyzing experiences and discourses fleshes their multidimensionality through both the content and form of research.

Exercise 4

- Write a short description of your own or someone else's lived experience (based, for example, on an interview).
- Collect popular or scientific texts that describe the same or similar lived experience. Analyze the commonalities and differences between the 'real' lived experience and the texts. To what extent is the lived experience guided by the popular and scientific discourses? Does the experience challenge or criticize the discourses?
- If you have interviewed other people, ask them to analyze the discourses that you have found in the cultural texts and to reflect how they have impacted their lives. If you are discussing your own experience, introspectively explore the role that the discourses have played in shaping your sense of your experience.
- As a last step, discuss the personal and political implications of the discourses that shape the lived experience you are studying. What kinds of effects do they have on a personal level? What types of social or political ideologies or regimes do they support? Think carefully through the contradictions of the discourses on both personal and political levels.

Part III

Reading Discourses

5

Reading Ideology

Main questions

- **What are the possibilities and problems embedded in classical structuralist methods, such as semiotics and narrative analysis, which analyze the 'ideology' embedded in cultural texts?**
- **How do notions of intertextuality and contextuality enrich structuralist analyses of texts?**
- **How do postmodern or ironic texts complicate ideological analysis? What are the insights and blind spots of both postmodern texts and postmodern forms of textual analysis?**
- **Just like texts, methods for analyzing texts are 'ideological', in the sense that they are invested in particular historical, social and political agendas. How can one explore the ideological nature of modes of textual analysis itself?**

The trademark of cultural studies, both in its classic and contemporary forms, has been the analysis of texts or discourses, to the point that the paradigm has been accused of a tendency to reduce all social phenomena into texts (Ferguson and Golding, 1997). One could say, however, that the specific feature of cultural studies' approach to texts is that, rather than examining their formal or aesthetic features, the paradigm investigates the way in which cultural texts emerge from, and play a role in, the changing historical, political, and social context. Thus, what characterizes cultural studies' approach to culture is not 'textualism' but 'contextualism' (Grossberg, 1997).

The interest in texts within the social context is umbilically connected with an interest in power. Originally, the interest in power articulated cultural studies' attempt to reformulate the Marxist notion of 'ideology', which interpreted culture largely in terms of dominant ideology that distorts reality in a way that serves the interests of the powerful. While cultural studies continues to examine the relationship between culture and social domination, it understands cultural texts, such as popular culture products, not to be mere loci of domination. Rather, it views them as a site of contestation over meaning, where different groups compete to set forth their understandings of the state of the affairs in the world. In order to make sense of 'how' the world was made to mean, early cultural studies resorted to structuralist methods of analyzing texts, such as semiotics and narrative analysis. Even if the boom of analysis of ideology and the use of structuralist methods in cultural studies was in the 1970s, these approaches continue to be widely used, and they also underpin many of the later approaches. For this reason, the first half of this chapter is devoted to discussing ideology, narrative and semiotics, using analyses of the classical, yet still blockbusting, James Bond films as an example.

However, not only texts but also forms of textual analysis are political and historical. To illustrate this, in the latter half of the chapter I will critically reflect on contemporary 'postmodern' texts as well as postmodern forms of textual analysis. Rather than making claims about reality 'out there', postmodern texts refer to other media texts, making often ironic and critical statements about the mediated nature of our reality. Postmodern modes of textual analysis usually revel in this critically self-reflexive interest in mediation that characterizes postmodern texts. Through analyses of some recent advertisements that mock documentary photographs on the South and the cult-movie *Natural Born Killers*, I will address some of the possibilities, problems and politics embedded in postmodern modes of producing and interpreting texts that characterize our times.

My overall intention in this chapter is to underline the need to, and outline ways to, examine any given text as well as any form of textual analysis against the historical and political context. If one is to unravel the complex historical and political agendas and struggles embedded in texts and interpretation, one needs to analyze them from several different perspectives that flesh out their diverse commitments and blind spots. Illustrating how this type of multi-perspectival textual analysis works, is the task this chapter sets out to fulfil.

Signification and power

Cultural studies' specific approach to texts is partly explained by the fact that the Birmingham-period research on subcultures and popular culture coincided and became part of the golden age of the French semiotic movement, spearheaded by Saussure (1960) and then Barthes (1972) as well as the Italian Eco (1979[1965]). These structuralist theorists investigated linguistic structures, such as basic units and recurring tropes, that were understood to be universal or apply to all natural languages or, at least, to specific genres of texts. One of these universal units that semiotics delineated is the sign, constituting of the signifier (or 'sign vehicle' e.g. 'white') and signified (or mental image e.g. 'purity'). What was crucial, from a cultural studies point of view, was that the relationship between the signifier and the signified was understood to be arbitrary, a matter of convention or, as cultural studies would underline, a matter of politics. Furthermore, the stitching between a particular signifier and signified was understood to be open for negotiation or signs were understood to be poly-semic or multiaccentual, to borrow Volosinov's term (Volosinov, 1973). Thus, signs could be interpreted differently in different contexts and by different groups (whiteness could have both positive and negative associations, depend-ing on the situation).

What interested cultural studies was the politics embedded in the process of forging a connection between a signifier and a signified. The paradigm coined this process as 'struggle over meaning', seeing it as an arena where different social groups competed to make the world mean. The most famous example of such struggles is the Civil Rights Movement's slogan 'Black is beautiful', which aimed to reverse the negative associations of blackness (ugly, inferior, etc.) (Hall, 1982). A later example of a similar phenomenon is the use of the term 'nigga' in rap-music, which renders a previously derogatory meaning into a sign of tough pride and threat, turning the racist notion of vice into a new virtue as well as a reminder of a racist past and present (it can, however, be debated to what extent this machismo subverts, and to what extent affirms, the original racist sign).

In broader theoretical terms, the semiotic theory and method helped cultural studies in its reformulation of the classical Marxist notion of dominant ideo-logy, which was often interpreted in terms of dominant or bourgeoisie ideas, which 'becloud' people's understanding of social reality and inequality. Even if cultural studies would not deny inequality, it wanted to acknowledge the com-plex nature of culture and ideology that, rather than being a uniform strait-jacket imposed on people, constituted a shifting, contested terrain.

Texts and contexts

Meanings of Bond

Many of the early cultural studies, as well as semiotic literature, analyzed the way in which meaning is constituted in popular texts and images, such as photographs, films and popular culture. Perhaps the most famous one of these analyses is Barthes' discussion of the colonialist myth articulated by the *Paris Match* cover of a black soldier saluting the French flag (Barthes, 1972). However, to illustrate the structuralist framework, I will take a closer look at Eco's (1979[1965]) analysis of Ian Fleming's famous spy-novels on James Bond, which were later turned into a series of blockbuster movies. I have chosen to focus on Eco's analysis, because it was later complemented, as well as challenged, by the cultural studies scholars, Bennett and Woollacott (1987), providing a useful illustration of the difference between structuralism and cultural studies.

Making an ironic reference to the first novel, *Casino Royale*, where Bond's colleague comments that he should not become human as he is such a 'wonderful machine', Eco notes that, in his novels, Fleming himself has built a system that works predictably like a machine (Eco, 1979: 46). Using structuralist methods, Eco outlines this machine-like or mechanic formula that fuels Bond-stories:

A. M moves and gives a task to Bond
B. Villain moves and appears to Bond (perhaps in vicarious forms)
C. Bond moves and gives a first check to Villain or Villain gives first check to Bond
D. Woman moves and shows herself to Bond
E. Bond takes Woman (possesses her or begins her seduction)
F. Villain captures Bond (with or without Woman, or at different moments)
G. Villain tortures Bond (with or without Woman)
H. Bond beats Villain (kills him, or kills his representative or helps at their killing)
I. Bond, convalescing, enjoys Woman, whom he then loses
    (Eco, 1979: 156)

Eco's construction of the skeletal-plot, which he argues repeats in each Bond novel, is based on Propp's analysis of the morphology of the folktale, with its primordial Hero, who gets a Task, goes through various trials and torments fighting the Villain, and, finally, completes the task and gets his Reward (Propp, 1968). This recurring plot, Eco argues, is underlaced or stitched together by a series of binaries (M/Bond; Bond/Woman; Bond/Villain; Free World/Soviet Union; Great Britain/Non-Anglo-Saxon-Countries) (Lévi-Strauss, 1970). Eco's analysis illustrates how one can use structuralist tools, such as Proppian narrative-analysis and Lévi-Straussian notion of binaries, to break a cultural product into basic units, thereby exposing its underlying structure as well as the often dichotomous value-principles that suture it.

Eco's main goal is to uncover the formula underneath a mass-market novel. He acknowledges that Bond novels can be deemed racist (since the Villains are, by and large, non-Anglo-Saxons), anti-communist, and to buttress primordial notions of women as caught up between perversion and purity, finally succumbing to seduction and ending in death (161). However, rather than seeing Bond stories as a reactionary political conspiracy, Eco argues that the reactionary nature of the novels is not so much constituted by their content than their form. Fleming's tactic of using archetypes to construct a successful novel reproduces the Manichean formula, which views the world in black and white terms as made up of good and evil forces in conflict (162).

The greatest strength and weakness of Eco's analysis, and many others done along similar lines, is its clean-cut nature, which makes all elements of Bond novels fall into prescribed categories that 'make sense'. As such, the analysis illuminates certain key features of Bond that help to unravel aspects of its politics or ideology. Still, even if the neatness of Eco's analysis appeals to logic, it is also irritatingly predictable, in the same way as the many student works that I have read, which keep finding that images of women in popular culture fall into the primordial categories of Mother and Whore. While it is true that these archetypes saturate popular culture, focusing solely on them often renders the analysis sterile or not particularly illuminative, since it tends to miss the small shifts and variations, historical details and contexts, which often account for much of the appeal of these stories.

In fact, Eco makes an interesting comment that Fleming's Bond stories abandon 'psychological motivations' and apply a 'structural' or 'formalistic' strategy (146). However, this poses the chicken or the egg question of whether it is Fleming who introduces formulas into his Bond stories or whether it is Eco, who reads them into the novels. Structuralism as an enterprise was decidedly objectivist in that it presumed the scientist and the texts (s)he studied to be separate and saw its project to discern, in an unbiased fashion, the 'patterns' that repeat in the material. However, any methodological approach not merely represents its objects of study but also, in part, constitutes them. Thus, the formulaic nature of the structuralist approach easily reinforces the machine-like and Manichean mode of thought it aims to expose and criticize.

Bond and beyond

From what I would deem to be more of a cultural studies interpretation, Bennett and Woollacott (1987) have read the Bond-phenomenon somewhat differently. They argue against Eco, noting that he does not sufficiently take into account the intertextuality of Bond, that is, the way it can only be understood in relation to the wider cultural and social panorama, consisting of other texts. What this intertextuality underlines is that Bond looks different when examined from different perspectives or in relation to different texts and contexts. What Bennett and Woollacott argue is that, in the British context, Bond novels should be read against the early twentieth century 'imperialist spy-thriller', which concerned the exploits of an English gentleman and an amateur spy, who warded off a threat to Britain represented by a foreign villain, usually associated with anarchism or socialism (83). Even if there are similarities between the imperialist spy-thriller and Bond novels, there are also significant differences, which highlight the ideological specificity and complexity of Bond-phenomena, which Eco does not wholly capture.

For example, in the imperialist novel the spy is upper leisure-class and thwarts off foreign 'syndicates' that disturb life in London clubs and England's country houses. On the contrary, Bond is a middle-class professional, who takes orders from M, who (before the introduction of Judi Dench as M in the most recent films) represents the old England and its old-boy-networks and often ends up in tension with Bond. Bond's lifestyle, predicated on liberal attitudes towards sex and gambling and docking of martinis, is also decidedly cosmopolitan and modern. Thus, instead of simply reproducing inherited ideologies, Bond novels rework them, imagining an English hero in new terms of professionalism and competitive individualism (113).

Furthermore, the Bond 'girl' is also a departure from the imperialist novel, which did not feature women in prominent roles. The girl provides Bond with an enigma (usually lodged in some dark secret of her past), which he needs to solve, and action, in that he needs to put her (as well as the 'foreign' villains) back in her place. Yet, the Bond girl is not archetypically feminine, often acting violently and beguilingly, she is more 'equal' to Bond, and their relationship is not predicated on the codes of chivalry and romance, but mostly sex or, to borrow Bennett and Woollacott, their relation is one of 'pure cock and cunt' (123). As such, the Bond girl is a kind of male fantasy version of the sexually liberated, independent woman, whose only restriction is that she should submit to the phallus (118).

This rereading does not make Bond novels and films 'progressive'; on many basic levels they remain deeply racist, sexist, narrowly nationalist, anti-welfare, and anti-communist. However, read against the mid-century British class- and gender-structures, and their cultural manifestations, it becomes apparent that Bond novels not only reproduce, but also twist, them, giving the archetypical Englishness a decidedly modern flair. This, argue Bennett and Woollacott, accounts for the popularity of the Bond-phenomenon, because in order to appeal to a wide audience, it has to connect with some popular and critical sentiments (4), even if this does not make the phenomenon a harbinger of radicalism.

This sensitivity to complexity and the intertextual and social context enables a more nuanced and better grounded analysis of a popular text than the formalistic semiotics or narrative analysis. Analyzing texts or discourses from multiple points of view, in order to tease out the social contradictions and contestations embedded in it is one of the trademarks of cultural studies. Besides Bond, it has shed light on, for instance, how Thatcherism turned the traditional Labour and Tory imaginary upside down (Hall, 1988). At a time of an acute economic crisis and unemployment, Thatcherism managed to present itself as on the side of 'the little people' and against the 'Trade Union barons', by appealing to the lower middle-class and 'respectable' working-class values of self-reliance and self-discipline, encapsulated in her slogan: 'you can't spend what you haven't got' (Hall, 1988: 71). Thatcherism can be analyzed in terms of the dichotomies between 'Us' and 'Them' that it constitutes, such respectable people versus Trade Union barons, welfare scroungers, and tinpot dictators (in reference to the Falklands War). Yet, the most important feature of Thatcherism (or Reaganism), argues Hall, is how it managed to articulate everyone into 'Us' by tickling a number of social nerves, which can only be analyzed by paying keen attention to the nuances of historical, political and social context.

The methodological lesson learnt from this is that the structuralist toolkit of methods, such as semiotics and narrative analysis, is good in highlighting certain key elements in cultural texts. However, because of its formalistic and logical nature it may end up imprinting this formalism into the products it studies. More than 30 years after the landmark works of Barthes and Eco, semiotics remains the bread and butter of almost any book on methods in cultural and communication studies, sometimes outlined as if a bag of tricks, useful to crack the code of culture (e.g. Berger, 2000). However, if we are to make sense of the political underpinnings and implications of the way in which the world is made to mean, or the signifier and signified stitched together, we need to pay careful attention to the historical, social, emotional and so on economies at play in any given social moment and place. If we do that, we may begin to see the fussier side of the cultural and social world, which does not fall so neatly into dichotomies and plots, but where there are twists, tweaks and blurrings that may reflect and change meaning and history in quite consequential ways. Being sensitive to nuances and ambiguities is also necessary if we are to reach beyond the Manichean machinery that splices the world into heroes and villains and mothers and whores, and begins to push beyond straightforward judgements and to see, and learn from, the grey areas in popular phenomena, such as Thatcherism and James Bonds.

Postmodern texts and analysis

James Bond and Thatcherism, as social and cultural phenomena, can be argued to be predicated on 'modern' cultural and social logic. Both discourses split the world rather neatly into 'us' (respectable English) and 'them' (tinpot dictators, Russian spies or, as of late, Russian mafia). Even if they both are, on occasion, hyperbolic, they both seem to make claims about what the reality 'is like'. However, contemporary media products and discourses increasingly obey a 'postmodern' logic. Following Baudrillard (1983), they can be characterized by a 'floating signifier', which no longer refers to a signified but to other signifiers, such as media texts. Thus, for example, the cult-movie *Pulp Fiction* (Tarantino, 1994) can be argued not to be, first and foremost, about gangster violence (which it 'depicts') but about media-violence, referring not to, lets say, any criminal neighbourhoods or people but to a vast archive of previous gangster, horror, and other classic and obscure movies (Polan, 2000).

To illustrate both how to analyze postmodern texts as well as to outline a postmodern way of analyzing texts, I will examine a few images in a recent issue of a rave-magazine *The Ministry*. Before I move on to the images, however, a few words on the magazine and rave-culture are in order. The British version of rave or techno-culture appeals to a predominantly white youth of varied class-backgrounds, and it has been argued to be decidedly postmodern or 'artificial' in that it does not have 'organic' roots in any particular community or culture. Rather, rave-culture has its origins in a mass market package-holiday (raves are argued to have originated from dance-parties in the Mediterranean resort-town of Ibiza), and it is characterized by a music created by dj's, who mix elements of already existing music and computer-generated sounds, and the easy use of the controversial, 'clean', mind-altering drug Ecstasy (Melechi, 1993; Redhead, 1993). This somewhat extravagant artificiality and superficiality has been alternately eulogized and condemned as the epitome of millennial abandon, hedonism, commercialism, and anti-establishment counterculture. *The Ministry* magazine belongs to the more straightforwardly commercially oriented end of the rave-scene, being one of the many commercial spin-offs of a London based dance-club, The Ministry of Sound (Collin, 1998). It is a thick glossy magazine with many flashy ads, fashions spreads, reviews of records, and articles, which often take a liberal attitude to some controversial topic, such as cocaine (February 2000) or hard-core pornography (November 2001).

The image that I will analyze depicts a group of Thai street children, who seem to be between 2 and 7 years of age. When one first takes a look at it, it reads like a news photograph, having all the iconic features of a documentary image of 'The Third World': the children are bare-foot, wearing torn, dirty clothes, and set against an ambiguous backdrop of corrugated metal with graffiti. 'Hat Patong Road, Phuket', reads the copy in 'Thai'ish' letters. Some of the children just stand, staring at the camera, others are making martial arts and other 'street pose' type gestures. Looking at the image more closely, one can see that next to each child a small copy gives the brand names, such as Gap, Polo Ralph Lauren, Tommy Hilfiger and Blue Marlin, and prices of the caps the children are wearing (*Ministry*, February 2000: 072–3). The picture is part of a special issue on the then newly released movie *The Beach*, which is used as a starting point for a series of small articles and a fashion spread on Thailand, which was becoming popular among ravers, searching for new holiday venues besides the traditional Ibiza. Most of the images in the special issue follow the traditional Orientalist tradition of revelling in the exoticism and eroticism of the 'East' (Said, 1995[1978]), featuring young people and models against deep blue 'tropical' sky and sea. The picture of the street children forms part of a small set of 'mock realist' pictures, which also includes photographs on Thai elders and a group of young Thai boxers.

As discussed earlier, any given text can be analyzed in relation to different social texts and sensibilities in order to unravel its contradictory politics. Still, not only the content of texts but also the forms of texts as well as forms of textual analysis are political. If one is to unravel the diverse and multilayered politics embedded in any given text one needs to examine it both in relation to different social agendas and using different methodological approaches. In order to illustrate how this type of multiperspectival analysis works and how it helps to tease out the many political agendas within a given text, I will in the following analyze the image of the Thai children first from a semiotic point of view and second using a postmodern interpretative strategy.

Reading the meanings of 'street'

Interpreted semiotically, one can look at the ad on the children in terms of forging an association with the caps (the signifier or brand) and the children and what they stand for, namely being street-wise or having 'street credibility' (signified) (see Goldman, 1992; Bignell, 1997). This interpretation is supported by a small separate text-ad, featuring one of the labels and referring to the image of the children that reads:

> Tapping into the new vogue for things Cuban, *Blue Marlin* have just made hats for the Cuban national team while in spring, they are launching an international series with old team logos from around the world. Seeking some street individuality? They got it. (*Ministry*, February 2000: 061)

Read this way, the ad blends into a tidal wave of popular culture and products – ranging from interior design magazines and labels, such as Benetton, to various 'well-being' therapies and toiletries – which are infatuated with 'difference'. As Hall has noted, whereas the old Fordist, Thatcherite project embodied a highly defensive nationalism, such as Bond fighting Russian spies, the new global Post Fordism revels in difference, trying to 'live with, overcome, sublate, get hold of, and incorporate' it (Hall, 1997: 33; also Kaplan, 1995; Lury, 1996; Ahmed, 2000; Franklin, Lury and Stacey, 2001).

The specificity of the image of street children is that it does not evoke the usual associations between difference, naturalism and exotic beauty. Rather, it appeals to a tougher or more 'cool' notion of difference. Just like with the Bond texts, this fascination with street-cool becomes intelligible against the background of other social texts and sensibilities. There are (at least) two sensibilities that this 'streetwise' image articulates. First, it can be seen as part of the long-term Western Orientalist tradition, which is fascinated with difference, wanting to appropriate or consume it. In this sense, the particular appeal of images of marginality and 'the street' is that it allows white, Western middle-class youth to experience some of the thrillingly embodied intensity associated with the 'toughness' of ghetto life, of being on the edge, in danger, or close to death (Sernhede, 2000). As has been pointed out by hooks (1992; also Kaur and Hutnyk, 1999) this fascination does not so much aim to open up to different people and places but mainly serves to refashion the self. It becomes a practice of 'eating the other', rendering difference merely a hot spice to spark up 'the dull dish of Western culture', or as *Ministry* instructs: 'mix in a little of that Goa spirituality, add a dash of Ibiza sun, garnish with the contents of Shaun Ryder's medicine cabinet and serve on a beach' (*Ministry*, February 2000: 029).

However, the second interpretation of the image is that it signals an affinity with the 'street-cool' of black dance music, such as hip hop, expressing both a bid to expropriate it as well as to belong, of being a part of a wider youthful, multicultural partying and radicalism, with all its contradictory romanticism of things 'street' and 'black'. This partying also becomes intelligible in opposition to the Thatcherite respectable, little-England mentality, against which 'rough' images of difference, threatening street-poses, references to the traditional enemies of the Western mindset, such as Thai ghettos and Castro's Cuba, and use of recreational drugs is intended as an offensive.

Depending on the angle from which one looks at the picture, it seems rather different, appearing as if continuing an old racist tradition or questioning a certain rigid and racist nationalism. The methodological point this underlines is twofold. First, any text or image has multiple interpretations, looking different when examined in relation to different texts or social sensibilities. The task of analysis is not to decide which of these interpretations is most 'correct' but the goal is to explore some of the possible interpretations in order to flesh out the complex politics of the text. It can be added that one can never exhaust all the meanings of a text. Rather than a cause of concern, this should be interpreted as an incitement to try and look at any given text from different angles. However, it also invites us to be less arrogant, in the sense of acknowledging that we can never arrive at a 'complete' interpretation of a text, but our reading will always remain socially located and circumscribed and blind to other meanings and politics.

The second thing that the few interpretations of the image underline is that just like the 'content' of the image looks different from different angles, so does the 'form' of the image. Eco's analysis implies that particular textual forms, such as polarized plotlines, are intrinsically 'reactionary'. The image of the street children does not juxtapose good and evil, but plays with, and thereby obscures, what is deemed evil or, at least, a problem. This evasion of 'Manicheanism', however, does not make the image radical, as this kind of 'playing with' danger-ous difference has become the norm in much contemporary culture with all its associated possibilities and problems as discussed above. What this empha-sizes is that the 'ideological' nature of form is also different in different social contexts. Thus, less polarized and more nuanced and ambivalent interpretation may be laudable in many contexts (one is immediately reminded of the after-math of 'September 11'). However, in other contexts, such as in relation to the image of the street children, it may also breed 'cool' indifference, and in still others it may end up politically and ethically untenable, such as when taking a stance on Guatemalan genocide, as discussed in Chapter 3.

Postmodern readings

Reading the image of the street children semiotically usefully unearths some of its political contradictions. However, the image can also be read from another methodological perspective as a classic postmodern text. The reason it catches our attention is because it brings into mind countless news photo-graphs on street children, which seems out of place in a leisure-centred glossy magazine. Thus, in classical postmodern fashion the image does not only, or even primarily, refer to a 'reality' out there ('the street') but to other signifiers (news photographs of street children) (Baudrillard, 1983).

This two-layered nature of the image makes it both similar to, and different from, other 'new wave' ads, such as the famous Benetton image of a bird amidst an oil spill. While both the Benetton ad and the ad with the children refer to previous documentary photographs on 'catastrophe', the image of the street children is different in that it does not want to sell the caps through associating them with a concern for Third World children, that is, it is not selling the brands, trying to associate them with a 'global conscience', the way Benetton markets itself (Giroux, 1994b; Lury, 2001). On the contrary, the picture's power to address, irritate and surprise the reader derives from the fact that it frustrates or interrupts expectations that we generally have of documentary images of street children, which evoke empathy, pity and notions of the South as desolate. In this sense, it can be argued to interrupt the ideology embedded in the prototypical, condescendingly empathetic, yet appalled, Western documentary gaze on the South.

In fact, the same technique of disruption is used in other images in the magazine, such as a photograph of an old, barefoot Columbian woman crouched to pick coca-leaves, which accompanies a reportage on the increasing use of cocaine in clubs. The picture is identical to the countless photographs on drug-plantations in the South, associated with foreignness, danger and poverty. The text accompanying the image, however, shortcircuits these associations: 'Harvesting coca plants in Columbia. Bit like your gran's backyard, isn't it?' By rerouting the image to something banally homely (grandmother's backyard and notions of traditional English gardening that it immediately brings into mind) the picture mocks the expectations of danger and foreignness.

Read through postmodernity, the striking feature of these images is their analytical reflexivity. The photographs have been carefully selected: the iconic images of street children and drug-plantations dot our newspapers and news forecasts day and night in and day and night out. These everyday images that all carry a strong aura of global catastrophe, concern and danger are part of the ubiquitous (tele)visual apparatus that creates the contemporary universal 'real'. As Doane (1990) has argued, focusing on melodramatic images of catastrophe, particularly on graphic details of dead, dying or otherwise suffering, such as poor and wretched, and in particular children's bodies, the global televisual asserts its 'realness'. By inviting strong feelings, these images invite the reader to 'feel and feel' and, thereby, feel in touch with the real, so that Baudrillard has defined images of Southern despair as the West's 'hallucinogen and aphrodisiac' (Baudrillard, 1994: 71; Clough, 1997: 97).

Thus, the radical aspect of the images in *The Ministry* magazine is that they break the spell of this obsession with the 'real'. By offering a classically coded documentary image of the South to the reader, only to mock it, they make us conscientious of the coded and political nature of these traditional realist images. By refusing the reality-effect, the pictures break away with two classical Western tropes on the South, which view it as either a threatening subject or an object of our charity. By rendering the coca-harvesting woman a gardening granny, the image deviates the associations of Third World drug-fields, danger, threat and anarchy (Campbell and Reeves, 1994). The same way, the picture of the street children with the caps does not invite either empathy or fear, thereby disrupting any pious concern for children from the South, which allow the Western subject to construct him/herself as a charitable person, with its accompanying condescending sentimentality.

Ungrounded images

However, even if the postmodern reading of the pictures exposes how they challenge mainstream ideologies about the South, this textual strategy as well as interpretation has its problems. Thus, just as the 'content' of texts can be read from multiple perspectives and in relation to different politics, the 'form' of texts and textual analysis can be interpreted in different ways to tease out their contradictions.

Postmodern images, which work by self-reflexively challenging other images and texts, not to 'reality', have been criticized for leading to what Lury (2001) has called 'cultural essentialism'. This means that they disembed or unground culture, erasing historical links between people, products, places and practices (183). Thus, the image of street children may mock the conventions of Western documentary gaze on the South, but, at the same time, it erases the issues of global inequality and urban poverty from the agenda. The coolness and irony the image communicates refer back to the West's own imagery. This constitutes an instance of double-consumption, where the West first consumes catastrophic images of the South and then consumes the South again in the form of an ironic reference to its own imagery. By the time we get to the caps ad, the issue of poverty has become a style.

In this respect, the image of the coca-picker is slightly more interesting. The image forms a part of a reportage on cocaine, which discusses its health risks and users' experiences. A small by-text discusses the 'origins' of coca, comparing the prices the growers get to street prices, referring to Columbian paramilitary rule, the ineffective nature of US counternarcotics policy and favourably mentioning the more orderly rule of leftist guerrillas in some of the cocaine growing areas (Naylor, 2001: 034). In a small way, these 'facts' could be said to establish a connection between cocaine use in British 'club-land' and cocaine growing in Latin America. Thus, together with the image, the text also challenges the counterproductive tendency to 'victimize' people, such as coca-growers, which does little to improve the position of dispossessed groups, serving to criminalize them and to justify police and military action (Campbell and Reeves, 1994). However, even if the footnote on growers does touch on some of the social and global dimensions of cocaine-commerce, it mainly works as a piece of information or 'revolutionary' curiosity on the origins of the product within the context of a several pages long report from the consumer's point of view.

To further illustrate, with a different example, the politics of this postmodern 'ungrounding' I will look at a class-discussion that I once was a part of on the Oliver Stone film *Natural Born Killers* (Stone, 1994). The film is a postmodern classic and a road-movie about a couple, Mickey and Mallory, who go on a serial-killing spree in the US West, become popular media heroes, end up imprisoned, and, finally, escape amidst a prison-riot sparked by the occasion of a 'real-crime' TV-show (*American Maniacs*) coming to do an 'in-depth' interview on Mickey. What makes this film postmodern is that its relatively graphic and bloody depiction of violence has a dream-like or 'movie-like' nature. It blends flash-backs to Mickey and Mallory's pasts of incest and child abuse and cartoon sequences into an almost obsessive analysis of the multilayered, mediated nature of violence. The fixation on media or cameras is exemplified by a scene, where Mickey, desperately looking for anti-venom for a rattlesnake bite, shoots a pharmacist, who had been watching news on Mickey and Mallory on television. After the shooting, Mickey, viewed through the eyes of a security camera, glances at the television screen, sees the report on himself with security-camera footage on the open television and bursts into laughter. Appropriately, the film ends with Mickey shooting Wayne Gayle, the reporter for the real crime show.

Soon after the release of the film, we read it for a doctoral class on interpretative ethnography, and most of us embraced it as a postmodern irony of the violently mediated nature of contemporary American society. Our enthusiasm was, however, interrupted by an African-American student, Shirley, who said that she thought the film was awful. 'That's not the way killers really are', she stated. 'Real killers feel guilty', she added. Shirley's commentary provoked the entire class to attack her for reading the film too 'literally'. The discussion deadlocked. The majority of us argued that the film should be read as a parody of media violence and not as a depiction on killing. Shirley continued to be offended by the film and our reading and argued that she knew the issue better, because she 'knew' killers. Later, the instructor of the course, Norman Denzin, published a piece (Denzin, 1999) contrasting the interpretations of *Natural Born Killers* by his stepson Allan and his Latino/a students Manuel and Gloria. Allan embraced the movie, much like we did, as a parody of violence. On the contrary, Manuel and Gloria refused to go to see the movie, as it did not tell about their people and they had seen enough violence already.

What these different interpretations tell is not, whether we or Shirley were right or wrong about the film, or whether the film is 'good' or 'bad'. Rather, the episode underlines the fact that just as the politics of texts become intelligible against the wider social and political context, so does the political nature of interpretation become evident against the social and political situation and location. Thus, ours, and the predominant academic interpretation of a text, such as *Natural Born Killers*, through postmodernity is related to a specific white, Western, college-educated 'media-savvyness' and the fact that our only relationship to 'killing' is through television (by this I do not want to imply that other groups could not interpret the film this way). Shirley's 'literal' and moral reading of the film is mixed with her religious background and testifies for her anger with the fact that the film does not address the moral issue of killing, which affects Black Americans in extravagantly disproportionate numbers. I would read Manuel and Gloria's rejection of the film as not 'theirs' in terms of revealing how *Natural Born Killers* is partly predicated on the same 'insular' media logic, which obsessively reproduces itself, that it aims to expose and criticize. In this respect it works in a similar fashion as the advertisement on Thai children, which mocked Western media-images of street-children, yet erased the issue of Third World poverty off the agenda altogether.

Finally, the methodological point I want to make through this discussion is that any reading of a text, including an academic reading, is as 'political', or embedded in a particular social context and location and their agendas, as any of the texts we analyze. Therefore, textual analysis should not only focus on unravelling the politics encoded into the texts but should also pay attention to the politics embedded in the decoding or interpreting texts.

Between contexts and texts

This last point brings one to a conundrum in audience studies, already touched upon in Chapter 2, which illustrates a key methodological issue in any textual analysis. A frequent issue of concern in audience-research is how to distinguish between the scholar's reading of a particular media text and the audience's reading of the same text. The answer that positivist audience-studies have given to this quandary is that what makes the scholar's reading of a text more informed is the use of scientific method of analysis. Thus, Radway (1984) presumed that her reading of the plot-formula with the 'sensitive hero' in romance novels revealed the 'deep' structure of the novels, which accounted for their appeal for the 'Smithton' women, even if they were unaware of it. This presumption creates two orders of interpretation: first there is the scientific, objective and disembodied reading of the scholar, and second there are the socially located readings of audiences that reflect their social positions, such as their gender, class and race backgrounds and political orientations.

As Ang (1996) has noted, Radway's reading of romances is, however, by no means innocent. It is heavily predicated on her rationalistic feminist framework and its notion of 'good' or emancipatory and 'bad' or disempowering aspects of romances, which belittles the titillating nature of romancing. The same way, our reading of *Natural Born Killers* was heavily invested in our postmodern paradigmatic orientation and our social position, bent on disqualifying alternative interpretations and positions, such as Shirley's literal and moralistic reading. Thus, despite our critical attitude towards 'truth', we did not want to accept an alternative interpretation of the film but, in a definite bid for power, defined Shirley's view as 'wrong' or inferior in relation to our superior, sophisticated analysis.

Recently, both textual analysis and audience studies have begun to pay attention, not only to interpreting the politics embedded in the content (or its reading by audiences), but also to the politics embedded in our understanding of what texts and interpretations are all about (Alasuutari, 1999). This position acknowledges that the theories and methods, such as the formulaic nature of semiotics or the postmodern infatuation with mediation we use to analyze texts are as 'ideological', or invested in social, political and historical agendas, as the texts themselves. The repercussions of this acknowledgement in practical methodological terms are threefold. First, if we are to comprehend the political nature of any given interpretation we need to look at texts through several interpretative or methodological frameworks, such as semiotics and post-modernity. Second, one needs to critically reflect on one's own perspective in terms of submitting it to a similar political and social scrutiny as one would submit any text. This means being self-reflexive about our tendency to prefer certain textual or interpretative strategies and define others, such as romancing or reading texts 'literally', as inferior. Third, the politics of any text as well as its interpretation can only be understood in relation to the historical, political context and its contradictions, which may reveal, for example, that the academic fascination with mediation may reflect a privileged culturalist class-position, far removed from the 'reality' of gruesome violence and poverty.

In the end, the task of new generation analyses of ideology boils back down to the old goal of cultural studies to examine the nexus between texts, power and social context. The novelty that methodological 'new times' has brought to this classical enterprise is that scholars are increasingly aware of the way in which their texts and methods do not exist outside of this political landscape and its struggles for power but are an integral part of it.

Conclusions

The emergence of cultural studies as a paradigm coincided, and was fuelled, by the French structuralist movement. Thus, since early on, one of the standard features of empirical research in cultural studies has been structuralist textual analysis that examines tropes and patterns in texts. However, since early on cultural studies has emphasized that textual analysis needs to be context sensitive, and that purely formal analysis does little to help us understand the politics of a particular cultural product. This is illustrated by the way in which Bennett and Woollacott came up with a much richer interpretation of the contradictions and appeal of James Bond against the British historical, social and political background than Eco, who used formalistic plot-analysis.

However, contemporary media-texts are often qualitatively different from 'modern' cultural products, such as James Bond. Many contemporary media products are characterized by a postmodern logic that no longer refers to a 'reality' out there, but, in a circular fashion, refers to other media texts.

Postmodern media texts often give the impression of being self-reflexively critical of media images. However, read carefully, and in relation to contemporary social context, postmodern texts often harbour many contradictory agendas. However, the postmodern awareness of the mediated nature of all knowledge has drawn attention to the fact that our methods of analyzing texts are not any less political than the texts we are analyzing. This can be illustrated by the way in which Eco's analysis of Bond reproduces the dichotomous logic he criticizes, and how my class attacked a 'literal' interpretation of *Natural Born Killers*, which did not conform to our postmodern sensibility. The lesson to be learnt from the fact that not only texts, but also our readings of texts, are political is that we should try to read any given text from several perspectives, using different approaches. At the same time, we should humbly admit that we can never completely understand a text, because all our readings are socially situated. Rather than try to undo bias in our readings, we should aim to become more self-reflexive about the social commitments and roots of our interpretations and use this awareness to tease out the contradictory politics of texts and their interpretations.

Exercise 5

- Take a media text, such as a film or a magazine article. Choose an interpretative framework, such as semiotics, narrative-analysis or postmodern analysis of mediation, and analyze the text through it. What kind(s) of politics does the text support?
- Further analyze the text in relation to other social texts and social sensibilities. What different kinds of social or political regimes does the text support?
- Does the text appear to support different or more complicated politics when examined from the intertextual/social perspective than when analyzed through one method?
- Show the media example to other people, such as fellow students or your own students, for interpretation. Is their interpretation different from or similar to yours? What do the differences of interpretation teach you about the social and political commitments of your reading?

6

Genealogical Analysis

Main questions

- **How is genealogical reading of history different from traditional historical analysis?**
- **How does the genealogical method analyze the 'historicity' of certain taken-for-granted notions, such as 'poverty' or 'anorexia'?**
- **What are the challenges of genealogical analyses of contemporary phenomena?**
- **Genealogy's main aim is to 'problematize' the way in which we tend to think of social phenomena or problems, instead of providing solutions to them. How can, and cannot, genealogy help us find solutions to social situations?**

The discussion on the ideological analysis of texts called attention to the need for scholars to become aware of the historical and political underpinnings of their own theories and methods. Genealogy is a method that does precisely that, namely, it investigates how certain taken-for-granted, such as scientific, truths are historical constructs that have their roots in specific social and political agendas. So, if ideological analysis would examine, for example, different meanings associated with 'blackness', genealogical analysis would investigate the historical origins of these meanings in, for example, colonialist medical theories.

   This type of critical analysis of the roots of certain discourses seems logical from a critical, cultural perspective. However, doing genealogy is more difficult that one might initially think, as it goes against the basic social scientific logic of 'explaining' things. For example, whereas traditional social inquiry would examine 'anorexia' in terms of studying how it is informed or 'caused' by suffocating beauty ideals, genealogy would turn the tables on the entire investigation and ask: What historical processes and events produced anorexia as a mental disorder, caused by susceptibility to media images and parental and peer expectations to be thin and good?

The answer genealogy would give to this question is that contemporary notions of anorexia have their origins in the American postwar social psychological preoccupation with the newly affluent and socially conformist suburbs – marked by a sense of domesticity and femininity – which were feared to provide seeding grounds for a fascism or communism of sorts. The goal of genealogical analysis, then, is twofold. First, by exposing that certain ways of thinking are not timeless truths but historical constructs, genealogy opens up space to think about them differently. Second, by unravelling the social roots of certain ways of thinking it pinpoints the way in which they lend support to possibly problematic or contradictory political and social regimes.

In what follows, I will outline two ways of doing genealogical analysis. First, I will discuss how it can be used to analyze the historical formation of discourses and ideas. I will start off by illustrating how genealogy is different from traditional history through a discussion of Brumberg's (1988) research on the nineteenth-century history of anorexia, which both is, and is not, genealogical. I will then illustrate, in more detail, the characteristics of genealogical reading of history and historical documents in light of my own work on the constitution of anorexia as a disorder of an insufficiently 'autonomous' self, which articulated specific political, historical agendas in postwar American society (Saukko, 1999). Second, I will discuss a way of analyzing the 'historicity' of contemporary phenomena or of investigating how our current way of understanding certain issues is rooted in the political credos and practices of our times. I will do this through a discussion of the historicity of an emergent, psychological ideal self, which unlike the autonomous self, is 'flexible' or open to the world and change.

In the end, I will briefly discuss the debate on the political 'goal' of genealogical analysis. According to some scholars (Rose, 1996), genealogy is a method that helps to dismantle authoritative forms of knowledge and thereby clear space for people to re-imagine themselves and their lives in new ways. According to others (Bennett, 1998), genealogy points to the always compromised nature of academic knowledge, thereby, suggesting that, instead of pretending to be 'free intellectuals', we should get openly engaged with the art of governing through state and other public and private agencies. In my view, genealogy as a method of analysis is mainly designed to question established beliefs and practices. However, challenging existing forms of thinking and acting paves the way for suggesting alternative ideas that have learnt from the historical lessons genealogy teaches us.

History of origins versus genealogy

Much of genealogical research focuses on the historical constitution of social phenomena, ranging from poverty (Dean, 1990) to the idea that 'seeing' is a means to get an objective idea of reality (Crary, 1992) (on general discussion see Dean, 1994; Poster, 1997; Kendall and Wickham, 1999). To outline how to do historical genealogical research, one can start with explaining its somewhat paradoxical goal of studying history in order to shatter historical 'truths'. To illustrate what this means I will start with a discussion of Brumberg's (1988) landmark study on the emergence of anorexia as a modern disease. Brumberg's work is both akin to genealogy and a more traditional history of 'origins', highlighting the differences between the two.

Brumberg (1988) focuses on the nineteenth century, when notions of women's starving shifted from religious to scientific and psychiatric explanations. This was a time when the holy fasting of medieval female saints and seventeeth-century 'miraculous maids' – popular religious celebrities, who were understood to survive without food – were redefined as suffering from 'anorexia nervosa' a nervous disorder, typical of middle-class women. Brumberg provides a rich account of how 'fasting girls' became a site where the war between religious and scientific authority was fought. For instance, several fasting women, who were alleged to be living without sustenance, died after being put under a watch by doctors that made sure no one was smuggling food to them. Having proved the women's dishonesty, the doctors claimed that their starving was not a testimony of 'miracles of God' but of 'fits of hysteria', typical of adolescent females (71).

Brumberg's analysis of the way in which the notion of female starving changed from religious, miraculous fasting to a psychopathology of the adolescent female is genealogical, in the sense that it maps the way in which two different discourses constitute their object differently. Thus, Brumberg challenges the ahistoricity of contemporary notions of anorexia, noting that women's starving has, in a different context, been understood both by society and the women themselves as 'a miracle' rather than sickness.

However, after the discussion of the early history, Brumberg moves on to describe how anorexia started to become more prevalent among young middle-class women in Victorian times. She argues that this had to do with the invention of a new period, 'adolescence', between childhood and adulthood, which led to prolonged dependency. This, argues Brumberg, led to an intensification of the relationship between parents and their young adult children, giving rise to problems in individuation, and, subsequently, to a young woman's starving to assert her independence and defiance of parental authority. Brumberg also discusses a series of aesthetic and class-based sensibilities, which associated robust bodies with lower classes and hard labour and thinness with 'sublimity of mind and purity of soul', making wasting 'fashionable' in the nineteenth century (185). However, in this latter part, Brumberg's analysis is no longer genealogical. This is because she shifts from investigating the way in which certain historical and institutional discourses constituted anorexia to discovering the 'origins' of anorexia.

Brumberg's description of the family-dramas and notions of ideal body in the nineteenth century come very close to contemporary notions of anorexia. Brumberg, indeed, notes that the early doctors' observations on the family-life of anorexics 'anticipated' the later 'family system's theory' (128). Reading how the doctors began viewing anorexia as a 'family-problem' would fit within the ambit of genealogy, but Brumberg, however, goes further than that, arguing that this is what anorexia 'really' was about in the nineteenth century. This line of argumentation raises the question of whether Brumberg is reading nineteenth-century anorexia through 1980s theories of family dysfunction, or making the mistake, maligned by historians, of imposing the present onto the past (Poster, 1997). Brumberg's slipping between these two modes of analysis illustrates the specificity of the genealogical method. The traditional history of 'origins' legitimates the present by finding its roots in the past ('already the nineteenth-century anorexics starved in reaction to suffocating family-environment, the way contemporary anorexics do'). On the contrary, geneal-ogy studies history in order to challenge the present (the notion of female starving as a family-pathology, did not exist before the nineteenth century, when it was produced by the budding profession of family doctors and psychiatrists of the Victorian bourgeoisie).

To formulate this specificity of the genealogical method in more general terms, one can say that it is characterized by a careful reading of historical details, not in terms of the truths that they tell (What was madness like before?) but in terms of the truths that they constitute (How did we begin to perceive certain behaviors and people as 'mad'?).

Analyzing the history of historical truths

Genealogy, biography, context

Against the discussion of Brumberg's work, it becomes clear that the charac-teristic feature of genealogy is the way in which it reads history and historical documents. As Foucault has stated, the 'archaeological' research that forms the basis of genealogical analysis focuses on what historical documents say, rather than speculates on what they do not say (Foucault, 1972: 25). This means that rather than speculate about individuals' and institutions' past motivations, genealogy focuses on how those motivations are constituted.

What this means, and how it is done, may be illustrated by my genealogy on the contemporary diagnostic criteria and popular notions of anorexia nervosa, which used as a starting point the biography of Hilde Bruch, the founding mother of psychiatric research on eating disorders. Bruch established and canonized the still prevailing notion (referred to by Brumberg) that anorexia has its roots in 'overpowering' family structures that do not allow the anorexic girl to become her 'own self' but makes her overly obedient, trying to live up to social and parental expectations to be pretty and good. Thus, when I decided that I wanted to do a genealogy on contemporary diagnostic criteria of anorexia, Bruch's work seemed a legitimate, as well as suitably narrow, focus of analysis. Bruch also lent herself for analysis, as Texas Medical Center Library hosted an archive of her personal, professional papers, which provided a good place to explore the historicity of her ideas.

However, when beginning to examine Bruch's papers, I had to clarify to myself the relationship between traditional biography and genealogy as well as the way in which genealogy approaches an archive. The classical, or 'wig history', approach to biography is to search for the origins of great ideas or deeds in the personal history of the great individual. This is the way in which the catalogue of Bruch's archive framed her in that it introduced her as not only the pioneer in research on eating disorders but also – in reference to Bruch's history as a German-Jewish refugee – as an individual, who 'suffered great emotional, and intellectual as well as physical pain in her lifetime', knowing what it meant to be 'second-class citizen' and a 'refugee' (Frazier, 1985, xi). Thus, from the point of view of classical biography, the frequent references to Germany in Bruch's archive and in her reminiscences would be read as establishing an 'origin' of her theory of anorexia as a dis-ease produced by authoritarian parenting. Her personal history could be understood to have made her a particularly critical individual, who was quick to spot and fight against 'authoritarianism' in its political as well as psychological 'manifestations' (see Preston and Decker, 1974[1975]; Hatch-Bruch, 1996).

Read genealogically, Bruch's history as a German-Jewish exile does not 'explain' her particular vision but contextualizes it within her personal as well as wider (inter)national history. To give an example of what this means, one can analyze the following commentary in her life-history interview:

> There is something very peculiar in this rather rigid political setting at least earlier in my life and then came the free-for-all of the Weimar republic and the school system had also this rather rigid – we were taught what the curriculum prescribed. Apparently there are two things that you can do – completely submit and become a conformist and that is the famous title of Heinrich Mann's book, Der Untertan, the subject, the underling. It can't quite be translated because only Germans have that concept and the Kaiser is the man on top and the others are the Untertan. ... But there is the other development and that is quite frequent – namely do the surface behavior but with the underlying thought 'I am free'. Okay, you don't get into trouble, you don't do things to make trouble but I think my thoughts were free. (Bruch in Preston and Decker, 1974: 57)

To begin to analyze this statement, it is good to bear in mind Foucault's (1972: 102) argument that discourses constitute their objects through 'repetition'. Thus, from the point of view of genealogy, this statement does not mean that Bruch 'was' a free-spirited individual. On the contrary, it 'constitutes' Bruch as a 'free' persona through a nearly compulsive reiteration of the characteristics of lack of freedom ('rigid political setting', 'rigid school system', 'submit', 'being a conformist', 'underling', 'Kaiser on top', 'Untertan'). Thus, Bruch's interpretation of anorexia as resulting from a lack of personal autonomy did not emerge from her personal experience of 'imposition'. Rather, her personal aversion to 'imposition' stems for a wider historical discourse on freedom, which both in her personal as well as general US history got articulated in relation to Germany. So, it is safe to say that besides telling about Bruch's personal aversion towards the culture of the Weimar Republic, the quote tells about a more general postwar American discourse that asserted the US as the harbinger of individual freedom in relation to both the former Axial powers (Germany, Italy, Japan) and the communist bloc. Thus, the elaboration on the intrinsically authoritarian aspects of German culture ('rigidity') fits with the historical political discourse that defined freedom in opposition to fascism and communism.

Still, Bruch not only found the German but also the American culture lacking freedom, as illustrated by the following commentary:

> One may look upon this [American] demand for 'psychological understanding' as the latest and sophisticated facet of the search for rules of conduct that have characterized American life [as an immigrant country]. Sometime ago I was interviewed by a newspaper reporter. He asked me: What, in your opinion, accounts for the widespread neurosis amongst our children and your people? My spontaneous answer was brief: 'The pursuit of happiness and the compulsion to be popular. ... The compulsive need for popularity is, of course, an expression of the inner uncertainty, that one knows about one's adequacy only by finding acclaim from others'. (Bruch, 1961a: 223–4)

Also this statement can be read in relation to both Bruch's personal as well as general national US history, although in this case the two become even more umbilically intertwined. Rather than attributing Bruch's criticism to her insights as an 'outsider' in American culture, her argument appears almost identical with the ideas of prominent postwar American thinkers, such as David Riesman (which Bruch cites). According to Riesman, Americans have become 'other-directed', people for whom 'their contemporaries are the source of direction (Riesman, 1976[1950]: 21) in contrast with the older American personality for whom the source of direction was 'inner'. To appreciate the politics of Riesman's book it is useful to note that his examples of typical 'inner-directed' people – the banker, the tradesman, and the small entrepreneurs (20) – constitute the mythologized characters of American liberal democracy and entrepreneurialism. However, Bruch's statement not only buttresses Riesman's liberalism, but it also has echoes of left-wing Frankfurt School's theory of 'authoritarian personality' (Adorno et al., 1950), which they argued was a particular type of personality that was becoming more and more prevalent in postwar American 'mass society'. The link between Bruch's work and the Frankfurt School was no pure coincidence either, as Bruch's analyst, Frieda Fromm-Reichmann was the former wife of Erich Fromm, one of the members of the Frankfurt School.

Thus, in this instance Bruch's personal history – such as her link to the fellow Jewish refugees of the Frankfurt School and the links established by her references – and general national history blur, as the anxiety over the eroding individualism in American society was a discourse that was both decidedly intellectual as well as political. On one hand, this discourse articulated anxiety over social conformism, which leftist intellectuals like the scholars of the Frankfurt School associated with a new type of fascism that manifested itself in middle-class complacency and hostility towards social critique and reform. However, the fear of conformity was also associated with anti-communist para-noia and a mixed position harking back to early American culture for its pioneer spirit. During and after the war this agonizing about mass culture mobilized a small army of mainstream social scientists who investigated media effects, public opinion formation and the infamous suburbs, all in the name of democracy (see Rose, 1996). Bruch's statements simply form a small part of this tidal wave of scientific and political concern over individuality.

Eventually, read genealogically, Bruch's biographical statements appear strangely 'impersonal'. Thus, rather than an original persona, Bruch is analyzed as a node in a historical network of ideas, events and processes. Her personal history as a German-Jewish exile in America and connections with the criti-cal exile-culture of the Frankfurt School coincide to 'produce' a particular version of the discourse on the ideal autonomous self that then formed the basis of her work on eating disorders. Even if the historical events that speak through her statements are rather general, it can be argued that the way they come together in Bruch's oeuvre is also somewhat unique and specific. Genealogy examines this historical 'specificity' for two reasons. First, genealogy examines how a particular idea, such as the idea of autonomous self and anorexia, emerged from very specific historical circumstances in order to demonstrate that it is not a timeless 'truth'. Second, it examines what historical circum-stances and agendas gave rise to the idea or practice, in order to be able to eval-uate what kinds of social and political projects it supports.

Genealogy and institutions

However, Bruch's theory of anorexia is not only related to her personal or the general US national history but also to the institutional context of postwar American psychiatry. Bruch had been interested in family dynamics already in her early studies on obesity (see Saukko, 1999). However, immediately after the Second World War Bruch underwent psychoanalytic training, which paralleled a general turn to Freud in American psychiatry after the war. The war traumas afflicting previously healthy men aroused psychiatrists' interest in the role of (childhood) traumas in forming the personality. The interest in family dynamics also fitted and reinforced the postwar family-centred atmosphere (Grob, 1991). Bruch's interpretation of the dysfunctional nature of the anorexics' families is in the following:

> The patients were described as having been outstandingly good and quiet children, obedient, clean … The need for self-reliant independence, which confronts every adolescent, seemed to cause an insoluble conflict, after a childhood of robot-like obedience. They lack awareness of their own resources and do not rely on their feelings, thoughts and bodily sensations. … Once this lack of autonomy has been defined, detailed histories will reveal subtle earlier indications of the deficits in autonomy and in initiative. (Bruch, 1973: 255)

Thus, what Bruch saw as the lynchpin of the anorexic's lack of autonomous sense of self was the oppressive family environment, particularly overpowering mothering. Drawing on Fromm-Reichman (1940), Bruch established that the roots of eating disorders were established in the early infant feeding experience. When the mother did not respond appropriately to the infant's cues, by, for example, overstuffing her to keep her quiet, the infant becomes incapable of recognizing her true needs and to act in a self-directed manner (Bruch, 1961b: 470–1).

Thus, from her general political commentaries on the nature of German and American social and political systems, Bruch's work on anorexia plunges into psychoanalytic interest in the minute detail of the infant-feeding experience. This is specifically how discourses work – they knit together, through repetition, different knowledges and discourses into a broad political and social agenda. The task of genealogy is precisely to unravel the way in which a discourse, such as the notion of an autonomous individual, weaves together psychiatric and political agendas. Furthermore, Bruch's focus on mothers and politics is far from unique but resonates with a general postwar political fixation on the middle-class family and its central character, the mother. On one hand the newly affluent 'ranch house and a refrigerator' family with its homemaker mother was used as a proof of the superiority of the American system of morals, politics and economics. On the other hand, the suburban home became a source of cultural agony, and amidst TV dramas embracing family values, such as *Father Knows Best* there were movies such as the James Dean film *Rebel Without A Cause*, which depicted the middle-class home as a loveless place reigned by passive-aggressive mothers devouring their children (e.g. Susman, 1989; Skolnick, 1991).

This discourse on the suburban home as a seedbed for psychological and political malaise also framed this locus as decidedly feminine. Thus, it was the prototypically or supposedly feminine values of being subordinate and compliant, which were seen to be making the American society and people 'sick'. Thus, anorexia, as a nearly all-female condition, seemed to epitomize this social, gendered disease of compliance, as illustrated by Bruch's comment:

> I for one thing think that the outburst – and that's what it is – of anorexia has to do with the women's movement, that the inner contradiction of having grown up as compliant,

obedient, adjustive, fitting-in person and the need to be a woman of achievement and do something independent are so much in contrast that these girls are caught in it. (Bruch, in Spignesi, 1980: 15)

This thread on femininity in Bruch's work links it with still another major post-war discourse, namely, liberal feminism. Early on Bruch argued that the problem with anorexics' mothers, 'women of superior intelligence and education', was that they had given up promising careers in favour of family and children. This only left them unsatisfied, neurotically focused on their children, trying to inculcate them – and especially the anorexic daughter – to live up to their own frustrated dreams (Bruch, 1978: 28–31). The anorexic herself, in this context, is described as 'dreading' her mother's confined life; yet, trained obedient, she is described as not being able to face the challenge of being her own person either. Thus, Bruch's theory, and many feminist appropriations of it, renders the anorexic a tragic transitional figure marking the shift from the suffocating traditional femininity of the 1950s towards the liberated femininity of the 1960s. However, this feminist thread is undercut by the mass society theory Bruch espouses. The critique of mass culture and female docility get intertwined into the classic equation of mass society and femininity, which diagnoses female behaviours, such as consumption, beauty-practices, and caring, as signs of psychological and social pathology.

Genealogy and 'people'

The analysis of Bruch's work, however, raises the question, what was the role of real, flesh and blood anorexics in the formation of the discourse on the condition. The mainstream understanding of how doctors come up with diagnostic criteria is that they analyze their patients, and by tracing common symptoms, delineate a syndrome and begin establishing its causes and looking for cures. Bruch's archive is full of detailed descriptions of her patients both in her patient-notes and in her research-notes that trace common elements. The following is an excerpt from her patient-notes:

Obedient, industrious, conscientious child, lonely, timid, shy. Musically oriented. Good student. Fear of being sick. Always shy & at best a barely adequate socializer. Obedient to parents, totally unable to get angry at them.

However, read genealogically, and not diagnostically, this statement does not tell what this anorexic woman was like (obedient, shy, and so on). On the contrary, it is another instance where the discourse on the ideal autonomous individual 'becomes flesh' through repetition of statements, such as 'obedient', 'industrious', 'conscientious', 'good student', 'fearful', 'unable to get angry' and so on. In this case, the discourse becomes flesh in rather literal terms, in that it gets etched onto people, shaping their sense of themselves and their actions.

This intersection between discourses and lived lives makes genealogy cross paths with the analysis of discourses that shape individuals' lived experience, as discussed in Chapter 4. Genealogy focuses on the part of this process, where discourses 'inscribe' individuals, that is, it reads something like the patient-notes not as telling about the individual but the operation of the discourse. Looking at my own hospital records from the time I had anorexia, this notion of discourse feels eerily true. The nurses' observation on how I was doing my homework in 'very neat handwriting', seem, very foreign or 'not me', and I recall how tremendously insulted I was by the description of myself as a petty pedant, when I once happened to read the notes the nurse had left on the table. Still, on other occasions I recall that the discourse literally got etched onto my self-consciousness. For example, once my psychiatrist asked me to draw a place 'where I would like to live'. After I had drawn the Smurf village, she lifted her eyebrows in curiosity and asked me, whether all the smurfs were boys (as the theory of anorexia presumes that anorexics do not want to grow up into an independent womanhood but want to stay children/androgynous). I fumbled that there was one girl in the village the Smurf Girl but that I didn't want to be the Smurf Girl, since she only caused conflicts. I recall the poignant look on her face when I rejected the identity of the Smurf Girl, and to this day, I conceive of myself as the 'smurf' or as having an element in my personality that does not want to be treated as a woman, particularly by men. However, it is impossible for me to tell, whether I was a 'smurf' already before or only after being defined as such by the psychiatrist.

The point I want to make with my personal anecdote is that, when doing genealogy, one should resist the temptation to start excavating 'real people' from archives. What these files tell about is not the people but the discourse that is being inscribed on them. Even reading my own patient records I have a strange sense that, even if I recognize myself in some of the descriptions, my recognition probably tells more about the medical discourse that I have internalized than about any 'me' that existed before I entered the hospital. In his early works, Foucault (1988[1965]) occasionally entertained the idea that, in between the lines of the early asylum documents, one could hear 'the murmur of the mad'. However, he later acknowledged that the asylum documents on the mad only told about the discourse on madness.

The methodological point that this underlines, is that trying to 'rescue' the mad from the archive is likely to slide from genealogy to the history of origins, as in Brumberg's case when she ceased reading the documents in terms of what they told about the early psychiatric discourse and began reading from them 'what was really wrong with the Victorian anorexics'. This does not mean that one cannot introduce some human element to doing genealogy. There are two basic ways of doing this.

First, one can study how people being inscribed by the discourse 'resist' it (for an example of a study done this way see Terry, 1999 on homosexuals). It becomes, for example, graphically clear from Bruch's archives that the anorexic women frequently and violently resisted their defining and treatment, being described as 'obstinate', 'defiant' and so on. Thus, in doing genealogy one can study resistance, but one needs to bear in mind that this is an activity that acquires its meaning simply in relation to the discourse, that is, it does not, again, tell about the 'people'. What this means can be illustrated by my own patient records, which chronicle the fact that my treatment ended when I escaped from the hospital and never returned. Thus, the final page of my records, written after my escape, notes that Paula has 'clearly lost her sense of reality', to the extent that it might be warranted to change the diagnosis from neurosis to 'psychosis'. This sentence tells nothing about 'me' or the motivations of my escape, or whether I was going 'mad' or not. It simply chronicles my very straightforward resistance to the medical inscription (I run out), and the way in which the medical discourse brands this as evidence of how I was 'outside of the true'.

The second way of introducing some 'human' elements to genealogy or combining it with some more human methods, is to combine it with critical analysis of the discursive constitution of lived experience, as discussed in Chapter 4. Thus, an analysis of the historicity of a particular discourse that has constituted people as, for example, 'anorexics' may help a critical analysis of lived experience, in that it contextualizes the discourse that shape people's lived sense of themselves. Thus, knowing the roots of the contemporary notion of anorexia in postwar American, both highly political and highly gendered fascination with individual freedom, helps to make critical sense of women's experiences of definitions of anorexia as being caught in an unproductive dichotomy between being 'strong' or a 'victim', as discussed in Chapter 4.

Genealogy and politics

Overall, the question this analysis begs is: What are we to make of all this? That is, what is the point of doing a genealogical analysis on something like the emergence of the postwar discourse on autonomous individuality and anorexia. The answer to this question is that it not only destabilizes this notion of anorexia as simply a 'truth', but by unravelling its historical and social roots and commitments, it also helps to evaluate the political and personal repercussions of this discourse.

On a political level, one can say that Bruch's theory draws critical attention to many problematic developments in postwar America. Like members of the Frankfurt School she draws attention to the conservative, conformist and uncritical nature of the suburban middle-class culture, adding to this picture a critique of the docile and domesticated femininity that this culture fostered.

However, by rendering the middle-class suburbs and women the lynchpins of social and psychological malaise, Bruch also singles out a particular social stratum as pathological. Even if this group is not particularly underprivileged in class-terms, it is so in terms of gender. Furthermore, if we look at the ideal personas that Bruch and others set forth as model personalities – the critical intellectual or Riesman's entrepreneur and banker – it is relatively clear that the theory of 'mass society' not only attacked lack of social critique but also articulated the agony and rejection of older middle-classes towards the newly affluent 'masses'. This becomes all the more complicated, if we look at Bruch's (Bruch and Touraine, 1940; Bruch, 1957; also see Saukko, 1999) early work on obesity, which focused on poor, mainly Eastern European and Mediterranean families in New York City. In that study, Bruch singles out the 'culture' of these people – such as extended families, 'autocratic' family structures, and focus on food – as being the cause of the children's lack of autonomy and, subsequently, obesity. In this case it becomes even clearer how the coupling of a notion of a lack of autonomy and eating problems produces a discourse that singles out social groups, such as women and poor ethnic minorities, as well as nations, such as Eastern Europe and Germany, as antithetical to the postwar ideal American 'free' individuality and society. The obvious political goal of this free world and free individuality is to 'naturalize' certain social and personality systems and their values as inherently superior to other systems or ways of being.

The repercussions of Bruch's theories for people's personal life are revealed by the fact that her theories of obesity and anorexia are virtually the same. One of the reasons anorexics starve is to assert their will-power and to stave off the qualities medical profession, including Bruch, in the early twentieth century associated with fatness, such as dependency, weakness and low class position. However, when diagnosed with an eating disorder, the anorexic has those very same abhorred qualities of weakness and dependency projected upon her, fuelling her sense of never being strong and independent enough. Studying the genealogy of eating disorders helps to understand how notions of obesity and anorexia move in a vicious circle, defining women as perpetually lacking in relation to the elusive and highly gendered ideal of individual autonomy. Pinpointing the fact that the ideal of autonomy is not a timeless truth about a healthy human psyche clears the ground for imagining and validating other, less agonizing modes of being.

Doing genealogy on the present

New times, new selves

It is fair to say that the ideal of an autonomous self still prevails in the contemporary Western world, and many women, for instance, view feminist empowerment in terms of gaining independence and full participation in public affairs, rather than being delegated into subordinate and support roles in the domestic sphere. However, there is also a new discourse on the self that is emerging, not only in psychology, but also in management speak as well as in the growing New Age lifestyle realm (e.g. Thrift, 1999, 2000).

What this self looks like, and how it is different from the old autonomous self, can be illustrated by my experience of attending a seminar in a private US hospital on new methods for treating eating disorders. As part of the programme all of us participants were introduced to a new treatment regime, the ropes course. Ropes course is a kind of adult playground, consisting of wires or ropes that are strung between trees and poles to construct a maze that people have to get through. The only way one could get through the 'elements' was through cooperation, and the main point about the course was to train people to break away from individualist or isolationist thinking and to begin to act together. Another aim of the ropes course was to increase participants' mutual self-confidence, and anyone who made a derogatory comment on either her/his own or someone else's performance, was immediately 'beeped', that is, the entire group stopped their activities and shouted 'beep!'

In comparison to the ideal autonomous self, this new 'connective' or 'flexible' self is characterized by an openness to the world. Thus, in a very 'physical' or embodied manner the ropes course aimed to cultivate a behaviour that would seek the company and help of others, instead of striving for independence from other people's influence. Furthermore, whereas the old autonomous self-ideal believed in a kind of one-size-fits-all individuality that aimed to impose a relatively uniform, white, male, middle-class individuality on others, the new flexible self aims to foster diversity and tolerance of difference. Thus, one of the goals of the ropes course was to teach people not to pass negative judgements on others that were not doing the same thing, or as well, as others. Furthermore, the course was designed so that people would have different functions (some had to support, others had to climb and so on), in order to teach participants the value of 'difference', in that everyone could help in the common project, even if in different ways (also Martin, 1994).

From the outset this new self seems rather attractive, as it promises to overcome some of the problematic features of the autonomous self, such as the stubborn idealization of independence and strength and inability to recognize alternative values or lifestyles. However, genealogy alerts us to studying a new discourse, such as flexible self, the same way as one would study a historical discourse: by following statements that begin to recur in diverse areas of life, weaving together a discursive formation with its specific social and political connections and effects.

Thus, just as we were getting ready to leave the ropes course, a group of business managers, who had come there to learn teamwork, entered it. Therefore, one way of beginning to analyze the contemporary psychological ideal genealogically is to explore how it is being employed in another area, where it has become increasingly popular, namely, management theory and practice. To illustrate both the possibilities and particular challenges of trying to make critical sense of an emergent phenomenon, I will discuss two different studies that try to make sense of the flexibility-discourse in management.

Going with the flow

The first piece of work, which tries to come to terms with a new, presently shaping discourse on 'flexibility' and its social implications, is Davis-Floyd's essay based on an interview with Betty Flowers, who creates corporate visions or 'myths' for Shell. The interview-study forms part of a collection that aims to reflect on the formation of a new 'corporate form' that, from the outset, seems to be using a language very similar to critical cultural studies (Marcus, 1998). Thus, the collection is a kind of genealogy of the present, trying to pinpoint the way in which a discourse that academia is very enthused with gets articulated in the realm of business management.

So, to give an example, one can look at Davis-Floyd's exploration of the practice of creating 'myths' in a transnational corporate setting:

> *Davis-Floyd*: So then you can make your business decisions based on those probabilities that you're seeing emerging?
>
> *Flowers*: Then it gets even more mysterious, because then you begin to see that the future is what you use to create the present, and that the present that you then create will create the future that you want. I mean, it's chicken/egg. It gets very curious....
>
> *Davis-Floyd*: ... What values were stressed in those stories, these self-consciously created myths?
>
> *Flowers*: In one, the value of individual/group ethnic diversity – 'doing it my way'. An in the other, the environmental values of cooperation and a long-term good future for everyone, because we're all in this together. ... The first scenario stressed nationalism, bettering your own group acting in your own self-interest, but your self-interest was more enlightened, or broader and included other people than yourself. So there was much freer access on all sort of levels – many more horizontal linkages, much more cooperative interaction.
>
> *Davis-Floyd*: While the other, 'the bad story', is more vertical, more about one group dominates, that sort of thing? (Davis-Floyd, 1998: 159–60)

Reading this interview, one can trace the basic elements or statements that belong to the flexibility discourse. The first element of this discourse is the notion of 'creating' realities, so that Betty Flowers ponders how myths 'become' real. This is very much in line with the notion that there are no universal or essentialist 'good' human or social qualities ('autonomous individuality') that somehow need to be uncovered or upheld, but that the point is to 'create' new futures, selves and so on. The second, closely related, element that Flowers underlines is the need to respect diversity and to act together to build a better future for all (which is then juxtaposed to the 'old' or 'bad' values of self-interest and competition).

The elements espoused by Flowers are clearly the same as I found in the ropes course, namely, the emerging ideal self is someone, who is able to connect with other people, respect their differences and build common futures.

However, despite its critical exploratory goal, Davis-Floyd's piece ends up a kind of anti-genealogy. She does not pay critical attention to a statement that is beginning to recur compulsively in different realms (such as the world of business and academia) and try to evaluate the social practices and agendas that this discourse is linked with. On the contrary, Davis-Floyd buys into the discourse or goes with its flow, ending up celebrating its potential with Flowers. This is an indication of the difficulty of doing genealogical or critical analyses of an emergent discourse as we, as intellectuals, are often so invested in it that it is very difficult to see its underbelly. This may have been the case with the postwar discourse on autonomy, which probably appeared unquestionably right and true to all the social scientists engaged in the myriad 'democracy' studies in the 1950s.

Going against the grain

An example of a different kind of analysis of the flexibility-enthusiasm within business management is an article by Calas and Smircich (1993) who discuss the sloganeering about 'feminine' forms of management. They start their discussion with a mock ad:

HELP WANTED

Seeking transforming manager. Impatient with rituals and symbols of hierarchy. Favours strengthening networks and interrelationships, connecting with coworkers, customers, suppliers. Not afraid to draw on personal, private experience when dealing in the public realms. Not hung up by a 'What's in it for me?' attitude. Focuses on the whole, not only the bottom line, shows concerns for the wider needs of the community. If 'managing by caring and nurturing' is your credo, you may be exactly what we need. Excellent salary and benefits, including child care and parental leave.

Contact: CORPORATE AMERICA
FAX: 1-800-INTRUBL
(Calas and Smircich, 1993: 71)

What this article does is that it analyses the newly forming discourse on feminine or flexible forms of management against, first, the history of discourses on women in the corporate world as well as the exigencies of globalization. It connects the new talk about femininity and management with an older, turn-of-the-century discourse that justified women working as secretaries, defending the innovation in terms of making the office into 'a more pleasant, peaceful and homelike place' (73). What Calas and Smircich argue is that the new discourse on management is quintessentially the same as the earlier one in that it envisions women's role in terms of lending 'support' to the 'real' male business.

What they argue the new discourse tells about is the weakening of the position of particularly middle managers in the national front, as the decisions are increasingly made on global scale. The role of the feminized national and middle managers in this scenario is to 'pacify' the workforce, gel them together behind corporate plans and to respond to their emotional and spiritual expectations in a situation of increasing global competition, continuous downsizing and decreasing expectations (77). Thus, the openness to difference and embracing of change becomes understandable in a volatile corporate context, where people are continuously made redundant and have to change their paths and roles accordingly. Furthermore, the ideal of 'togetherness', embedded in the discourse, is often articulated not in terms of solidarity but in a decidedly 'instrumental' way, captured by the idea that we need others to survive (Rothschild and Ollilainen, 1999). This sense of survival is embedded, for example, in the ropes course where the teamwork element encourages people to think of other people as instrumental to achieving the common goal (completing the course) and saving everybody from the imaginary 'sea of sharks'. The entire exercise cajoles people to complete the set task, and despite the empathetic beeping and encouragement, it never invites people to question the task at hand together.

From a methodological point of view, the critical discussion of Calas and Smircich illustrates the way in which one can critically interrogate 'new' and possibly exciting concepts and ideas by examining their historical roots (discourses on female secretaries) and the way they relate to a particular social context (global economy). However, the work of Calas and Smircich is not necessarily genealogical in the full sense of doing a detailed analysis of the key moments or texts that gave rise to the discourse on flexibility. Their essay is more like a first stab on making sense of the ideal flexible personality in management theory, and this kind of exploratory work is, perhaps, what one needs to do when beginning to make sense of a new and ongoing phenomenon.

The indeterminate nature of genealogy

Discourses in context

The main lessons to be learnt from the discussion above is not only how difficult it is to be critical of currently fashionable ideas but also that the wider meaning and implications of any given discourse become visible when one looks at its connections to different realms, from psychology to management theory, economy and labour practices. Establishing the interdiscursive connections of, for example, anorexia or management, and their shifts, enables us to see them as part of wider social regimes and their transformation. This was Foucault's (1978, 1979a) project, and one of his central arguments that he advanced through detailed studies on medical, psychiatric and criminological texts was that unlike premodern societies, which were governed through fear of 'death' (the scaffold), modern societies were governed through enhancement of 'life' (medicine, rehabilitation, education and so on). Even if not every empirical research project aims to map such epochal shifts, understanding and elaborating how one's own study relates to wider social developments, is always part of genealogy.

Based on his long-term research on official and popular psychology and social theory, Rose (1985, 1996, 1999) has analyzed the larger social ramifications of the shift from an autonomous to flexible individuality. Rose argues that the postwar mode of governance – articulated, for instance, in Bruch's work – was committed to a particular notion of healthy individuality that was seen to fit everyone. This idea of one-size-fits-all underpinned a host of contradictory social programmes, associated with the welfare state that aimed, for instance, to bring levels of health and education of the population at large up to a certain common standard. This ideology drove not only public education and health care systems but also the US network television and European public broadcasting companies' aims of creating a broad-based national audience that would sit down and watch *Bonanza* or *Coronation Street*, followed by the evening news (Lavery *et al.*, 1996). This social regime had its undoubted beneficial effects for poor and marginalized people who benefited from the welfare reforms. However, it was also attacked as imposing a politically invested common standard, such as the 'autonomous self', and of declaring other, gendered, ethnic and so on modes of living and being as substandard, unhealthy, or simply wrong.

The regime based on flexibility is different. One could say, to borrow Deleuze (1992), that whereas the old regime aimed to 'mould' people to fit a relatively fixed standardized form, the new regime works through 'modulation' that standardizes but also differentiates people as well as induces constant change. This new regime of self and society is no longer, or solely, characterized by the welfare state but by privatized healthcare, self-help groups, community care, and alternative therapies and pedagogies. Gone is also the prime-time, national family-audience, which has given way to the multiplicity of cable and satellite channels and the Internet. This is a regime that is more tolerant towards difference, often thrives on it, and gives more choices of, or forces more choices on, the self. At the same time, the regime is undercut by both normalization and inequality. The new communal regimes of the self, such as neighbourhood watches, may be more tailored but they continue to foster normalizing behaviour (see Rose, 1999). Furthermore, while there may be more diversified treatments and media-products available for those who can afford it, many people have to make do with eroding public provisions.

However, despite this dark underside of the flexible self, it cannot be seen in terms of just the latest 'capitalist plot'. The developments that brought about the new regime were contradictory, in that the transformation was spearheaded not only by conservative, monetarist attacks on the welfare state, but also new feminist and Civil Rights movements' claims for greater equality and recognition, which the welfarist and nationalist project of 'all' had muffled (Rose and Miller, 1992). Thus, just as the postwar welfare regime, the new flexible zeitgeist is riddled with contradictions. This underlines the fact that genealogy as a method is focused on the complexity of discourses, that is, it aims to get beyond declaring them simply 'bad' or 'good', but aims to enable us to see that they are always 'dangerous'.

Politics of research

The last statement about 'dangerousness' captures the most interesting as well as irritating feature of genealogical analysis, which is its indeterminacy. This means that the genealogical aim to 'challenge' preconceptions is not particularly useful for suggesting social or political alternatives (Fraser, 1994).

In fact, there are (at least) two interpretations of what the social and political goal of genealogy is. Drawing on Foucault's idea that we should make our lives 'work of art' (Foucault, 1985a), Rose has argued that at the core of Foucault's genealogical work is a manifesto against moral codes, universal truths, and authorities, or, in short, anything that 'stands in the way of life being its own telos' (Rose, 1999: 283). This somewhat anarchistic agenda 'for life' is truthful to Foucault's research project of challenging all forms of authority, discipline and domination. However, this project is articulated mainly in negativistic terms, being 'against' something, leaving it unclear, whether, or what, it stands 'for'.

In a different vein, Bennett (e.g. 1998) has pointed that Foucauldian analyses expose the fact that intellectuals do not exist 'outside' the apparatuses of power, illustrated by, for example, the fact that the corporate scenarios of Shell and the theoretical scenarios of cultural studies are similar. The lesson to be learnt from this, according to Bennett, is that academics should abandon their romantic self-image of being against 'establishment'. Instead, they should get their boots muddy and begin to fetch alternative policies, and modes of government and management, so that, for example, besides criticizing the imperialist fantasies that organize museums (Bennett, 1995), one could envision new, more egalitarian, ways of managing them (see Clifford, 1997). Having an effect on some of the practical decision-making in different levels of society is, in my view, one of the central aims of research. However, the idea that all research should be directly relevant and proposing alternatives for government agencies, therapeutic practice or local or global businesses is also problematic.

In thinking through my own research on anorexia, I would say that being engaged in the 'art of governing' is by no means foreign to academics. The postwar flurry of social scientific and social psychological research on 'democracy', 'suburbs' and 'opinion formation' was all very much done under a government umbrella and with state funding. What this research illustrates is that while it may have produced many interesting results, it remained blind to the political nature of the fundamental question that structured it, namely, that the American version of democracy and autonomous individuality were values that should be upheld at any cost. The same way, as discussed in Chapter 4, research that has a straightforward 'therapeutic' or institutional goal of improving medical practice often remains incapable of questioning the basic premise that drives it, such as 'safe sex counselling' or 'anorexia'. For this reason, I would rather see genealogy as a method that teases us to think beyond governmental logics, even while admitting that we can never wrestle ourselves out of socially compromised thinking.

Against this background, I would see genealogy as a method that helps academics and other social and cultural experts to become more aware of the historical and political commitments of their work. In the case of research on anorexia, genealogy helps to illuminate the historical and social roots as well as personal and political repercussions of medical and also feminist notions of anorexia as a dis-ease of an insufficiently autonomous self. Becoming aware of the somewhat problematic commitments of this particular notion of anorexia may encourage the development of new ways of approaching the condition and the self that would be less predicated on stubbornly isolationist notions of 'freedom'. However, as the analysis of the discourse on the flexible self demonstrates, the new alternatives fetched tend to be no less invested than the old ones. Therefore, genealogy as a method of analysis is best seen as a shrapnel that shatters taken-for-granted, as well as new and seemingly liberating, modes of thinking and acting by exposing their historical and always politically invested nature. Becoming aware of the contradictory politics underpinning our most cherished concepts may pave the way for new ways of thinking about ourselves and the world. Yet, coming up with these alternative ideas is not the task of genealogy, which remains a tool to continue challenging the basic premises of ideas both old and new.

Conclusions

Genealogy, as a method, investigates how certain taken-for-granted, such as scientific, truths are historical constructs that have their roots in specific social and political agendas. Thus, whereas traditional social and cultural inquiry would examine, for example, 'anorexia' in terms of studying how it is informed or 'caused' by suffocating beauty ideals, genealogy investigates what historical processes and events produced anorexia as a mental disorder, caused by susceptibility to media images and parental and peer expectations to be thin and good.

There are two main approaches to genealogy. First, the historical approach to genealogy investigates the 'history' of taken-for-granted concepts or states-of-affairs, such as anorexia or poverty. It does this through examining historical documents with the aim of tapping into moments when particular statements begin to recur, thereby producing a discourse, such as the postwar discourse on anorexia as a dis-ease of an insufficiently autonomous self. Mapping the statements of a particular discourse, such as examining Hilde Bruch's archives, leads to an interdiscursive exploration, where connections between a particular discourse, such as anorexia, and others, such as the Cold War preoccupation with freedom and democracy, emerge. These connections help to establish, first, the historicity of the phenomenon in question, in that it becomes apparent that certain conceptions of, for example, eating disorders are not timeless truths about people's behaviour but historically specific and always political explanations. Second, analyzing the connections between different discourses also helps to illuminate the wider social and political agendas that they form a part, so that definitions of anorexia not only refer to a certain psychological ideal but play into and out of a wide social, political and international regime founded on American notion of freedom.

The other way of doing genealogy is to investigate the historicity of phenomena that are forming in the 'present'. An example would be a critical investigation of the social or economic commitments of the emerging ideal 'flexible' self, which strongly resonates with many cherished concepts of cultural studies, such as the idea that selves are formed in interaction with the social environment and that the ideal self aims to continuously 'reinvent' itself. Because the emergent discourses often appear seductively 'fresh', a critical analysis of them may be more difficult than analyzing older ideas and practices. In any sense, the analysis of emergent discourses highlights the 'never ending' nature of genealogy in that it provides a critical intellectual tool that helps to unravel the political commitments of our thoughts and actions. Genealogical unravelling of the compromised nature of our ideas and practices may give rise to new ones, which, however, will have their own social investments and blindspots, underlining the importance of cultural analysis that is continuously reflexive about its commitments, working in the critical space between total compromise and absolute freedom.

Exercise 6

- Think of a social phenomenon or social problem you would like to study. Instead of setting out to 'explain' the phenomena, the way most social and cultural research does, do a 'genealogy' on it.
- Identify a pivotal moment, person or text(s) that have played a decisive role in defining the phenomenon. Locate some texts (archival texts, popular or scientific articles, biographic material) that articulate these founding definitions.
- Analyze the texts for recurring statements. Identify key themes that the definition of the phenomenon you are studying reiterates.
- Are there obvious clues in the texts (e.g. citations of other texts, references to prominent people or policies) that point to their relationship with other social texts and wider historical and political agendas? Follow these clues and analyze how the definitions of the phenomenon you are studying are related to agendas in other areas of life.
- Based on your analysis, discuss what wider social and political projects does the definition of the phenomenon that you study either support or challenge. Learning from the history, suggest some possible new ways of understanding and acting in relation to the social problem or phenomenon.

7

On Deconstruction and Beyond

Main questions

- **Why is deconstruction particularly useful for unravelling the complex and contradictory nature of social dichotomies interlacing, for example, images and discourses on the female body?**
- **How does deconstruction help to make sense of the logic of media texts, such as *South Park*, which may be considered deconstructive? How does it enable one to unravel the values, often associated with 'freedom', that tend to underpin deconstructive texts?**
- **Why does the deconstructive impulse of continuing criticism of dichotomies sometimes end up reinforcing dichotomies?**
- **How can the deconstructive impulse be turned 'constructive', that is, how can we move from criticizing culture towards suggesting better alternatives?**

Deconstruction, which is a theory, methodology and a method, at the same time, is one of the most popular devices to critically analyze texts in cultural studies. Most frequently associated with the thought of the French poststructuralist theorist, Jacques Derrida, it is closely related to both semiotics and Foucauldian genealogy. Like genealogy it challenges taken-for-granted or naturalized concepts and practices. Similar to semiotics, it is interested in uncovering the binaries that underpin the language and culture we use to make sense of reality. Semiotics works to expose the values embedded in relatively apparent binaries, such as Bond versus the Villain (Bennett and Woollacott, 1987), that interlace cultural texts. Somewhat differently, deconstruction aims to destabilize binaries by unravelling the way in which binaries render the other side of the equation invisible and natural. An example would be Said's (1995[1978]) analysis of the way in which nineteenth-century discourses on 'the Orient', as irrational, despotic and erotic, first and foremost, work to construct the self-identity of 'the Occident' as rational, democratic, and puritan – a benchmark against which all peoples should be measured.

This chapter outlines and discusses deconstruction as a methodological approach, particularly as it applies to analyzing the female body as well as popular texts, such as *South Park*, which themselves can be considered 'deconstructive'. The reason why I have chosen to focus on the body is because it is the locus of one of the most profound, naturalized and often contradictory cultural dichotomies (nature/culture; body/mind; object/subject; woman/man; beautiful/ugly). I have chosen to analyze *South Park* as an exemplar of a text that itself works to shatter core cultural binaries, while, at the same time, affirming another underlying set of core-values. The examples have also been chosen with equal opportunities in mind in that the focus in the section on the body is femininity, whereas *South Park* is arguably a more masculine media form.

I will also discuss some of the problems that deconstruction as a method and a practice has a tendency to run into, even if these problems are not necessarily the fault of the approach itself but its application. The first of these problems is that the deconstructive drive to challenge dichotomies may sometimes end up consolidating them, as happens, for example, in feminist disputes over beauty-practices. The second is that the criticism of naturalized norms may lead one to embrace a romantic notion of (male, childlike) freedom, as happens in *South Park*. While deconstruction as a practice may sometimes cultivate these problems, it also helps to unravel them. However, there is a third shortcoming that is embedded in the deconstructive method *per se*. This is the fact that deconstruction is not a 'positive' science (Spivak, 1976), but that it is a useful tool for social critique but its critical nature does not yield itself for suggesting social alternatives. To outline a more 'constructively' deconstructive methodological framework, I will, in the end, resort to the works of Pierre Bourdieu and Mikhail Bakhtin. Bourdieu makes sense of structures of inequality that underpin the different cultural binaries uncovered by deconstruction, whereas Bakhtin's idea of dialogues helps to build bridges or alliances between different forms of subjugation. This framework helps research to be more constructively critical and to get beyond stagnated debates over, for example, whether it is feminist for women to engage in beauty-practices or not, or whether *South Park* fosters puerile sexism or poignant political critique.

Deconstructing the female body

Contradictory dichotomies

The female body constitutes a good topic for deconstructive analysis as it is unusually saturated with meanings, underpinned by binary-logic. Early critiques on the discourses depicting the female body often focused on the 'stereotypical' representation of women in the media as either sex objects or caretakers (e.g. Kilbourne, 1995[1989]). This line of inquiry usually has been predicated on notions of 'wrong' kinds of images (housewives, blond bombshells, etc.), in opposition to 'right' or more egalitarian ones (women as news anchors and so on). These modes of analysis have their insights. However, the advantage of deconstruction is that it draws attention to the dichotomous nature of these critiques that suppress one way of being (housewives) and elevate another (news anchors), without paying attention to the way in which women can be subjugated not only by denying them masculine modes of existence but also by denigrating feminine ones.

To illustrate these contradictions one can take a closer look at a loaded contemporary symbol, that of a thin female body. In one of my classes on the body, I have taken the habit of asking students to come up with all the associations that come into their mind, when faced with a thin body. Students usually quickly come up with a relatively complete list of associations, unravelled by feminist scholarship (e.g. Chernin, 1994[1980]; Bordo, 1993, 1997; Malson, 1998) in the area, such as: beautiful, sexy, professional, intelligent, independent, strong, powerful, androgynous, healthy, fit, frail, feminine, asexual, vain, unthreatening, weak, dependent, powerless, mentally ill, sick. This list of associations tells about the highly loaded, fundamentally dichotomous, and inherently contradictory nature of associations attached to the thin, female body. What the list enables one to comprehend, in the first instance, is why the thin female body is so attractive, as it is associated with a host of highly desirable attributes (intelligence, beauty, and so on) that suppress highly undesirable attributes (stupidity and ugliness). What deconstruction does is that it unearths the binaries that interlace these associations as well as helps to expose the way in which they prey on old cultural associations, such as negation of the body (thinness) and mind (intelligence). By unravelling this social and binary-driven logic, it shatters or 'deconstructs' our tendency to presume that these qualities are 'naturally' linked with thin bodies.

However, as the list indicates, the associations we attach to thin bodies are by no means uniform. Thus, the second thing that deconstruction enables us to do, is to analyze the contradictions of the list, which makes the thin body to stand both for qualities associated with, for example, maleness (professional, independent, strong, powerful, androgynous) and for qualities associated with femininity (frail, unthreatening, weak, dependent). Hence, the contradictions embedded in the discourse on thin female body is similar to the schizophrenias characterizing Orientalism, which, for example, both feared the Oriental 'barbarian' sexuality and fantasized about its wild eroticism. These contradictions illustrate the beguiling and seductive nature of discourses that render the thin female body attractive, because it ambivalently embodies both the modern strong or ballsy femininity and the classical female frailty or daintiness.

To make matters even more complicated, the list reveals that the thin body is not only associated with qualities deemed desirable or ambivalent but also qualities that are outright negative, standing for pathology (sick, mentally ill). These negative notions tell about traditional associations between being thin or wasted and bodily sickness, but they also testify for the increasingly common associations between being thin and excessive dieting and eating disorders. Despite their feminist edge, these negative associations provoked by the thin body often prey on ancient associations between femininity, vanity and weakness of mind. They play into notions that women are particularly prone to 'suffer' from mental illness (hysteria) and are easily carried away, or 'duped', by other people's opinions and mass ideologies, such as media images, all of which are qualities that stand in opposition to the robustly healthy or independent and unpenetrable male mind. What this illustrates is the complex nature of discourses, which leave no 'safe' or righteous ground on which to stand, as whether we aspire towards the thin body or criticize it, we end up reproducing normative and highly gendered dichotomies. Thus, the third advantage of deconstruction is that it enables us to unravel the indeterminate or maze-like nature of discourses, where criticizing the binaries that underpin women's beauty practices is bound to produce another binary, that of a vainglorious and weak-minded woman who stands in opposition to the self-determining man.

Criticizing the thin body

To illustrate, in more detail, how the unravelling of contradictory dichotomies works, I will take a closer look at the feminist analyses that, first, criticize the thin body ideal and, second, criticize the criticisms of the thin body ideal and other beauty practices. To start off with the first point, one can look at Susan Bordo's (1993, 1997) analysis of the slender body, which was one of the first ones to point out that the thin body does not merely signify prettiness, but that images of slenderness often have a strong air of 'emancipation'. Reading a series of fitness ads and ads featuring businessman-like women from the 1980s, Bordo notes that these images give a new spin to the age-old associations between femininity and the flesh or the body. Thus, thinness and fitness promise women a way to surpass the traditional associations of feminine body, reproduction and objecthood and of articulating a mastery of their flesh, or of mind over body, a decidedly masculine character trait (the attributes of 'professional', 'strong' and so on, on the list before, refer to this association). However, Bordo argues that besides this 'emancipatory' flair, notions of thinness also play into and out of ancient fears of female largeness, hunger, and desire. Thus, being thin, or small, not only articulates will-power but also diminishes the person, making her less intrusive and invasive or, intrinsically, closer to the ideal understated femininity (the attributes of 'frailty', 'weakness' and so on, on the list, refer to this association). As Bordo states in her analysis of ads using thin women, dressed in conservative business-suits:

The buxom Sophia Loren was a sex goddess in an era when women were encouraged to define their deepest desires in terms of service to home, husband, and family. Today, it is required of female desire, loose in the male world, to be normalized, according to the professional (and male) standards of that world: female bodies, accordingly, must be stripped of all psychic resonances with maternal power. From the standpoint of male anxiety, the lean body of the career businesswoman today may symbolize such neutralization. With her body, and her dress she declares symbolic allegiance to the professional, white, male world along with her lack of intention to subvert that arena with alternative 'female values'. (1993: 208)

The fact that the thin female body evokes associations that are both decidedly masculine (strength, will-power) and quintessentially feminine (frail, small) account for its power to attract and seduce both women and men. The both seductively contradictory and gendered nature of the thin female body is something that would be difficult to decipher using more conventional forms of analysis of 'stereotypes'. Analysis of stereotypes cannot easily grasp contradictions, as it is predicated on a notion of enlightened and less enlightened images (Pickering, 2001). If one was looking for stereotypes, one might note that while women appear in business suits ('good'), they still have to look pretty ('bad'), which, would, however, leave unexamined the both seductive and problematic nature of both symbols of masculinity (business suit) and femininity (beauty).

Still, even if Bordo uses the deconstructive logic (with a Foucauldian spin) to analyze the thin body, she also attacks deconstruction for its drive to destabilize binaries, such as gender binaries. She particularly criticizes the theorization of Judith Butler (1990, 1993), who uses deconstruction to challenge the fundamental gendered dichotomy between male and female bodies, arguing that there is nothing inherently natural or biological about gender but that it is thoroughly 'performed'. This conclusion makes Butler embrace practices, such as butch/femme identities and drag, which reveal the nature of gender as a performative act. According to Bordo (1993: 294–5), Butler's theory is oblivious of the fact that such a 'destabilized', androgynous or ungendered body may be quickly becoming the norm in contemporary societies. The 'Other' that this playfully unstable body suppresses may be just the primordial, devouring and stubbornly stable and fleshy female. This deconstructive critique of deconstruction points out that deconstruction needs to be context-sensitive, so that it is wary of historical shifts in binaries (attacking gender-binaries may have been radical a few decades ago, whereas gender-bending has become one of the cultural norms by early twenty-first century).

Criticizing critiques of thinness

However, the criticisms of the dichotomies underpinning the thin body ideal and other beauty practices have been attacked for buttressing a different set of polarizations. Thus, critical investigations of the way in which women modify their bodies through, for example, diets and cosmetic surgery, may subtly affirm a dichotomy between nature and culture in two senses. First, they may embrace the ancient ideal, unmodified and natural body, usually associated with the unadorned and unmade up male body, which stands in opposition to the culturally constrained, artificial, decorated and vainglorious female body (Davis, 1995; Felski, 1995; Tseelon, 1995). Second, it may also buttress the opposition between a culturally constrained mind that is 'doped' by beauty ideals and the strong or independent 'true' mind that is unaffected by cultural ideologies. The latter dichotomy also boils back down to a fundamental and highly gendered social dichotomy between an active and independent, ideal male subject – a hero and commander of his life – and a passive, dependent female subject, defined and subjugated by others. On my students' list on qualities attributed to the thin female body, these associations correspond to the notions of 'vain', and '(mentally) sick'.

Thus, while criticisms of the thin body ideal are driven by a feminist agenda, they also harbour sexist dichotomies, which has not gone unnoticed by other feminists. Thus, it has been argued that rather than yearning for a presumably 'natural' female body, feminists should acknowledge that bodies and body-ideals are always constructed and try to construct them differently. This has led many scholars to analyze popular and high-brow body-art or performances that aim to imagine a different kind of female body. One of the art-forms that has attracted feminists' attention is Orlan's work, particularly her performance cosmetic surgeries. In these staged, yet real, 'cut-into-the-flesh' surgeries surgeons reconstruct Orlan's face to resemble the most famous Western pieces of art, such as Da Vinci's *Mona Lisa* and Botticelli's *Venus*. Her stated aim is to both reappropriate the qualities associated with the paintings – such as transsexuality, as Mona Lisa is understood to be Da Vinci's self-portrait, and fertility and creativity associated with Venus – as well as to expose the gruesome way in which women have been, and continue to be, 'constructed' to fit the male gaze (e.g. Davis, 1999; Ince, 2000; Zeglin-Perry, 2000). As Davis describes Orlan's deconstructive project:

> For Orlan plastic surgery is a path to self-determination – a way for women to regain control over their bodies. Plastic surgery is one of the primary arenas where man's power can be most powerfully asserted on women's bodies, 'where the dictates of the dominant ideology ... become ... more deeply embedded in the female flesh'. Instead of having her body rejuvenated or beautified, she turns the tables and uses surgery as a medium for a different project. For example, when Orlan's male plastic surgeons balked at having to make her too ugly ('they wanted to keep me cute'), she turned to a female feminist plastic surgeon who was prepared to carry out her wishes. (Davis, 1999: 459)

What is at issue here is that Orlan's aim is to expose the way in which women's bodies have been graphically reconstructed in patriarchy, while, at the same time, try to come up with an alternative, or self-defined, way of constructing the female body. From the point of view of deconstruction, Orlan's project is interesting in that she does not commit the *faux pas* of claiming that her work exists outside or is 'free' from patriarchy or argue that cosmetic surgery is 'good'. Rather, she uses the patriarchal tool, cosmetic surgery, to expose its own logic as well as to use it for her own means, thereby acknowledging that her project both depends on and opposes the male gaze. In this sense, Orlan's art has affinities with the popular image of Madonna, who throughout her career has both embodied and deconstructed the iconic blond bombshell and the Madonna/whore dichotomy. Thus, she has both used and parodied, for example, the Marilyn Monroe bleached blond image, remaking it to work 'for her', not merely as an object of the male gaze, but as a woman in command of, taking pleasure in, her body, beauty, and sexuality in an almost autoerotic manner (Schwichtenberg, 1993).

However, as the story goes, the analyses of female attempts to both deconstruct and reconstruct the female body have been counter-attacked by other commentators. Even if someone like Orlan takes great care to both criticize cosmetic surgery as well as use it for her own ends, she still comes across as being in charge of her operations. This attitude has been attacked by commentators, such as Bordo (1997), who has argued that it buttresses the contemporary individualist zeitgeist, according to which people are having liposuction or 'sleeping rough' out of their own 'choice' and not because of structural constraints. Thus, one could say that while the idea that women who engage in beauty practices are victims of culture, or 'bimbos', has its problems, the idea that cosmetic surgery is an act of self-definition is problematic as well.

To put to a preliminary rest these ongoing, and possibly never-ending, feminist deconstructive debates around the female body, one can say that all the positions have a truth to them, while none of them is without its blind spots. From a methodological point of view, the greatest advantage of deconstruction is that it exposes this slippery terrain, where all positions are suspect. It helps to unwrap the beguilingly complex and contradictory nature of the dichotomies, saturating notions of the female body (male/female; mind/body; nature/culture; genuine/artifice; and subject/object). By fleshing out these contradictions, it helps to destabilize the multiple dogmas that perpetuate women's relations with their bodies and illuminate the double-binds, where women are damned as ugly, if they do not change their bodies, and also damned as vain and easily influenced, if they do change their bodies. However, even if the indeterminate nature of deconstruction is its greatest strength, it is also its greatest weakness. In a nutshell, deconstruction leaves us short of a methodology that would be able to build dialogues between the different, and also similar, ways in which women are cajoled by contradictory discourses (identified by my students in less than ten minutes) that define women as too ugly, too vain, too big, too small, too strong, too weak, too much sex, too little sex, too natural and too artificial.

I will come back to the issue of how to make deconstruction more constructive at the end of this chapter, but before that I will look at how things seem from the other side of the fence and discuss a decidedly deconstructive and decidedly masculine debate on another form of media images: adult cartoons.

Deconstructing deconstruction

On quiet, redneck mountain town

When looking at the various images, tackled in the previous section, such as images of thin women in business suits, Madonna, or Orlan, they come across as challenging gender but also intent on making a statement. The deconstructive logic of the adult cartoon, *South Park* is different in that it breaks binaries in a kind of jolly smashing or careless sense, fuelled by male adolescent or puerile humour, characterized by constant cursing and prolific references to sex and excreting. The deconstructive logic of the cartoon also seems rather relentless, challenging and ridiculing everything from right-wing conservatism and nationalism to political correctness and any kind of gender, race or sexuality based identity politics and from parental, school and religious authorities to popular, media and consumer culture.

I was first introduced to *South Park* when my British undergraduate students started bringing tapes of it to class in the late 1990s. It is safe to say that, of those people that I interact with on a regular basis, the cartoon has a particular appeal to both male students and academics, both of whom consider it incredibly funny and witty and having a sharp, critical political edge. The cartoon is constructed around the antics and adventures of four 8-year-old third graders, Cartman (a fat son of a single mother), Kyle (a Jewish boy), Stan (a 'regular' boy), and Kenny (a welfare-kid, wearing an orange parka, who humorously gets killed in every episode). The boys live in a 'quiet, redneck mountain town', South Park, populated by ineffectual parents, teachers, school counsellor, the Mayor, militarist Vietnam War veterans and Jesus, who hosts his own talk-show. The only adult authority in the series is Chef, an African-American fat cook, who is the only one that understands and defends the children, while also being, in a decidedly stereotypical way, a superior 'sweet and tender' lover, and a kind of male, subservient and understanding Mammy for the children (Gardiner, 2000). The cartoon is decidedly 'postmodern' in that it is saturated with intertextual references to other media and much of the humour as well as criticism of the series draws on the blurring of boundaries between reality and media, so that the main plot of the episodes often centres on the town being frequented by media and folk icons, from Barbara Streisand to Satan, aliens and popular news crews. The cartoon has, obviously, provoked controversy, being accused of using offensive language, buttressing nonchalance towards violence, being sexist, racist and denigrating towards ethnic and religious customs and even of being one of the incentives behind the Columbine high-school killings (the real Colorado town of South Park is only a few miles from Columbine high) (Slade, 2001).

In order to illustrate how deconstruction can be used to unravel a media-text, such as *South Park*, I will read one of the South Park films, *Bigger, Longer, Uncut* (1999), in two different ways. First, I will unpack the deconstructive logic – or the breaking up of key social binaries that bind together and legitimate a certain culture – of the film, which accounts for its critical edge. Second, I will analyze the way in which the film, despite its deconstructive bent, affirms a set of normative values, the most central one being the romantic notion of an unruly male child. I will then discuss how deconstruction helps to unravel both the critical or 'deconstructive' potential of the film as well as the values underneath this criticism. I will also address the fact that deconstruction, as a method, cannot provide a way of fleshing out values that would get beyond both non-normativity and one-dimensional normativity.

The reason I have chosen to study the particular South Park film is that it is a 'meta-story' in which *South Park* reflects on itself, or on the criticisms levelled against the TV-series and its identity as a media and social product. The film's plot is constructed around an outrage provoked by a movie, *Arses on Fire*, an offshoot of the children's favourite adult cartoon series *Terrance and Philip*, an alter ego of *South Park* itself. After seeing the film, which according to their parents is nothing but 'foul language and toilet humour', the children start cursing profusely at school. The parents get outraged and organize themselves into a coalition, 'Mothers against Canada' (Terrance and Philip are Canadian), which eventually leads to a war between the United States and Canada. Meanwhile, Kenny gets killed, when, being influenced by the movie, he lights his bottom on fire, goes to hell and finds out that Satan and Saddam Hussein, who are having a gay relationship, are planning to take over the world, if Terrance and Philip (who are held captive by the US forces) are executed. The four children end up saving Terrance and Philip, just before their public electrocution as part of a large show-biz event, featuring, for example, Winona Ryder. Having saved Terrance and Philip and the world the children return home with their parents.

Deconstructive criticism

The humour and criticism of *South Park* is largely based on juxtaposing and mixing usually unrelated phenomena in a way that breaks away from their original meaning, exposing its politics and rendering it humorous. For example, in the opening sequence, Stan walks across South Park singing, reminiscent of the all-time family-favourite musical *The Sound of Music*:

> There's a bunch of birds in the sky
> and some deers just went running by
> and the snow's pure and bright
> on the earth rich and brown
> just another Sunday morning in my quiet mountain town

Stan ends up in the rhinoplastic surgery, where his mother works and where a row of mute people always sit in the waiting room with bandaged noses, and asks her mother for money to go to see the Terrance and Philip movie. He then continues to pick up his friends, and together they pass by a church choir and jump over a homeless man. Along the road, Stan's mother refers to him as an 'angel' and likens him to Jesus with a mind 'so open and pure', and the welfare kid Kenny's mother shouts that, if he misses church, he is going to go to hell and has to answer to Satan himself. As a whole, the juxtaposition of nature (deer, snow) and artifice (plastic surgery), devoutness (church) and lack of compassion (homeless man), angels and Satan all work to undermine one another and concoct a humorous melee on the contradictions of the 'quiet, little, white trash, redneck mountain town' (as the rhyme of the song that is developed and repeated throughout the opening sequence states) of South Park.

Sandwiched between the main plot, the film has a series of minor disturbing juxtapositions that work to undermine the meanings of institutions and cultural myths. In the mid sequence on hell, Satan is pictured reading a book, entitled 'Saddam is from Mars' (in reference to John Gray's self-help, bestseller *Men are from Mars, Women are from Venus*), trying to make sense of his communication difficulties with his gay-partner Saddam Hussein. When the parents organize themselves against the movie, they, similar to various protest movements as well as vigilante groups, print themselves T-shirts with a 'ban' sign on it with letters 'MAC' (Mothers Against Canada). This mixing of elements – such as Satan and feminized self-help, the 'anti' of both radical and conservative protest movements and the boring and benevolent US-neighbour, Canada – render their original meaning absurd.

The film is also rife with more straightforward parody of, for example, individualism, masculinity and racism. When the school-counsellor takes the task of 'curing' the children's cursing, they end up tap-dancing and singing the pop-psychological self-reform mantra: 'We can do, it's all up to us, we can change our lives today ...'. When Mr Garrison, the school-teacher puts on an army uniform, he states, in a poignantly cheeky voice: 'This makes me feel like a tough brute male'. When Chef starts protesting against the 'Operation Human Shield', which puts all black soldiers to the front row of the attack, a general shuts him up by saying: 'I don't listen to hip hop'. One could say that *South Park* even mocks itself, or its alter ego Terrance and Philip, as part of a decidedly 'stupid' media culture. When Terrance and Philip make jokes, asking 'What did the Spanish priest say to an Iranian gynecologist?', and the audience pauses in expectation of a clever answer, the cartoon characters start farting and laughing. Equally stupid is a news report on Terrance and Philip topping the charts with their music video, 'Shut your f****ing mouth, uncle-f****er', where the cartoon figures wiggle themselves in silvery overalls, like countless boybands and rapbands.

The basic deconstructive aim of the film is encapsulated in the last scene, when, on the battlefield amidst dead bodies, Satan, who is supposed to take over, if Terrance and Philip are executed, says to Mrs Broflovski, Kyle's mother: 'You brought enough intolerance to the world to allow my coming'. Remorsefully, she responds: 'But I was just trying to make the world a better place for children'. Thus, the bottom-line of the film is to break the mainstream, conservative, American middle-class culture by revealing its own hypocrisy, violence and intolerance, which it accuses others perpetuate. Deconstruction helps to unravel *South Park's* 'logic' of smashing into pieces and rendering dubious and ridiculous the constitutive binaries that hold the white, conservative middle-class ideology together, such as the difference between good and evil, Jesus and Satan, black and white, purity and contamination, pure nature and corrupt culture.

Core values

However, despite the seeming wholesale attack on key values of American society, *South Park* also affirms a set of values. As indicated in the previous chapter, even deconstructive texts, which aim to challenge, for example, the idea that there are any intrinsic, unchangeable qualities to the body, embrace a value, namely that of malleability. The values embraced by *South Park* are, however, slightly different or less deconstructive, I would say.

Slade (2001) has argued that even if *South Park* as a series has been accused of being immoral, it has a deeply moral message. One of the moral messages that Slade identifies is the fact that the parents are not interested in their children. This is definitely the case in *Bigger, Longer, Uncut.* When, in the opening sequence, Stan and his friends approach the movie-theatre they sing: 'movies teach us what our parents don't have time to say'. Equally, in the closing sequence, after the total war, Kyle says to his mother that the problem is not television but that 'you never talk to me'. While this idea may reveal a problem in the family life of contemporary busy society, the values it sets forth are poignantly double-edged, particularly in relation to the dubious gender-agenda of the film and the series.

When taking a closer deconstructive look at the film, against the backdrop of feminist critiques of developmentalist child psychology (Walkerdine, 1993, 1998[1989]) and feminist critiques of *South Park* (Gardiner, 2000), one can see that it affirms one of the key values of modern culture: the romantic notion of the 'playful', white, male, healthy child. This mischievous and playful male child, who is resistant against constraining discipline is, in developmental psychology as well as in popular common sense, constituted as the ideal, autonomous and active 'subject', against whom the normality of other subjects is measured (Walkerdine, 1993). Thus, the way in which the four central children resist the normalizing agencies and institutions in their lives, such as parents, school, counselling, army, religion, mass media, consumerism and political correctness, is very much in keeping with the notion of the romantic male child, such as Rousseau's Emile, that resist restrictive authorities.

Along similar lines, what has been deemed as the 'offensive' features of the series, such as cursing and obsessive interest in excrements (farting, 'poo' and so forth) and sex, can be argued to present a certain male form or appropriation of 'anality' (Gardiner, 2000). 'Anality', or being interested in and playing with faeces, is understood to be a regressive personality feature, but it can also be seen as a particular, anarchistic or 'expulsive' form of resisting authorities. Furthermore, anality or fascination with things 'gross' is also a particularly male form of expression, a traditional way for men to demonstrate their superiority in relation to women by being able to handle 'disgusting' things, such as rodents and faeces, and to be able to be nonchalantly cruel by, for example, killing small animals (these features are also played out in similar cartoons, such as *Beavis and Butthead* (see Kellner, 1995; also Beneke, 1997).

Against this background, one can read the depiction of Terrance and Philip in *South Park* differently. In the previous section, I suggested that the fact that Terrance and Philip appear relatively 'stupid' demonstrates the deconstructive nature of the series in that it does not justify even its own alter-ego, but constructs it as another instance of 'banal' popular culture. However, if one looks at, for example, the joke about the 'Spanish priest' and 'Iranian gynecologist', the fact that the punch-line is a fart is both a commentary on the stupidity of popular culture (and the countless talk-show jokes like the one on the priest and the gynecologist) and an instance where this stupidity is surpassed by mocking it. The same way the Terrance and Philip music video, 'Shut your f****in' mouth, uncle-f****er', and the continuous repetition of the f-word in the Terrance and Philip film as well as in *South Park* generally reads not only as a commentary on popular culture that relies on obsessive cursing and sexism – such as much rap and other 'cock-rock' forms (Dimitriadis, 2001) – but perpetuates its logic of 'taking the piss out' of everything.

While this male form of resisting social norms may expose and criticize social constrictions and institutions, such as militarism, it brushes under the carpet the fact that this male unruliness is exercised at the expense of those groups, who have to put up with it or even have to cherish it, particularly mothers and (mostly female) teachers. Walkerdine (1998[1989]), for example, has discussed how the developmental psychological ideal of the romantic male child, whose natural, playful naughtiness should not be constricted by finicky regulations, plays out in 'real' everyday primary school life:

> Annie takes a piece of Lego to add to a construction she is building. Terry tries to take it away from her to use himself and she resists. He says: 'You're a stupid cunt, Annie.' The teacher tells him to stop and Sean tries to mess up another child's construction. The teacher tells him to stop. Then Sean says: 'Get out of it, Miss Baxter paxter'.
>
> ...
>
> Terry: Get out of it, Miss Baxter the knickers paxter knickers, bum.
> Sean: Knickers, shit, bum.
> Miss B: Sean, that's enough. You're being silly.
>
> ...

Sean: Miss Baxter, show your knickers your bum off.
Sean: Take all your clothes off, your bra off.
Terry: Yeah, and take your bum off, take your wee-wee off, take your clothes, your mouth off.
Sean: Take your teeth out, take your head off, take your hair off, take your bum off. Miss Baxter the paxter knickers taxter.
Miss B: Sean, go and find something else to do, please. (63)

What this excerpt exemplifies is the way in which being 'naughty' not only works to challenge authorities but also legitimates an abusive subjugation of others. Thus, this particular form of childlike or childish male naughtiness is both socially reprimanded and celebrated as an expression of the intrinsic human 'unruliness' that resists the shackles of cultural constrictions. The shackles that the four male children in *South Park* aim to shake off, represent not only the traditional conservative forces, wanting to suppress any youthful rule-breaking, such as the army, teachers and religion, but also the new forces, such as consumerism, popular culture, feminism, gay rights and civil rights movements, that have challenged the white male time-worn prerogatives of male supremacy, racial and Western supremacy, and homophobia.

Deconstruction as a method enables one to analyze not only the critical logic of the series, but also the constitutive core values of the series. Derrida acknowledged that the 'danger' of the deconstructive method is that it may end up embracing an always value-laden notion of romantic 'freedom', even if the romantic notion of natural freedom was one of the key focuses of Derrida's criticism. However, deconstruction does not offer ideas of how to get beyond the relentless critique of all values and embracing of one-dimensional core values or icons, such as the natural female body or the romantic male child.

Towards constructive criticism

Despite the attack on binaries, deconstruction as a method has a tendency to reproduce them. This happens in scholarly and popular discussions on both the female body and *South Park* that tend to get articulated in polarized terms over whether or not it is feminist to engage in beauty or other body-modification practices, or whether *South Park* fosters puerile sexism or sharp political critique. As deconstruction would have it, all these positions are both tenable and untenable, each criticizing a particular norm while suggesting another, equally problematic one. As a method, deconstruction is highly effective in unravelling the problematic underside of also positions that, on the surface, appear 'progressive'. However, it does not have much to offer for politics that tries to come up with better social alternatives.

Thus, in order to outline a methodological framework that would render the biting deconstructive edge more constructive I will resort to Pierre Bourdieu's work on inequality and Mikhail Bakhtin's notion of dialogues. What I hope to outline is a research framework that facilitates dialogues, not stalwarts, between the various forms of subjugation or social inequality revealed by deconstruction.

Like Derrida, Bourdieu is a poststructuralist and also his theory examines the way in which symbolic structures consolidate social ones. However, unlike Derrida, who focuses on language, Bourdieu (1984) investigates the way in which structures and struggles in different areas of life, or 'fields', are both different and similar. Thus, for example, Bourdieu points out that a high-brow musical taste usually corresponds with, as well as consolidates, a secure economic position. However, sometimes a low-brow music, such as jazz, may subvert the rules of the game and constitute itself as avant-garde or subversive, achieving a higher status than the group, urban poor blacks, with which it was originally associated. What Bourdieu's theory draws attention to, in methodological terms, is that there are different forms of and struggles against inequality, which may both corroborate and challenge one another.

Applying this framework to the analysis of the female body, one can note that it involves (at least) a couple of fields. First, one could argue that there is a general field of beauty, where the closer one's body conforms to the Western ideal of white features and slender body, the higher one's status on that field is. However, there is a second field structured around a class-based bodily disposition or style, which may be in an antagonistic relationship to the field of beauty. In short, while being beautiful may enhance a woman's power and desirability, her attempt to be beautiful and desirable may also diminish her power status by rendering her vainglorious and irrational ('bimbo'), qualities associated with women in general but lower-class women in particular.

The clash of these two powerfields is not only embedded in the sexist discourse that demands women to be both asexual mothers and sexual whores, but also underpins feminist critiques of beauty. This contradiction can be illustrated by the history of the middle-class suffragettes' rallying against the corsette in the nineteenth century (Montague, 1994). As Montague argues, suffragettes' rejection of the corsette was a statement against 'oppressive' beauty ideals as well as a bid towards a less 'curvy' and, thereby more androgynous, female body ideal. From this moment onwards the 'non-curvy' body has become fashionable every time the feminist movement has raised its head, in the 1920s and in the 1960s, leading to dieting, a kind of 'natural' corsette. However, more interestingly, Montague points out that the suffragettes' argument against the curvy body did not only articulate feminist but also class-based endeavours, namely, it can be seen as an effort to distinguish the middle-class respectable and androgynous female body from the curvaceous or sultry body of the lower class prostitute as well as from the oversexualized body of the black woman. Thus, the body-politics of the suffragettes, according to Montague, did not only aim to establish equality between genders, but also aimed to distinguish the middle-class 'rational' women, worthy of the responsibility of vote, from the overly feminine and sexual women of lower classes and races.

Against this background the criticisms of beauty ideals very easily reinforce the middle-class ideal of respectable body that aims to do gender in a 'modest' way (Skeggs, 1997; Fraser, 1999). Thus while the criticisms of beauty may challenge the inequalities embedded in the field that judges people based on their looks, they may also subtly reinforce the norm of the respectable body that condemns attempts to beautify or sexualize one's body as articulating vanity, vulgarity and stupidity, all signs of 'lower' social and moral positions.

One could say that the feminist attempts to 'reimagine' one's body through gregarious activities, from Madonna's use of whorish gear to Orlan's performance surgeries, articulate a politics that deliberately wants to attack the constrictions of the respectable body. However, while these practices may have established a new style of emancipated and sexual women, it is questionable whether this style is available to all women or just those with high symbolic capital. I would argue that the style, popular among some feminist university students in the 1990s, of donning black leather and lace gear and heavy make-up, would not be interpreted as a statement on emancipation, if appropriated by a working-class woman in a working-class style. Rather than seen as 'camp', the working-class women in black leather, such as heavy metal girls, are most likely to be interpreted in the opposite way as simply subordinate 'vamps'.

Deconstruction, as a method, helps to unravel these different forms of subjugation. The advantage of Bourdieu's theory of fields is that it helps to tie these symbolic subjugations and prohibitions to other, sometimes contradictory and clashing, forms of social inequality. However, if one wants to foster conversations between these different positions and forms of subjugation one needs to go beyond deconstruction and analysis of different forms of inequalities. Bakhtin's (1981, 1986; Volosinov, 1973) notion of a dialogic text or novel provides a useful heuristic to begin to think of ways of analyzing texts that cultivate conversations between different symbolic and social forms of subjugation. According to Bakhtin, the artistic and political potential of the nineteenth-century 'dialogic' novel was that it provided a forum, where different social 'accents' were brought together and into a conversation with one another. The novel was a new and unique art form – reflecting the revolutionary and democratic ambitions of nineteenth-century social movements – in that it fomented discussions between different views, without allowing any one of them to impose itself on others (normative view) or without allowing the views or voices to splinter into a cacophony where they would talk past one another (non-normative or deconstructionist view). Bakhtin, therefore, invites a way of analyzing texts, not in an either/or, but in an and/and mode.

This dialogic mode would acknowledge that women can be subjugated both by beauty ideals and by notions of them as being morally or intellectually inferior if they engage in beauty practices. In fact, many women are acutely aware of the tension between the demand to be beautiful and respectable, trying desperately to find a balance between looking attractive but in a way that would not be considered overdoing it or being 'tarty'. I would also argue that the tragedy of many anorexic women is that, while their main goal in starving may have been to attain the non-curvy, emancipated or respectable body, after they are diagnosed as having an eating disorder, they are often defined as having fallen into the trap of vanity and vulgarity and 'dopism' – precisely those qualities they wanted to stave off through starving. Modes of analyzing cultural phenomena that excavate underlying binaries from multiple points of view flesh out these contradictions. However, analyses of the different norms surrounding body-practices often get entrenched into between positions that argue that women are *either* oppressed by beauty ideals *or* oppressed by norms that punish them for paying attention or 'meddling' with their bodies. What dialogism suggests is a way of doing research and politics that acknowledges that women can be oppressed *both* by beauty ideals *and* by norms that condemn women for beautifying themselves.

If one would interpret *South Park* in light of Bourdieu's fields, it can also be located at the crossroads of several fields of power. In the field of masculinity, it may be seen to articulate a young male position against, and frustration with, conservative, right-wing, and often religiously articulated, disciplined, militaristic and authoritarian maleness. However, when looked at from the point of view of wider powerfields of struggles over gender, race and ethnicity, *South Park* occupies a more defensive posture, belittling and ridiculing women's and black's attempts to politicize issues, such as sexual harassment, as 'naff' political correctness. As a media product, *South Park*, together with other adult cartoons and forms of music, such as rap or 'indie', occupies a position that defines itself in opposition to, or as distinct from, the 'mass' or mid–low brow culture, often associated with femininity (talk-shows, self-help, Barbara Streisand, Britney Spears, and Winona Ryder).

Thinking of how to bring into a dialogue the different attacks on, and bids for, power that *South Park* articulates one can think about some of the contradictions of contemporary masculinity. In my classes, where we read both *South Park* and a lot of feminist literature, many of my male students enjoy the cartoon but often implicitly or explicitly express that feminist literature bypasses the fact that also men can be subordinated by social structures, institutions and in human relations. In this context, *South Park* may be seen to vent out the frustrations felt by generation-X males in terms of older, rigid codes of masculinity, imposed by traditional patriarchal institutions, such as the military, family, church and the school. Thus, *South Park* is an instance of a kind of masculine critique of institutions traditionally considered the bulwarks of patriarchy, and condemning the series as sheer sexism does not do justice to the complex pleasures and radical social agendas that the series offers. The constant mocking of feminized consumer and media culture in the series – epitomized by Cartman's mother, who in an amusing as well as draconian fashion keeps stuffing him with cheesy puffs and muffins – is a more contradictory trope, expressing a male yearning beyond the massifying and pacifying consumer culture, often associated with general feminizing as well as overpowering and fundamentally 'uncaring' mothering. However, the jokes that ridicule any pleas for equal treatment by women and ethnic minorities and revel in, for instance blatantly racist depictions of, for example, the Middle East (*Not Without my Anus*) and Central America (*Rainforest Schmainforest*), however, are not offending authorities. They are nothing but a defensive move against challenges to the traditional, white, Western, male superiority. Thus, a constructively deconstructive analysis would neither condemn nor celebrate *South Park*, but flesh out its contradictory power-politics, embedded in the binaries it both deconstructs and consolidates. It would acknowledge the way in which the series attacks and mocks conservative, authoritarian suppression that pushes down white young men as well as other groups, while it would also acknowledge the way in which it is an attempt to usurp power in relation to other groups by ridiculing and denying the legitimacy of their grievances. It would call for a politics that would analyze and fight against subjugation of men and women, blacks and whites, avoiding both one-eyed claims of 'victimization' and denial of inequalities and struggles that exist between different groups.

Conclusions

Deconstruction as a method is useful for unravelling binaries that underpin our thinking, constructing complex normative mazes, such as the ones created around the thin female body. Thus, feminists have used deconstruction to unearth the way in which the thin body stands not only for beauty but, most importantly, for emancipation, strength and intelligence (or mind) qualities that stand in opposition to the voluptuous, reproductive female body. However, other feminists have argued that the critiques of thin beauty ideals and other beauty practices easily affirm an ancient notion of women as vain and easily influenced or 'dopes'. In the end, the feminist debates around body-ideals have often become stagnated between feminists who criticize beauty ideals and feminists who argue that these critiques deny women's agency or frame them as bimbos. In a similar vein, the deconstructive adult cartoon, *South Park*, mocks a series of conservative, middle-American binaries between good and evil, Jesus and Satan, purity and contamination and so on. However, at the same time *South Park*'s rallying against all norms ends up embracing the romantic ideal of a white, mischievious natural male child, the prerogative of which is to subordinate people that stand in his way towards freedom, particularly women and racial and ethnic minorities with their 'naf' demands of obedience and political correctness.

   Thus, scholarly and popular uses of deconstruction easily end up reinforcing dichotomies or embracing an unarticulated ultimate value of freedom such as the romantic male child. Against this background it is suggested that deconstruction be complemented with Bourdieu's theory of different fields of inequality, which helps to unravel the way in which different binaries may articulate different inequalities. Bakhtin's theory of dialogues, furthermore, provides tools for thinking how to bring the different inequalities and grievances into dialogue with one another, in order to begin to imagine complex feminist politics capable of addressing the fact that women may be oppressed both by beauty ideals and by the way in which they are deemed as dopes or vain, if they engage in beauty practices. Dialogic theory also acknowledges that men may be subjugated by conservative, parental, religious and militaristic authorities, but that the rambunctious white, male, mischievious child, who does not tolerate any restrictions, may also buttress steep gendered and racial and national inequalities.

Exercise 7

- Choose a cultural text for analysis (this could be anything from a media text to a policy-document). Analyze what kinds of binaries underpin the text. What do these binaries suppress/prohibit?
- Are these binaries contradictory?
- What kinds of social issues and inequalities do these dichotomies tell about? Do they articulate diverse kinds of social subordination or bids for power?
- Think how you could present your analysis so that it would foster dialogic politics that would be able to tackle the different, and possibly contradictory, forms of social and cultural subordination revealed by your analysis.

Part IV

Analyzing the Global Context

8

Analysis of 'Reality' and Space

Main questions

- **Cultural studies has recently been attacked for focusing on culture and identity, at the expense of global economic inequality. How does the analysis of 'space' help to answer this criticism?**
- **What are the advantages and blind spots embedded in realist/materialist approaches to studying space, such as Manuel Castells's treatise on The Information Society?**
- **How does a multimethodological analysis of material, discursive and lived dimensions of space enrich more traditional analyses of globalization?**
- **Why is 'network' a better metaphor for studying space than a 'map'? What are the pitfalls of the network-metaphor?**

The relationship between cultural studies and 'political economy', which refers to usually leftist, macro-analysis of economy, has traditionally been a torn one. On one hand, both paradigms belong to the same critical leftist tradition. On the other hand, scholars interested in political economy have accused cultural studies of focusing on symbolic processes, arguing the tradition diverts attention from increasing global economic inequality and exploitation. In media studies, it has been argued that cultural studies' interest in media texts and their interpretations has buttressed a neo-liberal ideology that wants people to imagine themselves and their lives in terms of consumer-choice and leisure, diverting attention from the critical areas of media ownership, and work or labour

(Murdock, 1997). Cultural studies has also been challenged by a broad materialist 'rainbow' front, criticizing that it has turned issues of ethnicity, gender and sexuality into questions of identity, style and difference, bypassing the grim material forms of inequality and discrimination facing women, gays, and black and brown people in the South and in the North (Ebert, 1993; Dirlik, 1994; Morton, 1996; Walby, 2001).

In this chapter, I will discuss ways of incorporating an analysis of global, political and economic reality to cultural studies, drawing on critical geographers' work on 'space'. The reason I have chosen to focus on space is that it has recently been the focus of much interest and theorizing in the social sciences, and this flurry of research has produced innovative methodological ideas and practices, which will be discussed both in this and the following chapter. On one hand, scholars have been attracted to studying space, because it seems more tangible or material than, lets say, time or culture, and it also promises to give a broad overview of global developments taking place across the earthly surface. On the other hand, scholars have criticized the materialist, objectivist approach to space, 'from above'. They have pointed out that the way we perceive space is always discursively mediated and political, and that instead of trying to get a broad overview, we should pay attention to different perceptions of space, including lived views on space 'from below'. These latter theorizations have paved the way for multimethodological approaches that analyze the material, discursive, and lived aspects of contemporary global space and reality. As such, they point towards ways of bringing together the study of lived experience and discourses, discussed earlier in the book, and the analysis of the global, social, political and economic context.

In what follows, I will start with discussing the materialist/realist approach to space through a discussion of the advantages and blind spots embedded in Manuel Castells' (1996, 1997, 1998) three-volume landmark treatise on the Information Society, which describes how the world really 'is' at the end of the second millennium. In the second section, I will critically discuss the way in which the binary-driven terms Castells uses to categorize social phenomena partly – such as his division between reactive and proactive social movements – undermine the politics he suggests. In the third section I will, drawing on Edward Soja's notion of 'Thirdspace', sketch a multiperspectival mode of studying space that examines its material, or 'real' aspects but that also critically reflects on the always political and partial nature of the terms that we use to describe or, more appropriately, 'inscribe' space. The final section of the chapter illustrates multiperspectival analysis of space through a discussion of feminist geographic works on women's role in new economic structures. These works examine both material and lived perspectives on new economy, while being acutely reflexive of the politics embedded in the terms or discourses they use in, and conclusions they draw from, their studies.

To conclude, I briefly discuss why the metaphor of a 'network' is, perhaps, better suited to analyze contemporary spatial developments than the traditional metaphor of a 'map'. I will also make a few critical remarks about our current fascination with networks in general and network methodology in particular, to underline that no methodology is perfect or without its political blind spots.

Materialist/realist analysis

Analyzing the Information Society

To start discussing how to analyze the global space from a political and economic point of view, I will turn to the, perhaps, most authoritative statement in that area: Manuel Castells's three-volume treatise on The Information Society (Castells, 1996, 1997, 1998).

To give an overview of Castells's trilogy, in a nutshell, it argues that the global space has increasingly been split into the 'space of flows' (or the sphere of The Net) and the 'space of places' (or the sphere of the Self). The Net refers to material time-sharing activities that are no longer bound to a particular place, such as electronically mediated communication and financial transactions as well as the quickly moving global, managerial elite (Castells, 1996: 412). This global space of flows begins, in a sense, to live a life of its own, surpassing earthbound material social realities. This happens, for example, in megacities, such as New York or Mexico City, which are externally connected to financial and other networks while internally disconnecting local marginalized populations (404).

Most people do not inhabit this ungrounded space of flows but are caught in a 'space of places'. In this sphere of The Self, people construct identities that feed into social movements that contain the seeds of social transformation. Castells distinguishes between three types of identities. A 'legitimizing identity' validates the authority of dominant institutions; an example is trade unions that bargain with the welfare state. A 'resistant identity' resists The Net by isolating into communes, ranging from Mexican Zapatistas to religious fundamentalism and American patriots. Finally, 'project identity' reaches outward to constitute a new global civil society and change history. Castells (1997) sees the potential for this project, for example, in feminist struggles against patriarchy and environmental movements' 'holistic' worldview.

Castells constructs this broad argument through examining a number of developments, from changes in labour structures, industry and technology to transformations of family-patterns, the state and politics, and the emergence of global criminal economy, Asian 'tiger economies, and' the ghettoized 'fourth world' in both North and the South. He bases his analyses of these developments on large quantities of statistical data on, for example, Internet connections, female labour patterns, fertility rates, income distribution and incarceration rates in different parts of the world. Castells's approach is a classical macro-sociological one in that his main aim is to build, or to 'suggest', a 'cross-cultural theory of economy and society in the information age'. The extensive empirical 'data' he has collected and analyzed serves to probe, or to use Castells's words, to 'constrain', the theoretical argument (Castells, 1996: 26–7). Castells does not explain his methodology much, but he does refer to his use of statistics in the opening sequence of the trilogy:

> I am aware of the limitations in lending credibility to information that may not always be accurate, yet the reader will realize that there are numerous precautions taken in this text, so as to form conclusions usually on the basis of convergent trends from several sources, according to a methodology of triangulation with a well-established, successful tradition among historians, policemen, and investigative reporters. (26)

Thus, making the usual reservations about the use of international and national statistics, which may be biased or inaccurate, Castells states that he has triangulated the data through consulting multiple sources. What this basically means is that, according to Castells, give and take a small margin of error, his data and therefore his analysis of global developments that give rise to the information society are 'accurate'. Thus, Castells's trilogy obeys the logic of basic positivist and realist social scientific research, which is based on a rigorous analysis of 'data', using a scientific method. The aim of research in this tradition is to establish a hypothesis or theory about the way things in the world 'really are' and then find out whether this is so or not. In essence, Castells's theory suggests a grand narrative or a 'truth' about how the world stands at the end of the second millennium. Period.

Discussing Castells's entire oeuvre would be too large an undertaking. So, in what follows I will focus on his analysis of women's position and the feminist movement, which he identifies as one of the 'proactive' social movements, as well as on his discussion of some of the 'reactive' movements or responses to globalization. My intention with this discussion is to reflect on the strengths and blind spots embedded in Castells's analysis that result from the methodological position he adopts.

The flexible women

Castells (1997) devotes a relatively large chapter to what he calls 'the end of patriarchalism', which refers to global transformations in women's economic position, the achievements or impact of the feminist movement as well as various trends that undermine the traditional patriarchal nuclear-family.

In the chapter Castells traces a worldwide development of women's increasing role in paid labour. So, across the Western OECD-countries women's participation in labour force has, in the past 20 years, risen from around 50 per cent to around 65 per cent, while men's participation has either stagnated or mildly decreased (155). This development is not restricted to Western industrialized nations either, and women's economic activity nearly doubled in India between 1970 and 1990 (160–1). Castells attributes these changes to transformations in the economy and the labour market, so that women's interpersonal skills, their flexible work-patterns as well as their lower pay fit the requirements of contemporary postindustrial economy. However, he notes that advances in reproductive technologies, particularly in contraception, as well as the global presence of the feminist agenda and imaginary have also fuelled the process.

The transformations in work-patterns parallel equally fundamental changes in family-structures. Divorce rates are doubling in many parts of the world, and fertility rates are dropping in both developed and developing countries, with the exception of Africa, where rates have plateaud (140–1). At the same time births out of wedlock have dramatically increased in, for example the United States, where currently 20 per cent of first babies of Caucasian women are born out of wedlock, and 40 per cent of Hispanic and 70 per cent African-American first babies are born out of wedlock (147). As a consequence of these developments, the standard or normative image of a 'married couple with children' constituted only a quarter of US households in the mid-1990s.

In conjunction with these profound structural transformations, Castells reviews a series of national and international feminist movements and analyzes how they are interwoven with other politics, from human rights to sexual rights movements. For example, Castells discusses how feminism has been part of the anti-Franquist coalition and later part of the socialist state apparatus in Spain, identified with communist affinities and later cultural concerns in Italy, and articulated a number of North/South issues as well as discrepancies in the UN Women's Forum in Beijing. It is this ability to attach itself, or open up, to different political sensibilities that Castells argues is the strength of the feminist movement, constituting it as a possible 'project' identity. It makes the movement capable of connecting various concerns together into a 'flexible network' of ideas and identities and thereby reinvigorating a global civil society, powerful enough to respond to the Net (199).

The strength of Castells's analysis is its incredibly wide scope that marshals a dizzying array of statistics from all parts of the world to pinpoint crucial developments in women's position across the global landscape. By and large these developments point to increases in women's economic power and the concomitant erosion of the normative, heterosexual patriarchal family. However, these developments also have exploitative features, such as low-wage and hazardous labour in the flexible sweatshop and electronics industries, and the fact that the number of children living in poverty is increasing, partly due to single parenthood. What is most remarkable about this kind of analysis is its ability to identify trends that happen, albeit in somewhat different form, in many parts of the world.

If one compares Castells's methodological approach to the modes of inquiry discussed elsewhere in this book, its ability to connect, for example, gender with wide economic and global trends and developments is unsurpassable. Castells's discussion of, for example, the growing economic, and concomitant emotional, independence of women, coupled with the stark statistics on the educational and economic marginalization and criminalization of black men, sets Jones's new ethnographic discussion of the both violent and caring relationship between white Andrea and black Andrés within the wider social context (Jones, 2000; and see Chapter 3). Andrés' words on how 'the only meaningful relations in my life have been with women' are cast in a wider light against the statistics on the fact that 70 per cent of African-American women give birth to their first child out of wedlock, creating strong female-centred cultures particularly in poor, black, urban neighbourhoods. The impact of this on heterosexual relations is illustrated by data, according to which 60 per cent of adults in Chicago's inner-city have never been married (Castells, 1998: 143). While the 'cold' statistics do not tell how these issues are 'lived' (the way Jones' new ethnography so powerfully does), they do locate interpersonal, interracial and heterosexual relationships as part of wider, global structural changes.

In the same way the romantic, frustrated and rebellious white, male subjectivity constructed in *South Park* becomes intelligible against the changes in the relative weakening of men's position both in the private familiar and public, economic realms. These developments have sparked, particularly in States like Colorado (the location of 'real' South Park) (Castells, 1997: 88–90), a militarist, religious, white male reaction in the form of militias and Christian fundamentalism, which *South Park* both challenges, and in a more subtle way, also supports. While deconstructive analysis of *South Park* (see Chapter 7) may reveal the contradictions of this popular discourse on masculinity, reflecting on it against the backdrop of the changes in the family and economy, highlights the wider social landscape from which, and to which, the series speaks.

As discussed in the previous chapters, what the sad and fatal violence of Andrés towards Andrea and the contradictions of *South Park* call for are dialogues between different forms of subordination and frustration. What a materialist/realist perspective brings to these discussions on dialogues is an analysis of how conflicts between different groups and perspectives not only have to do with understanding and ideology but also with very real, and possibly conflicting, material interests. Understanding the structural conflicts, between men and women, blacks and whites, and beginning to negotiate them should be conducive of the kinds of 'project' identities, which Castells argues could articulate diverse interests together into a flexible oppositional coalition, capable of providing a counterforce to the sinister aspects of globalization. However, I would argue that his work and its methodological commitments both work to facilitate the kind of dialogic politics as well as, in another sense, undermine it.

Political space

The inflexible others

Castells's theory has been widely acclaimed and has also provoked criticism. On one hand, critics have argued that Castells gets caught up in the networking hype, believing that we are living in an entirely new era that carries the promise of increased levels of productivity and equality, if we manage to avoid certain tribalistic scenarios (Golding, 2000; Smart, 2000). On the other hand, scholars have criticized Castells for presenting a too gloomy picture of a steeply divided world. For example Stern (1999) points out that Castells's picture of the destitution of African-Americans does not take into account that in terms of income and educational levels, they are better off than ever, even if ghettos (in many ways) are cut off from mainstream life and economy.

These critiques obey the same 'realist' methodological logic as Castells' work, that is, they argue that Castells has got the 'facts' wrong or interpreted them erroneously. However, another line of critique has challenged the binary-driven logic of the concepts that the trilogy uses, such as envisioning a world polarized between the big, bad Net and the brave or poor little Self (Waterman, 1999; Friedmann, 2000). A similar stark dichotomy characterizes Castells's analysis of 'new' social movements, which are seen as either 'reactive' or 'project'. What makes this division particularly suspicious is the fact that nearly all the movements that Castells deems to have the greatest potential to become project identities (feminists, environmentalists and the European Union) represent 'nice' social forces that we in the Western world are comfortable with. The reactive or 'resistant' ones (Mexican Zapatistas, American patriots, and Islamic and other fundamentalists) represent groups that may be nice or not so nice but are nevertheless less privileged than the proactive ones.

To begin to unravel the problematic nature and political investments of Castells's analysis, one can resort to a discussion I had with my undergraduate students on what or who have become the Other in the post-Cold War era. 'Those that run around with guns', was an instant and unanimous answer. The specific groups the students came up with included Serbs, American militia, Islamic fundamentalists, terrorists, and other 'fanatics locked up in a particular mindset'. My undergraduates' list and its underlying logic are conspicuously close to Castells's discussion of those movements and identities he defines as the most reactive. These dichotomies, resonating with contemporary popular and political sentiments, which emerge out of Castells's analysis of social movements, reveal the limit of his methodological realism. The limit of the realist quest to 'describe' how the world 'really is', is that it ends up blind to the political or constitutive nature of the concepts it uses. Thus, Castells brilliantly pinpoints the ways in which the global economic and political networks empower some people while disempowering others. Yet, he does not pay attention to the way in which his juxtaposition of the 'reactive' movements, closed upon themselves, and the 'project' ones, which are open and connecting with others, ends up consolidating the steep inequalities and hostilities between people that he writes about.

If one is to problematize the concepts Castells uses to make sense of the world, one needs to shift methodological gears and complement his materialist/realist analysis of the uneven global space with a discourse-analytical approach, such as deconstruction. Deconstruction can help to unpack the contradictory politics embedded in, for example, this description of the nature of the 'reactive' movements:

Religious fundamentalism, cultural nationalism, territorial communes are, by and large, defensive reactions. Reactions against three fundamental threats, perceived in all societies ... in this end of millennium. Reaction against globalization ... Reaction against networking and flexibility ... And the reaction against the crisis of patriarchal family ... These defensive reactions become sources of meaning and identity by constructing new cultural codes out of historical materials. Because the new processes of domination to which people react are imbedded in information flows, the building of autonomy has to rely in reverse information flows. God, nation, family and community will provide unbreakable, eternal codes, around which a counter-offensive will be mounted against the culture of real virtuality. Thus, against the informationalization of culture, bodies are informationalized. That is, individuals bear their gods in their heart. They do not reason, they believe. (Castells, 1997: 65–6)

This excerpt is illustrative of three features of Castells's mode of analysis. First, it links the various 'fundamentalist' movements to wider developments, such as the emergence of the global Net and concomitant erosion of patriarchal structures, illuminating their contradictory global and social roots. Second, it sheds critical light on cultural studies' romantic interest in the 'local' and 'marginal', pointing out how the marginal can also be a locus of defensive intolerance. However, the third and problematic feature of Castells's analysis of new movements is the way in which it is tightly interlaced by categorizing binaries, such as defensive/proactive, history/future, autonomy/connectivity, culture/body, and reason/belief. Castells's analysis of the social and global dimensions of the fundamentalist movements points to their contradictory roots in increasing global inequality as well as loss of traditional patriarchal power. However, when defining the movements' attitude or strategy, contradictions drop out of Castells' analysis, and his definitions turn relentlessly negative. The movements are positioned as representing forces of the 'body', 'belief', and as harking back to tradition or history, affirming a set of fundamental binaries, such as body/mind, belief/knowledge or irrationality/irrationality, and history/future. As such they affirm the classical white, male, Western, Enlightenment values of rationality, culture and being 'modern' or future-oriented, standing in opposition to the wild, natural or embodied Other, steeped in archaic traditions and irrational superstitions. The political problem with these polarizing taxonomies is that they fuel the kinds of hostilities and inequalities that separate people in the Information Society and make envisioning common alternatives to it difficult.

From space to spaces

From divisions to dialogues

Deconstruction as a method enables one to uncover the problematic nature of the binaries underpinning Castells's analysis of the global space. However, as discussed in Chapter 7, deconstruction is a useful tool for criticizing texts, but it is not as useful for helping to imagine social alternatives. Thus, to begin to think of a mode of study that could preserve the insights of Castells's structural analysis but would also trouble his binaries, one can turn to Ang's (2001) recent discussion on the nationalist populist politics of Pauline Hanson in Australia.

The populist politics of Pauline Hanson, 'a divorced mother of four and a former small-businesswoman' (Ang, 2001: 154), definitely belongs to the kind of 'reactive' reactions to globalization that Castells writes about. Hanson's political rallying against 'the Aboriginal industry' and arguments about Australia 'being swamped by Asians', appeal to what she terms 'ordinary Australians', such as white, both rural and suburban, working-class and lower-middle-class people. To make sense of Hanson's politics, Ang, initially, draws on Castells and identifies the movement as a resistance to globalization, such as borderless, volatile global markets and transnational migration that have eroded both the economic and cultural power of these, by and large, uneducated people. In agreement with Castells, Ang also points out that the 'absolutization of a strictly localized, exclusionary "us", and the symbolic warding off of everything and everyone that is associated with the invading "outside"' is not only violently xenophobic but also clearly counterproductive, making the Hansonites incapable of entering any political coalition and further disinvesting them of the contemporary economic and symbolic hard currency of multicultural ease and flexibility.

However, Ang also points out, how in contemporary Australia her identity as an immigrant of 'Asian' origin, puts her into a curious position in relation to the Hansonites. This is because it puts her squarely at the centre of the dominant political discourse, re-imagining Australia as a 'multicultural Australia in Asia'. This discourse – that was spearheaded by the charismatic 'new labour' prime minister, Paul Keating in the 1990s and embraced by the corporate world and the intellectual class – was part and parcel of the aggressive neoliberal politics of restructuring. The aim of this restructuring of the economy and culture was to enable Australia to better compete in the global markets, particularly the lucrative Asian one. Reflecting on her personal and academic identity in relation to this discourse and the Hansonite resentment, Ang concludes:

> As a relatively recent immigrant into Australia and a person of 'Asian' background, I had (and have) a personal cultural stake in the redefinition of 'Australian identity' as an open space for diverse influences, traditions and trajectories and as the intersection of multiplicity of global cultural flows … Such a postmodern nation would be more rather than less prepared than others in the world to feel comfortable in the globalized world of the twenty-first century. It would be a future-oriented nation which is not just capable of change but actively desires change, turning necessity into opportunity in times of altered economic and geopolitical circumstances. (2001: 155)

Thus, in a self-reflexive move, Ang problematizes her own position as a feminist, multicultural intellectual as being too close for comfort to the discourse and policy that justifies the marginalization of Pauline Hanson and xenophobic, inflexible 'white trash' like her. Thus, unlike Castells, who sees himself as the objective scientific observer describing the state of affairs of the late-twentieth-century world, Ang critically reflects on the situated and political nature of her own knowledge in relation to Pauline Hanson and her supporters.

Ang acknowledges the structural or 'real' roots of Pauline Hanson's movement in the contradictions of globalization. Like Castells, she also defines Hanson's strategy as largely counterproductive and unethical. Yet, Ang also questions the hegemonic discourse idealizing cosmopolitanism, in which she herself is implicated as an intellectual of Asian origin, pointing out that it fuels the antagonism that characterizes the structural and symbolic relationship between the cosmopolites and Hansonites. Thus, instead of being locked in binaries, such as 'global versus local, privileged versus marginalized, progressive versus reactionary', she suggest viewing relationship between people like herself and people that would support Hanson in 'more negotiated, conciliatory, exploratory terms, terms in which no singular antagonism is allowed to saturate the entire significance of the relationship' (157).

Reading Castells against Ang's discussion on Hanson, points at four crucial methodological issues in studying contemporary global world or space, shot through with economic, political and symbolic divisions and inequalities. First, it underlines the need to understand the broad, global structural developments and processes that produce the winners and losers of our times. Second, it draws attention to the fact that we can never describe global developments objectively or in an unbiased manner, as any description of the global is mediated by political discourses, partly shaped by the scholar's location within the global landscape (s)he is studying. The always political and situated nature of all knowledge emphasizes the need for self-reflexive awareness of the discourses and positions that drive our thought. The always both 'real' and political nature of descriptions of the global leads to the third, and most important, methodological lesson: The need to be aware of the political consequences of one's research, that is, the need to be aware of what kinds of 'real' worlds we are, not describing, but producing. Comparing Castells and Ang, they both express a concern for global inequalities. However, Castells's taxonomic logic writes certain underprivileged movements, people and worldviews 'off' from progressive politics. Slightly differently, Ang's critically self-reflexive and more ambivalent stance gestures towards a more reconciliatory and open space that invites a dialogue between different inequalities, perhaps, asking everyone to have another look at the terms they are using to make sense of themselves and their situation.

Thirdspace

In order to begin to think how to combine a 'materialist' analysis of global, social space and an acknowledgement of the political nature of the concepts we use to describe or constitute it, one may resort to Edward Soja's (1996, 2000) notion of 'Thirdspace'. Soja is a critical geographer like Castells, but his postmodernist bent renders his theory useful for expanding the realist/materialist methodological framework.

Roughly put, Soja argues 'space' has three dimensions. What he terms 'first space' refers to its material qualities that render certain actions impossible and facilitate others, so that, for example, the process of urbanization fuels itself by making certain nodal or rich regions capable of fomenting interaction and wealth and increase their importance, power and attraction. First space also refers to a realist, positivist mode of analysis, such as Castells's work, that aims to measure and map developments across the global space, often using quantitative methods.

By the term 'second space' Soja refers to popular, political and intellectual discourses and images we have of space, which may idealize certain spaces and demonize others. Within this view, Castells's theory on the global information society is not a 'description' but a discourse that creates a certain vision of global space and its developments, lamenting the emergence of certain types of spaces and celebrating others. An example of a more practical discourse that envisions and produces space is urban planning and its fashions that have produced, for example, the theme-park-like neighbourhoods in Los Angeles and other global metropolis, which sell themselves with an ethnic or cultural theme and a reconstructed past.

The third and most interesting space aims to undo the oppositional nature of realism and social constructionism and to understand space as both-real-and-imagined (Soja, 1996: 73–5). To borrow Donna Haraway (1997), one could say that Soja's notion of 'Thirdspace' refers to the way in which space is materially-and-semiotically produced, so that the different planning, policy, intellectual and grassroots 'visions' work or interact with the material space, producing cities, natural preserves, spatial divisions and social inequalities as well as riots, such as the Los Angeles riots in 1992, that alter the landscape. Thirdspace then calls attention to the both real and political nature of discourses on space in that they 'transform' it.

Furthermore, Thirdspace also encompasses the lived dimension of space. In a sense the lived space refers to the ways in which space is viewed and produced at the local and embodied everyday level. However, as Soja notes, the lived view on space 'from below' and the material view of space 'from above' should not be perceived hierarchically as general and particular (Soja, 1996: 310). The grounded, lived approach to space offers a different perspective than the 'aerial' view from above, but the everyday, lived space can say as much about 'the global' as the planners' or theorists' view. An example of the interlocked nature of embodied, everyday space and the global one is provided by bell hooks's discussion on 'dark' spaces:

One of my five sisters wants to know how it is I come to think about these things, about houses and space. ... I tell this sister in a late night conversation that I am learning to think about blackness in a new way. Tanizaki speaks of seeing beauty in darkness and shares this moment of insight: 'The quality that we call beauty, however, must always grow from the realities of life, and our ancestors, forced to live in dark rooms, presently came to discover beauty in shadows, ultimately to guide shadows toward beauty's end'. My sister has skin darker than mine. We think about our skin as a dark room, a place of shadows. We talk often about colour politics and the way racism has created an aesthetic that wounds us … In the shadows of late night, we talk about the need to see darkness differently, to talk about it in a new way. In that space of shadows we long for an aesthetic of blackness – strange and oppositional. (hooks, 1990: 113)

This poetic analysis of hooks (also Soja, 1996: 104) calls attention to the way in which the most intimate, embodied experience of one's skin is related to the cruel transnational practice of slavery, which confined blacks into a life of shadows and dark rooms. It illustrates the way in which the 'lived' approach to space is also global and political, even if differently than a political economic analysis. The quote from hooks also draws attention to the oppositional or utopian potential of lived space or Thirdspace. It highlights the way in which a particular lived view, such as hooks' 'space of darkness', may challenge or disrupt more general or mainstream descriptions of space by pointing at their blind spots and, thereby, carrying the potential to transform or disrupt the politics as usual of space. This happened, for example, during the Los Angeles riots in 1992, when disenfranchised groups, confined to living in the shadows of this world-metropolis, took over the segregated urban sprawl, questioning its legitimacy and breaking its boundaries. However, one should bear in mind that a lived or local view of space is not necessarily radical or egalitarian, as illustrated by Pauline Hanson's imaginary space of 'ordinary Australians'. Still, one needs to be reflective of the political consequences of simply demonizing the space inhabited or created by the Hansonites.

Methodologically speaking, Soja's notion of Thirdspace suggests a multiperspectival approach to studying 'space'. It underlines the need to, first, study the global, material macrostructures and processes of space, such as the contradictory economic and political developments outlined by Castells. However, second, it also calls for a careful analysis of the political nature and implications of the concepts or discourses we and other institutions use to make sense of space. Third, Soja's model draws attention to the need to examine space also from 'below', from the point of view of local, lived space, which may challenge the view from above or the concepts we use to describe space.

Looking at Soja's material, discursive and lived spaces, they parallel the three sections of this book on 'contexts', 'texts', and 'lived experience'. Soja's Thirdspace, just as this book, calls for a mode of inquiry that examines, or at least keeps in mind, the different dimensions of space or social reality. While the lived, discursive and contextual aspects of space and reality can be studied in separation, both analytically and empirically, they intertwine with one another. This 'intertwining' also points beyond viewing these approaches in a linear fashion, as if leading from the 'small' (even, if perhaps, romanticized) lived view to the medium-range focus on mediation and all the way 'up' to the analysis of global context that gives us the 'big' picture. Rather than imagining the perspectives to proceed vertically from small to big, they are best envisioned horizontally, or as a web, where views from different nodes open up a different view on space, but these views cannot be organized hierarchically. This means, that global developments do not simply 'explain' local spaces or identities, but that lived views on space may trouble or even turn the tables on global views. Thus, rather than searching for linear explanations and clean-cut categories, the methodological metaphor of a web is sensitive to complex or multidimensional explanations and contradictions that defy taxonomic categories. This is exemplified by Ang's discussion, which refuses to impose her 'cosmopolitan' worldview on the Hansonites and define them as simply misguided, dangerous and wrong. On the contrary, she allows the Hanson-phenomenon to fundamentally question the cosmopolitanism, in which she as a person and as a professional is invested, while also acknowledging the deep problems in the Hansonites' worldview. Ang's discussion, however, is not an empirical study but a theoretical and political meditation. Thus, in order to illustrate and discuss how multidimensional research on space is done in practice, I will turn to the works of feminist geographers.

Feminist geographies

Gendered spaces

Feminist geography has been paradigmatically and politically positioned in a way that has made it likely to both draw on theories of space and to challenge traditional concepts of space and modes of studying it. This is because male geographers' notion of space has often reflected a very masculine understanding of the world. So, for example, in urban geography women's spaces, such as suburbs and homes, are usually understood in terms of private, consumption and reproduction (Wilson, 1991). Feminist scholars have challenged this real-and-imagined gendered geography by both criticizing women's confinement in the suburban 'safe' space as well as drawing attention to the fact that the home is not simply the private sphere of reproduction but also a locus of often exhausting production or work as well as politics (Gibson-Graham, 1996). To complicate things further, the feminist critiques of the confining nature of home have been found decidedly middle-class biased, blind to the many women who do not have a place they could call 'home' (Pratt, 1999).

Because feminist geographers, perhaps, more than others have had to 'contest' many taken-for-granted notions of space, they have been in a position to see, unusually clearly, that theories on space are not 'descriptive' but 'inscriptive' or political. Therefore, for instance, drawing on Judith Butler's (1990) theory, Gibson et al. (2001) have suggested that we see theories of space as 'performative', that is, instead of describing states of affairs they construct certain kinds of spaces and identities and politics that go with them. This underlines the need to reflect on how our modes of study and theorizing suggest or facilitate certain kinds of spaces and politics and render other kinds of politics unfathomable. Furthermore, it also emphasizes the need to approach space from different directions in order to get a sense of different ways of living and understanding space.

The political nature of space, and the way in which looking at it from another perspective may make things seem rather different, can be illustrated by, for example, feminist geographers' work on economic restructuration. In this area, male critical geographers' have often focused on transformations in heavy industries, such as mining, as their rise and fall have been associated with the emergence and disappearance of radical, (male) working-class politics. Feminist geographers, however, have pointed out that these studies frequently omit women, the miners' wives, from their analysis. Studying the restructuring of traditional English mining towns, Massey (1994) has pinpointed how the traditional gender structures in the areas redirected future developments in unexpected ways. Thus, after the collapse of mining, when regional policy incentives began to attract 'new' industries to previous mining towns, they did not employ the ex-miners, but their wives. This was because the women, who had largely been homemakers, provided an ideal flexible pool of labour, which was largely non-unionized, ready to work part-time and flexible hours and for small pay. This development stood in contrast to the 'cotton mill' towns, which, equally suffering from restructuration, did not attract new industries, even if they also offered a large pool of female labour. This was because the vast female unemployment was partly belittled and went partly unnoticed by statistics and, concomitantly, regional policy incentives (because the women did not necessarily register as unemployed but simply 'returned home') as well as because the strongly unionized female labourforce was not so attractive to the new employers.

Massey's discussion epitomizes a long policy and theoretical discussion that, drawing on statistics and also on ethnographic work, tried to make sense of 'why' the regional policy incentives did not work as expected, that is, provide jobs for the ex-miners. It illustrates how the academic and governmental presumably 'objective' analysis of the regional situation proved to be seriously flawed and highly political in that they simply omitted half the issue, that is, women. It also illustrates that looking at a (regional) space from a different perspective may make it seem very different and that the perspective one adopts has straightforward political consequences, so that the male-bias of government's regional policy initiatives turned them upside down for better and for worse.

Flexible economy, flexible theory

To illustrate, in more detail, how to analyze and understand global developments, the political nature of discourses that describe them, and the 'from the ground' views that challenge them I will look at a recent study on Filipina contract workers (Gibson et al., 2001). The notion of Filipina contract workers refers to migrant women who work, usually as domestic workers, in places, such as Hong Kong, Singapore, Japan, the Middle East or in the West. As Gibson *et al.* note, these women are often comprehended through the oppositional discourses of either being 'national heroes' or 'victims of globalization'. The notion of 'national heroes' was coined by the president Cory Aquino and has its roots in the Philipino government's official attitude and programme to encourage overseas employment, as it brings much needed hard currency to the country. The idea of 'victims' illustrates the attitude of many Western non-governmental organizations that provide help and aim to organize the women, seen as being economically exploited and often abused by the migrant-labour system.

What Gibson *et al.* note is that these notions or 'theories' are not necessarily 'right' or 'wrong'. Rather, what one needs to ask is what kinds of political possibilities they open up. They argue that neither the national discourse, hailing the women's entrepreneurialism, nor the NGO-discourse, rendering the women helpless victims, is particularly useful for imagining the transnational migrant space in a way that would foment the women's political agency or identity (8). The authors argue that neither of these discourses do justice to the complexities and contradictions of the contract-working women, who occupy multiple positions in the global landscape and its inequalities.

To illustrate the complexities, Gibson *et al.* turn to the story of 'Luz', who had worked as a domestic helper in Hong Kong for seven years. She went to Hong Kong soon after she had married and had a son, in a situation where, even with a college degree in Home Economics, she worked as an agricultural worker on her husband's parents' farm. Her experience with the first Chinese family was not very good; Luz worked long hours and the children verbally abused her as 'just a maid' who could be 'sent back' (Gibson *et al.*, 2001: 8). She then found work, through her network of Philipina friends, with a British family, which worked better in terms of pay and work, and later for an Australian couple, who allowed her to do extra work for a Canadian family. When the Canadian family was returning, they wanted to take Luz with them. Luz's husband, to whom she had been sending money regularly, however, confiscated her passport:

> 'He is holding my passport. And I must write to my Canadian employer and tell her it cannot be …', Luz explained with sadness. 'Here it is not the same, nobody understands me, my life in Hong Kong …'. (9)

This quote troubles any easy notion of Luz as a victim or a hero, as she sees her former employers as offering her a more lucrative life and her husband as the villain. However, Luz's situation is still more complicated than that, and Gibson *et al.* note that her migrant earnings had consolidated her household's position within the local elite. So, Luz's money allowed her husband to buy some cars for hire, and later an auto-repair shop. Luz had also put some money aside for herself, which she used to buy some agricultural land that was cultivated by distant relatives. Thus, rather than being a simple victimized domestic, Luz was also a petite-capitalist, running her own business and employing a no mean number of other people, while also being restricted by the patriarchal structure of her own family.

Acknowledging these multiple roles, paints a different picture of Luz than captured by the hero or victim narratives. However, most important of all, it suggests different political strategies. Gibson *et al.* suggest that a more contradictory understanding of the contract workers' life calls for or creates more complex political responses that aim to both improve the women's lot 'abroad' and work towards enabling their income to contribute to general well-being and development at 'home'. An initiative that addresses these issues is the Hong Kong Asian Migrant Centre's 'reintegration programme', which helps contract-working women to save and pool their resources for an investment at home. The aims of this programme were twofold. First, it aims to enable the women to break the cycle of migrations and 'go back' as well as honour the women's desire to improve their economic position. Second, by suggesting the pooling of resources and the funding of, for example, cooperatives, the scheme also aims to break away from the individualist entrepreneurialism and channel the women's money to purposes that foster national, sustainable development (13–14).

The study on Luz and the other feminist geographies illustrate four methodological points in analyses of space. First, they emphasize the need to understand broad, both transnational and national, developments, such as the restructuring of regions, unemployment and migrations figures and patterns and government policies and their interaction. One would not be able to understand the way in which the lives and fates of the miners' wives and Luz are connected to wide social and global developments, politics, and policies without investigating policy documents, discourses, and statistics and patterns.

Second, even if seemingly concrete things, such as 'space' or statistics seem to call for an analysis of the hard and fast 'facts' of social life, all analysis of space or developments remains political. All the different studies discussed in this chapter in their own particular ways testify for the way in which we go about theorizing and discussing space 'construct' it. Thus, the negligence of gender in some forms of geographical analysis and policy-talk misses out on fundamental developments, which not only brush under the carpet of the concerns of a particular group but also undo the original aims of a policy-programme both for better and worse. Instead of considering the political nature of our research an outrage, this calls for modes of inquiry that are critically reflective on their own political impact.

Third, as the alluring image of the disembodied, objective view of space from above is revealed to be a chimera, studying space needs to accommodate an analysis or consideration of possible alternative spaces and views of/from space. This encourages combining ethnographic or other 'ground' methods with the more general political economic analysis of social processes and structures. Gibson *et al.* could not have come up with their powerful reconsideration of the migrant-worker experience, if they had not consulted people like Luz.

Fourth, in keeping with Soja's notion of Thirdspace, multidimensional research on space has a strong utopian element to it. By trying to both find out what 'is really going on' and, at the same time, break away from traditional descriptions and politics that dictate the 'goings on' in the contemporary world, multidimensional analysis of space tries to create or facilitate new and more egalitarian spaces. Part of this more egalitarian project is also an attempt to create more egalitarian research spaces that acknowledge the political and partial nature of our own analyses and work to expand and pluralize our sense of space or spaces.

From maps to networks

One could say that Manuel Castells's way of studying the global space is close to the traditional geographic endeavour of 'mapping', which aims to get an 'accurate' overview of vast stretches of space and, thereby, yield 'knowledge' of or facilitate control over them. Castells's analysis and theory has its undeniable and remarkable merits, offering an overview of both similar and different social, political and economic developments across the world. In this sense, it offers insights into large processes that help to contextualize 'on the ground' issues explored by, for example, new ethnography, such as violent relationships between men and women.

However, the shortcoming of the desire to map the 'big picture' is that it runs the risk of producing the colonialist cartographer's myopia, who thought he was 'mapping' the non-European space, but ended up inscribing a cruel colonialist space that annihilated other radically different notions of spaces as well as 'real' spaces and peoples (Kirby, 1996). Thus, the problem with the objectivist view on space is that it denies its political nature and, thus, may silence alternative notions of space in the name of 'truth'. This accounts, for example, for the polarized drive to categorize social movements into outdated and inward-looking, and upbeat and forward-looking ones that steepens mistrust and inequalities between these groups.

A more multidimensional mode of studying space acknowledges that any description is always also an inscription or contains a political agenda and, for its small or big part, transforms space. Thus, instead of a vertical, top-down 'map', it views research on space in terms of a horizontal or 'flat' 'network'. The metaphor of a network draws attention to three methodological issues. First, it points out that the scholar does not exist 'above' the space (s)he is studying, but always observes the world from a particular location or node in a network, underlining the always partial and particular and never objective nature of our positions. Second, it provides a framework that does not privilege certain perspectives, such as the political economic or geographic view 'from above', but acknowledges that lived, scientific, policy and so on views on space may be different, but they cannot be organized hierarchically as they observe the space from a different position. Thus, microviews do not simply 'prove' or 'disprove' macroviews but can confound them and provide alternative scenarios and vice versa. Third, the metaphor of networks views reality in a more 'messy' way, not in terms of clear categories but more as a tangle of interconnected events and issues that call attention to complexities and contradictions.

Returning to Castells's (1997) analysis of patriarchy, it has a relatively upbeat tone. Castells does point to contradictions and the perseverance of sexism, but, overall, women's marching into the workforce across the globe as well as their abandoning of heteronormative families seems inevitable and laudable. If one looks at the works of Massey (1994) and Gibson et al. (2001), the picture seems rather different. In both the cases of British former mining-towns and Philipina contract workers the issue is women's entrance into the workforce. In these studies, the women appear as the 'winners' of the new economy, as exploited cheap labour, subjugated by gender structures, as well as structurally or directly marginalizing other groups (unionized women, men, the distant relatives working on the contract-workers' farms in a semi-feudal relationship). The picture that these studies paint on women's entrance into the workforce is significantly different. One cannot do away with the difference by saying that the feminist studies 'zoom' to the details of women's work in the new economy and, thereby, present a more 'fine-grained' picture of the wider developments the broad shapes of which Castells captures. On the contrary, the different studies partly support and partly complicate one another. What this aims to say is that one cannot say that one yields a 'bigger' and another one a 'smaller' picture, but that the studies view the issue of women and new economy from different positions that are always partial and political.

Comparing the basic differences of the political repercussions of Castells macroview on global space and Gibson et al.'s more microview, one can say a few words about the political project Castells openly embraces: The European Union. Castells envisages that European identity could become a project in that it could stand for the 'defence of the welfare state, of social solidarity, of stable employment and of workers' rights, and the concern about universal human rights and the plight of the Fourth World' (Castells, 1998: 353). I would say that, in principle, the goals Castells envisions for an international organization, such as EU, are highly laudable from a leftist cultural studies perspective. However, the way Castells writes about the EU renders Western Europeans as saviours of all the world's plights, and it smacks as awfully patronizing. On the contrary, the solution Gibson et al. propose to the contradictions of Philipina contract-workers' situation is a non-governmental initiative that works to help the women save in order to return home and establish cooperatives or other 'socially' oriented business-ventures. This is a laudable goal that is true to the women's own desires to improve their economic position, while working to find ways to blunt the individualist entrepreneurialist edge of this desire and channel it towards more community oriented projects. Still, the spirit of 'think globally, act locally' that these kinds of initiatives echo, easily divert attention away from wider state or inter-state oriented solutions, thereby, ending up partly buttressing the kind of petite-entrepreneurialism, albeit with a social conscience, that the authors criticize.

Again, this does not make one or the other of the positions 'right' or 'wrong'. The wide systemic solutions, such as EU, easily end up imposing their policies on weaker groups, much like Castells's analysis does. However, it can also effectuate large-scale programmes, such as certain minimum equal opportunities laws in the entire Europe (the beneficial effects of which I have personally witnessed in Great Britain, one of the more sexist European countries that has had to change its laws to fit the general standard). The same way, a nongovernmental initiative, such as the one discussed by Gibson *et al.*, may end up suspicious of national or international policy-initiatives. However, they may be sensitive to the local specific needs and hopes that people have and that may challenge, for example, (inter-)national policies designed to 'help' them, much like the research of Gibson *et al.*

In the end, the different modes of analyzing the global social, political and economic space, spaces, places and peoples, testify for that, despite their apparent concreteness, 'facts' do not speak for themselves, but they have to be spoken for. This, however, should not be seen as a disincentive to study 'facts' but merely to cultivate a critical self-reflexive attitude towards studying them that acknowledges the political nature of the categories, 'data', and methodologies that we use. To say a final word about Castells and Gibson *et al.* one could hope for research and politics that would find ways to create dialogues between positions that approach the world as a map to be controlled or as a network to be plunged into. This might point towards global policy-initiatives that would be sensitive to differing views that call for altering, perhaps, the basic premises and terms of the policies.

Conclusions

Cultural studies has often been accused of focusing on culture and identity at the expense of important social and global economic inequalities and injustices. Learning from these criticisms, one of the ways in which the political economic has been brought into the paradigm is through an analysis of 'space', which provides an object of study that seems, at the same time, conveniently tangible or material and promises to give a global overview.

This chapter argues that a materialist/realist analysis of global spatial developments, such as Manuel Castells's treatise on the Information Society, can provide valuable insights on the structural processes and developments that shape the discourses and lived experiences that are discussed in other parts of the book. However, it is also argued that the fact that realist analysis is blind to the political nature of the concepts it uses may sometimes undermine its own politics. For example, Castells's entire oeuvre criticizes the often steep social and economic inequalities that the global economy and politics perpetuate. However, he remains unaware of the way in which his taxonomizing of the social movements of the underprivileged groups as 'resistant' or reactive, in juxtaposition to the 'project' or proactive social movements of the privileged groups, ends up steepening the social inequalities and hostilities he criticizes in the first place.

Thus, it is suggested that Edward Soja's notion of a three-dimensional space that encompasses both its material, discursive as well as lived and political dimensions provides a useful framework to preserve the insights of the materialist/ realist analysis, while enriching it with an awareness of the political nature of any description of space. A research approach that has been particularly prone to use the methodological heuristic of a multidimensional space is feminist geography, which is often decidedly interested in real spatial developments and acutely aware of the political or gendered way in which this space is described. Works done on British miners' wives and Philipina contract-workers in feminist geography have exposed the way in which discourses on space are political and have very 'real' effects', as when, for example, the new industries, expected to employ the unemployed miners recruited their wives, in a situation where regional policy had nearly completely ignored the existence of half of the people (women) in the region. The same way, Gibson *et al.* argue that Philipina contract-workers are often seen in terms of either victims or heroes, which does not do justice to the contradictions of these women's multiple economic, social and gendered positions.

All in all, feminist geographers present modes of analyzing space that acknowledge its material, discursive and lived dimensions. Studying space from these multiple dimensions often produces analysis that gives a more complex and contradictory view of developments. So, looked at from different perspectives, the Philipina contract-workers appear as neither victims nor heroes, but can be, at the same time, exploited labourers in a foreign country as well as successful and exploitative small capitalists in the Philippines, where their hard earned hard currency enable them to establish themselves as part of the petit bourgeoisie entrepreneurial elite.

Thus, Castells's materialist/realist analysis of space embodies a 'top down' mode of analyzing space, which often comes up with clear-cut categories and advocates 'top down' solutions to problems of space, such as European Union policies. On the contrary, the feminist geographers often view and study space in messier terms of a network of interconnected locales that make space look different from the perspective of different locales. As a consequence, these 'network' studies are more likely to suggest less 'systemic' and more local solutions to problems, such as contract-workers' cooperatives, which aim to both improve the women's position as well as to help them in investing in businesses that have more widespread developmental and less exploitative effects in the Philippines. However, in the end, advocating local, globally sensitive solutions is just as ideological as proposing systemic ones, which underlines that all modes of approaching space are political, while also calling for modes of study and politics that would combine these views from above and from below to a project that would be both sensitive to local specificities and capable of building projects with global effects.

Exercise 8

- Think of a social and global development that reconfigures 'space' (anything from global patterns of migrancy to media flows between different cultures). Locate statistics on this development and write a short description of the major trends.
- Complement your statistical analysis with an interview with someone, who is a stakeholder in the process you are analyzing. This can be anyone from a migrant or a media consumer to a representative of governmental or non-governmental organization tackling the issue. Discuss whether this view corroborates or contradicts your statistical analysis.
- Identify the key stakeholders in the issue or development you are analyzing. Design a research project that would compare the perspectives of the different groups on the issue ('perspectives' can be obtained from documents as well as, for example, through interviews).
- Return to your statistical analysis and think what kind of policies or politics it supports. Think whether analyzing the process from other points of view might complicate the policy or political implications.

9

Studying Multiple Sites and Scapes

Main questions

- **How does one study multiple 'sites'? How does one study multiple 'scapes'? How are the two research strategies interrelated?**
- **Why is it important to pay careful attention to what 'scape' or sphere of life one is studying?**
- **Why is it more feasible to study different sites in terms of 'montage' rather than tracing/constructing a coherent narrative to tie them together?**
- **How does the heuristic of multi-sited ethnography and multiple 'scapes' help to bring together the different methodological approaches discussed in this book?**

In this final chapter my intention is to outline a framework that facilitates bringing together, or into dialogue, different methodological approaches, using the notions of 'multi-sited ethnography' (Marcus, 1998a) and 'scapes' (Appadurai, 1997) as a guideline. Very briefly, what the notion of multi-sited ethnography refers to is a practice of studying how any given phenomenon takes shape in and across multiple locales or sites. Thus, a multi-sited study can, for example, examine the continuities and discontinuities in the politics and practices of 'tango' as it travels from Argentinian working-class neighbourhoods to European salons and to Japanese dancehalls (Savigliano, 1995). However, the different 'sites' do not have to be geographically separate from one another, and one can, to give another example, study multiple sites by investigating how 'amniocentesis' changes when one looks at it from the perspectives of science labs, antenatal clinics, and families of different ethnic origins in New York (Rapp, 2000). Studying different locations has two aims. First, it draws attention to the way in which a social phenomenon cannot be 'typified' but changes when one looks at it from different perspectives, so that amniocentesis seems and 'is' very different in different contexts. Second, it locates a social phenomenon within a wider social and, possibly global, context, pointing at connections that exist between what one is studying and other social processes or locations.

The notion of a 'scape' is a close sibling to 'site', and it refers to spheres of life, such as economics (financescape), media (mediascape), and people (ethnoscape), which layer social reality (Appadurai, 1997). Thus, if 'multi-sited' research would look at a phenomenon from different locations, the approach focusing on 'scapes' might look at, for example, amniocentesis from economic, media and everyday perspectives. The concepts of sites and scapes provide a heuristic on how to study social issues and events from two different dimensions. However, the ideas of sites and scapes are also closely related, and Appadurai's notion of 'flows' helps to connect the two concepts. Rather than seeing 'scapes' as static layers of reality, Appadurai argues they should be seen as flows (of people, media-images, things, money etc.) that connect different places and people. Thus, methodologically one can envision studying how different 'sites' are connected with, and disconnected from, one another by diverse flows that articulate diverse 'scapes'. So, the different sites in New York where amniocentesis is constructed and lived may be united by a new medical technology focusing on 'genes', but these genes are articulated very differently as they get attached to, and are transformed by, other discourses and practices, such as feminist notions of reproductive rights or disability rights activism.

The idea of sites, united by diverse flows, resembles the multidimensional analyses of space discussed in the previous chapter. There are, indeed, many similarities between the two approaches, and they stem from the same social and intellectual sensibilities, such as 'globalization'. However, whereas the multidimensional spatial analyses done by geographers tend to have a more 'systemic' focus, the multi-sited studies done by anthropologists and sociologists view the world more as a 'mosaic'. This means that the geographic analyses are more likely to come up with general, even if contradictory and multidimensional, statements or synthesis about issues and developments. On the contrary, multi-sited studies are more likely to juxtapose different sites – obeying a logic closer to cinematic 'montage' than traditional literary/scientific narrative (on montage see e.g. Chatman, 1978; Maltby, 1995; on ethnographic applications Denzin, 1997a). The distinction between a more 'systemic' and mosaic- or montage-like research should not be seen in terms of two different approaches but rather in terms of a continuum. However, from a methodological point of view, it is a significant distinction, as the studies that are pieced together in a looser fashion often deliberately highlight how different aspects of reality, such as history, everyday life and discourses, and different ways of studying them, may both complement and contradict one another, opening different angles on reality. As such, multi-sited research helps to respond to two challenges posed to research by contemporary social and political environment, namely, it allows one to both do justice to differences and to point at unities that exist across differences.

In what follows, I will first outline different ways of doing multi-sited research, drawing on Marcus (1998a), who has coined the term, as well as Burawoy *et al.* (2000; also Burawoy, 2001), who propose the concept of 'global ethnography'. In the second section, I will reflect, in more detail, how to analyze different 'scapes'. In the third section, I will discuss in more detail, how to study different 'sites' together. The fourth section, drawing on Hannah Arendt's notion of an agonistic dialogue and contrasting it to Jurgen Habermas's consensual dialogue, outlines a dialogic framework to combine analysis of sites, scapes, and methodologies that aims to do justice to their specificity while also bringing them into conversation with one another. In the last section of this book, I will briefly illustrate the advantage of multi-sited research approach by discussing why I ended up resorting to it to make sense of the contradictory personal and political dimensions of eating disorders.

Sites, scapes and the global

What goes under the term 'multi-sited ethnography' has its roots in anthropological and sociological recognition that the traditional local focus of the two disciplines, such as the anthropologist's 'village' and the sociologist's 'subculture' or 'street corner', is no longer feasible in the contemporary, global world (Clifford, 1997). It has been argued that villages and townships can no longer be studied in isolation, as, rather than isolated locales, they have started to appear more like crossroads, traversed by transnational flows of money, immigrants, tourists, images, influences, policies and politics.

Thus, in his landmark essay, Marcus (1998a) suggested that places should be studied in connection with other 'sites', in order to comprehend the way in which they are shaped by, and shape, the wider social, and global, context. However, besides providing a heuristic for social and cultural research to study global connections, multi-sited research highlights disconnections or disjunctures. This means it allows to break up what appears inevitable or common sense by illuminating that the same phenomenon may be attached to very different social agendas in different locations and contexts, to the extent it may begin to look as if one is no longer talking about the same phenomenon.

Marcus (85–6) also points out that multi-sited ethnography disrupts anthropology's romantic interest in the 'subaltern' (in cultural studies one could talk about an interest in the 'margin'). According to Marcus, the subaltern does not necessarily possess all, or even the best, information, and besides the margin, one may need to study the centre to understand the wider ramifications of the issue under study. In a similar vein, Burawoy (2001: 149–50) suggests that ethnography does not have to be limited to the, either disempowering or empowering, 'reception' of globalization (in the 'local') but can also study the way in which globalization is 'produced' by specific agencies, institutions and actors, which can be observed. An interesting and exemplary study on the blending of the local and the global is Ong's (1999) research on transnational Chinese, which highlights the interweaving of ethnicity, family, financial investment, culture and politics that creates a global force, such as the transnational Chinese economies and communities in Hong Kong and California. Studies such as Ong's also illustrate that multi-sited ethnography may usefully complicate what subordination or being from the margin is, illustrating different, potentially clashing, and potentially collapsing, forms of subordination.

Marcus outlines two basic modes of doing multi-sited research. The first way of coming up with the sites is to 'follow' one's object of research, whether this is a metaphor (such as the metaphor of 'flexibility', which Martin (1994) followed from neighbourhoods to science labs and management workshops), people (like the Afghanis that Edwards (1994) followed from Afghanistan to Washington DC and the Internet) or a medical technology or diagnosis (such as amniocentesis (Rapp, 2000) or anorexia (Saukko, 1999, 2000, 2002b)). The other way of constructing a multi-sited study is to trace the connections of a particular strategic site, such as map the connections stemming from a village or a shopping mall that lead to various political and economic institutions and social locales (Frow and Morris, 1992).

What Appadurai's (1997) notion of scapes adds to this picture is an understanding of the way in which different sites and their connections may correspond to different spheres of life. Thus, as Frow and Morris (1992) note, the connections of a shopping mall may lead one to study planning policy, job markets, consumption patterns, both in terms of culture as well as economy, and gendered lifestyles (who works in the mall, who visits it, when and for what purposes, such as spending an early afternoon with children and so on). The idea of scapes calls for a multidisciplinary focus that invites cultural studies to venture into exploring areas of life beyond analyzing the symbolic, such as policy, economy or ecology. Together the notions of sites and scapes also call for the use of different methodological approaches. Studying a particular site, such as an ethnic neighbourhood, may benefit from the use of new ethnographic methodologies that help the scholar to understand a different lived world, whereas making sense of past and present policies requires the use of historical and/or genealogical approaches, analysis of statistics and so on. In a similar fashion, capturing the different sites and scapes may require different genres of writing, so that discussing the lived and embodied experience of dancing tango (Savigliano, 1995) may require a different mode of communication than examining its history and production.

Multi-sited ethnography, thereby, provides a framework not only for analyzing a social phenomenon within the wider context but also invites the use of different methodological approaches to make sense of the different facets of contemporary global reality. The uniting methodological feature of these studies is that they all study multiple locales (sites) and explore different areas of life (scapes). However, studies vary in terms of the 'scape' they prefer, some are mostly focused on people or lived experience, others are most interested in the politics and economics and still others are geared toward studying texts or discourses. However, individual studies within the approach vary in terms of what methodological approaches they use, and how they combine them. Furthermore, studies also vary in terms of whether they stitch the different sites together rather tightly or relatively loosely; in the former case the studies are more prone to underline connections between sites, whereas in the latter case the studies are more bound to 'trouble' unifying explanations.

Overall, multi-sited and multi-scape analysis helps to imagine a research and politics that is capable of doing justice to difference and to point to unities across differences. This is because it provides a heuristic that draws attention to the specificity of different spheres of life (scapes) and different contexts or sites, while also pointing at connections between them. However, the balancing between unity and difference and singularity and plurality is a difficult act. The both difficult and promising nature of this research approach is illustrated in the way in which studies done within this perspective study different 'scapes', which I will discuss next.

Studying scapes: on passion and politics

Appadurai's (1997) notion of scapes is both close to, and somewhat different from, the distinction between 'lived', 'discursive' and 'contextual' approaches to studying social reality. Whereas Appadurai's distinction refers to different aspects or facets of reality, my division relates to different methodological approaches. The two may go together, so that studying Appadurai's 'ethnoscape' (the scape of 'people') may often focus on lived experience, whereas 'examining ideoscape' and 'mediascape' may correspond to studying discourses or texts. However, just like studying lived experience needs to be attentive to discourses (that interlace experiences) and contexts (such as social structures of inequality that mediate experience), studying 'ethnoscape' does not have to refer to exploring the 'lived' but can involve investigating demographics and so on. Thus, even if studying ethnoscape is more likely to employ the hermeneutic approach and studying financescape is more likely to apply contextualist or realist methodology, both the different methodologies and the spheres of life overlap with, and bleed into, one another.

This 'bleeding into' or intertwining of different spheres of life and modes of studying them is the most exciting aspect of Appadurai's theory and the methodological approach embedded in it. However, sometimes studies done under the banner of multi-sited or global ethnography give the impression that they are studying 'everything'. Thus, Appadurai's notion of scapes also provides an analytical tool that helps to keep in mind what areas of life a particular study is, and is not, studying. For example, a particular study may analyze discourses and claim that they resonate with certain economic policies or trends. This is fine, and one of the main goals of multi-sited studies is to pinpoint such 'resonances'. However, Appadurai's notion of scapes draws attention to the fact that such a study may not be studying economic activities and practices *per se*.

The other useful thing about Appadurai's framework is that it provides a way of delineating different areas of life. Thus, I do not view Appadurai's five scapes (ethno, ideo, media, techno and finance) as exhaustive, but more as a heuristic that allows one to distinguish further pertinent areas of life. In the following discussion I will distinguish also 'bodyscape' (referring to corporeality), 'politocoscape' (referring to social action that focuses on 'interests'), and 'sacredscape' (referring to the sphere of the sacred or spiritual). Proliferating scapes *ad infinitum* renders the concept useless, but I would argue that corporeality, politics and the sacred are broad categories that refer to distinct areas of life and help make sense of the specific 'aspect' of reality a study investigates, as, hopefully will become clear in what follows.

In order to illustrate the usefulness of paying attention to what 'scapes' one is studying, I will discuss two both different and similar multi-sited studies. The first one is Marta Savigliano's (1995) analysis of the changing face of the politics of tango, as it travels from Argentinian working-class neighbourhoods and red light districts to Parisian and London salons and Japanese dancehalls. The second one is Zsusza Gille's (2000, 2001) study on a dispute over the construction of an incinerator for hazardous waste in a post-Communist village in Hungary. Both of these studies examine the ways in which a phenomenon, such as tango and the environment, is tangled with both local human experiences and social divisions and global social structures of power and inequality. Despite this similarity, Savigliano and Gille end up studying the global/local nexus in very different terms. Thus, whereas Savigliano examines how tango embodies central gender, class and colonialist power struggles, Gille studies how the different local and global actors negotiate a conflict of interests. Thus, whereas the former studies how power operates through corporeality, or what I would term 'bodyscape', the latter focuses on a more conventional form of interest-based politics or 'politicoscape'. Discussing the similarities and differences between these two approaches illustrates the methodological difference that 'scape' makes.

'Bodyscape'

Savigliano's multi-sited study of tango traces the development of its contradictory politics from Argentinian working-class townships and brothels to the salons in London and Paris, all the way to Japanese dancehalls. Savigliano does not say much about her methodology, besides rejecting the notion of 'methods', arguing that these 'tools' alienate intellectual workers from their labour and politics (14). Rationalizing Savigliano's research strategy, she seems loyal to the 'bricoleur' or 'jack of all trades' approach to research that uses multiple materials and tools and makes do with whatever is at hand (Denzin and Lincoln, 2000). Thus, Savigliano's study is based on an analysis of historical material, some interviews as well as her own autobiography. Just like her research strategy, her narrative is a pastiche, composed of historical and discourse analysis, drama-sequels and autobiographic meditations. From these different materials, gathered from Argentina, Paris, London and Japan, she pieces together an analysis of tango as an 'erotic game played between unequal partners' (76) that articulates complex politics of race, class, gender and nation. As the title of Savigliano's book, *Tango and the political economy of passion*, indicates, it studies the way in which an economy of 'emotions and affects' parallel more material and ideological forms of power that characterize gender, race and class relations both locally and globally (1). To illustrate the contradictions of this economy of passion, Savigliano discusses tango as an epitome of *machismo*. As a dance, where the male drags the woman to dance and leads her through it (78), tango can be seen to capitulate the Argentinian *machismo*, or complex male competition and bonding effectuated through crass performances of superiority over women. However, Savigliano notes (47), the term *machismo* also becomes a way for distinguishing the bourgeois 'civilized' maleness from 'incorrect' and barbarian male–female relations, associated with tango and lower classes and races (so that *machismo*, with its 'Latin' roots, continues to be a shorthand for sexism on a global scale).

Further contradictions emerge, when the intense, erotic and tension-riddled dance becomes a spectacle for the fascinating and terrifying aspects of Otherness to be consumed by the 'genteel' people in France, Great Britain and Japan. Thus, in Japan, the dominance of the sanitized or 'civilized' British version of tango is legitimated by the idea that Japanese are 'reserved' and, thereby, the Argentinian ('body touch') tango is too 'raw' for them. Still, advocates of the Argentinian version argue for a deep affinity between the Japanese and Argentinians, claiming the distant nations share a profound sentiment of 'passion and melancholy'. However, as the notion of the 'rawness' of tango has its roots in the core countries' (England, France and the United States) discourse on the 'exotic', the figurative and literal dance of pulling apart and drawing together between the two peripheral countries, Japan and Argentina, is mediated by the colonialist legacy of racist (auto)exoticism.

To give a taster of the way in which Savigliano sees tangos to embody or enact wider social struggles and their contradictions, one can look at her description of the gender-dynamics of the dance:

> No smiles. Tangos are male confessions of failure and defeat, a recognition that men's sources of empowerment are also the causes of their misery. Women, mysteriously, have the capacity to use the same things that imprison them – including men – to fight back. Tangos

report repeated female attempts at evasion, the permanent danger of betrayal. The strategy consists basically in seducing men, making them feel powerful and safe by acting as loyal subordinates, and in the midst of their enchantment with total control, the tamed female escapes. ... This is the tension of the tango, the struggle condensed in the dance. (209)

As this excerpt illustrates, what Savigliano sees as the 'glue' or flow that binds the different sites and actors (Argentinian townships, prostitutes, pimps, wives, soldiers, Parisian and London middle-classes and Japanese learning 'Western' modes of socializing) together is a corporeal political economy of passion. This economy of passion operates through tango that enacts or 'performs' (Butler, 1990) the power-struggles, consolidating existing inequalities as well as challenging them, all in a decidedly embodied, flesh, blood, sweat, tears and sperm fashion.

'Politicoscape'

The specificity of Savigliano's perspective is highlighted, if one compares it with the multi-sited study of Gille. Gille sets out to study the both global and local forms of power and struggle through a case study on a dispute over the construction of an incinerator to burn hazardous waste in a Hungarian village, Garé. In order to understand the ramifications of the dispute, Gille, much like Savigliano, resorts to history. Thus, in addition to interviewing the inhabitants of Garé and the neighbouring Szalánta, she studied the history of the environmental conflict and the region and attended press conferences and demonstrations over the construction, which also involved the Hungarian government, a joint-venture French–Hungarian company Hungaropec (that wanted to build the incinerator) and Greenpeace.

To make the long story short, the plans for the incinerator had their origins in a toxic waste dump, located near Garé, which was the legacy of a communist-era state-firm, Budapest Chemical Works (BCW). The people of Garé originally learnt of the dump through the bad odours that were entering their gardens, as the deal to establish the dump was struck between the council of the nearby village of Szalánta (Garé was under the administration of this village and the two villages had a history of social struggle and rivalry) and the BCW. After the collapse of state-communism, the residents of Garé entered into negotiations with first the BCW and then Hungaropec (a joint venture between BCW and a French firm) in order to construct the incinerator. Both the newly formed transnational company and the villagers had an interest in cleaning up the dump and surviving in the new economy, which for Garéans meant tax-revenues and employment from the incinerator. However, the inhabitants of Szalánta opposed the incinerator – as they had nothing to gain, except for the toxic downfall – and joined forces with other neighbouring villages and local and transnational Greenpeace to launch a campaign to oppose the construction and to advocate the use of already existing and Western incinerators.

The dispute goes against any simple notion of poor little locals at the mercy of big bad globals. The small village of Garé was striking a deal with a multi-national company to advocate the construction of an incinerator, and drawing on discourses of 'Europeanization' to legitimate its cause (as the incinerator was marketed in terms of inserting Garé into the ambit of Western Europe and its companies). The local (Szalánta) and global (Greenpeace) opponents of the incinerator drew on an equally contradictory set of discourses and politics from NIMBYism ('not-in-my-backyard') to ecological colonization and environmental racism (drawing on the fact that Garé and Szalánta are both part of Baranya, a rural, peripheral and ethnically mixed region) (255).

To illustrate the thorny and surprising nature of the situation, having its roots in history, Gille discusses the unholy triumvirate between the inhabitants of Garé, the BCW and the French counterpart (EMC):

> The novelty of this triumvirate resides not so much in its unlikelihood (a victim and its victimizer – the village with its polluter) as in its direct unmediated relations between a village and an industrial firm, on the one hand, and between a small, disempowered village and a relatively powerful Western company, on the other. It is in stark contrast to the past in which the state held the remote control of Garé's life. (251)

What this quote and the discussion above illustrate, from a methodological point of view, is the way in which a multi-sited approach, which attends to diverse global and local issues and players, presents a nuanced and contradictory picture of this dispute. As such, this kind of methodological approach allows one to attend to multiple social, historical, regional, global and local dimensions of a dispute and respect and do justice to the diverse, potentially clashing inequalities.

However, what the quote also illustrates is the way in which Gille frames the dispute in terms of 'interest'. All the different actors and actions are invested in a struggle over power, money and principles, which is fought in relatively conventional 'political' terms of public hearings, demonstrations, campaigns and economic, administrative and local political (both official or governmental and unofficial or non-governmental) decisions. This is in striking contrast with someone like Savigliano's work, which, even if she also studies the global/local nexus in terms of power, examines this power in embodied, sensual and sensed terms. This does not mean that either Gille or Savigliano is 'right' or 'wrong'. It simply means that these, in principle similar, multi-sited studies, effectively study a different scape.

Blurring scapes

The methodological lesson learnt from reading Savigliano's and Gille's studies through Appadurai's concept of 'scape' is twofold. First, the concept of scape draws attention to the specific focus of the study and enables research to become aware of the sometimes disciplinary penchant to examine 'connections' in terms of a specific area of life (and the corporeal and political focuses of Savigliano and Gille correspond to their respective fields: dance studies and sociology). Clarifying the scape(s) the study is focusing on, may highlight its strength (exploring global power-relations in terms of an embodied dance is, after all, rather innovative and original). Second, the notion of scape also clarifies what areas of life the study is not focusing on, or what areas of life might be left in the shadow. This does not mean to suggest that studies should cover 'everything', it simply means that the idea of scapes makes research more conscientious of its partiality.

For example, the title of Savigliano's book, *Tango and the political economy of passion*, is, in a sense, an oxymoron. The book is a dense and fascinating account of the way in which tango becomes a scene for class, gender and race based, fundamentally embodied and representational struggles for power. Still, the book does not refer to 'political economy' in the traditional sense of studying the economy (production) or politics (direct use in political projects) of tango but explores, or gestures towards, the way in which 'economy' and 'politics' get played out in the embodied and representational politics of the dance. Savigliano is explicit about this. Referring to Wallis and Malm's (1984) political economic study on the music-industry of small countries, she notes that she has not been interested in the way in which 'technology and marketing' of this music is mediated by 'big people', but in the way in which the identities of the small people, such as Argentines and Japanese, are mediated through the 'exoticism' of big people (1995: 204). Both the 'properly' political economic, as well as the representational and corporeal aspects of global music are entangled with colonialist, gendered, class-based and raced structures of power and inequality. However, they study those structures from a different perspective or scape, which, from a methodological perspective, is important to note.

In some sense, one could say that it is legitimate to study the sphere of corporeality in relation to tango, as it is a decidedly corporeal activity, whereas 'politics' might be a legitimate focus in making sense of an environmental dispute, a phenomenon that could be deemed political. Even if I think that social phenomena may be closer to some 'scape' than others, I also believe that social phenomena can be studied from the perspective of different scapes, which yields rather different results. Thus, I would argue that the fact that Gille studies the dispute over the incinerator in Garé from the point of view of 'conflicting interests', does not 'reflect' the political nature of the dispute but 'constructs' it in those terms. It does not necessarily mean that the conflict 'is' a political one. To illustrate the idea, one can argue that there is a corporeal or embodied dimension to environmental disputes, which is hinted at in Gille:

> To make sense out of the smell and the slowly leaking pieces of information about the dump and its dangers, the villagers conjured up this absent Other. When animals died, BCW had killed them; when red snow fell, BCW had coloured it, when Szalánta got a

new road, BCW had paid for it; when trees dried out, BCW had desiccated them; when fruit tasted badly, BCW's poison had spoiled them ... . (2001: 325)

From this excerpt one can read an everyday 'embodied' threatening experience of environmental pollution, which seeps into different areas of life, interlacing our experience of the food we eat, our sense of our own and our children's bodies and their health, and our sense of our environment. However, Gille's interest-geared focus, as well as the language that she uses, bypasses this dimension of the environment. In fact, this reminds me of an aborted research-project that I once started on the various 'forest movements' in Finland. When working as an environmental journalist, I had frequently covered the disputes between logging companies, the government, and these movements. However, when I went to interview the members of the movements as a researcher, they wanted to talk to me about a topic that had never come up in the press conferences: spirituality. They told me that the reason they wanted to conserve the forests was because they felt the woods had a 'spirit', but that they could never express this to the press, the government or the companies as they would be written off as irrational. On the contrary, they had to present all manner of statistics on the economic unfeasibility of logging certain parts of the forests and of their unique ecological and recreational value (preferably in monetary terms). What this example illustrates is the way in which certain 'scapes' cannot be addressed in certain institutional contexts or through certain institutional forms of speech and writing. Thus, the activists had to 'speak' 'econoscape' and 'politicoscape', but they could not speak 'sacredscape' in the press conferences. This does not mean that the embodied or spiritual aspects of the environment are the most important ones. It simply indicates that research, just like journalism, often prioritizes a certain scape that may correspond to disciplinary or paradigmatic concerns. While it would be impossible to cover all scapes and sites that come together at any given phenomenon, the notion of scapes still suggests that we pay more conscientious attention to the kinds of 'flows' we are, and are not, studying.

Overall, the notion of scape helps to clarify the multi-sited projects, which often ambitiously set out to study local/global/social/political/cultural/economic aspects of the phenomenon they are studying. While this wide scope is the greatest strength of the approach, it may also lead to confusion. To return to the idea that multi-sited research highlights the tension between difference and unity, one can say that the idea of a scape underlines the specificity or uniqueness of different spheres of life and the need to do justice to this specificity and acknowledge their partiality. At the same time it also points at connections between the different spheres, while bearing in mind that these connections may often be best thought in terms of 'resonances' than direct relations. Thus, Savigliano points out how corporeal and representative forms resonate with global, economic and political aspects of colonial power, insightfully illuminating connections between corporeal and these other forms of power. However, she does not study political and economic forms of power *per se*. Thus, Gille studies how historical social relations and interests draw local and global actors together and pull them apart. As such, she studies the social and political relations that are forged in an environmental dispute but does not explore, for example, the sphere of the corporeal or spiritual dimensions of the environment.

Studying sites: montage and narrative

On difference and dialogue

Gille (2001) provides a useful segue from discussing scapes to discussing sites by arguing that the selection of the sites that a scholar studies should not be guided by the scholar's intuition or imagination but 'social relations' that exist between them. Gille argues against Marcus (1998a), claiming that the composition of sites should not be a matter of the scholar's jetsetting but follow the 'real' social connections that exist between sites. She also points out that coming up with the sites in a kind of haphazard way (Japan and Argentina), powered by the scholar's imagination, does little to help people understand how their fates are united, in real terms, and to come up with collective projects to change the world. Based on her research on the environment, Gille argues that studying sites in relative isolation, trying to capture their specificity, easily leads to a kind of NIMBYism where looking at the world from one's own narrow perspective is justified in the name of doing justice to difference.

I both agree and disagree with Gille. First, I disagree with her argument that we should study 'real' connections instead of forging arbitrary ones. This is, because, in my view, research always partly constructs its object of study, underlining our political and ethical responsibility for the realities we make or connections that we draw. Second, and related to the first point, I think that one of the crucial goals of multi-sited ethnography is to highlight links between different people and places with the hope of enabling social, and even global, projects that would begin to change our common world together. In this respect I completely agree with Gille in that pure fragmentation and celebration of difference may be deeply counterproductive. Third, however, I disagree with Gille in that multi-sited studies should try to highlight 'real' connections that would then point to 'a' political solution, such as solving environmental problems in a holistic manner. The reason I disagree with Gille on this account is that this kind of forging of 'consensus', through resorting to claims about 'real' connections, may work to silence discrepancies by arguing their arguments are not 'real'. The beauty of multi-sited ethnography is precisely the fact that it provides a mode of analysis that straddles the difficult terrain between, pointing at unities or connections and doing justice to differences and discrepancies.

To help conceptualize and concretize this goal of doing justice to difference and unity one can think it can be accomplished through strategies of writing. Far from being a mere technique (with ready-made formulas) to convey 'results', writing should be seen as a way of doing research that articulates its philosophical and political commitments. Thus, to illustrate a way of thinking, doing and writing research between commonalities and differences, it is useful to resort to a few basic distinctions between different narrative strategies. Thus, one could say that multi-sited research obeys the logic of montage and mimesis, typical of cinematic story-telling, rather than narrative and diegesis, typical of written accounts. To cut a long story or theory short, the distinction between mimesis and diegesis goes back to Plato, who distinguished poets that 'imitate' or mime by narration (performance) and that speak in their own person (report) (Chatman, 1978; Maltby, 1995). In a similar way, films construct their narratives through 'montage' or juxtaposing clips to one another, whereas in written narrative the narrator weaves the different parts of the story together through her/his authorial voice.

Thus, a research and writing strategy that follows the logic of 'mosaic' or montage juxtaposes different sites and scapes to one another, highlighting their specificity and piecing them together in a more tension-riddled fashion that does not produce closure. When exploring the different sites and scapes, this approach aims to find a research strategy and a mode of writing that is truer to the phenomenon or dimension under study, in a sense, 'miming' it, using more performative means, such as fiction or shifting genres (an example would be Savigliano's drama-sequels that are 'dances') (on performance see Polkinghorne, 1995; Denzin, 1997a). On the other hand research that obeys the logic of diegesis and narrative conforms to the traditional mode of doing and writing research that constructs a coherent narrative that is told by the detached and omniscient author and that produces straightforward 'results' and a closure. Rather than seeing these two modes of doing and writing research as separate either/or categories, they should be seen in terms of a continuum. Most multi-sited research arguably falls somewhere between these two positions, having elements of montage but also cohering in terms of writing and mode of analysis. The studies, which are most fragmented and closest to the 'raw' nature of the material, simply contrast different materials to one another. An example would be Laughlin's (1996) study on the Bhopal accident that merely juxtaposes press-releases and other material done by activists groups from different perspectives and for different purposes.

However, to understand how sites can be pieced together in terms of a mosaic or montage and what the methodological advantages of this strategy are, one needs to turn to 'real' studies. Thus, in what follows I will discuss Rayna Rapp's (2000) work on amniocentesis that is one of the most eloquent multi-sited studies in its sensitivity to differences and unities, even if it is not particularly 'avant-garde'.

On sites, genes and genres

Rapp initiated her study on amniocentesis after a personal experience with the procedure, which led her to choose abortion after her foetus was diagnosed with Down's syndrome. After her experience, she wrote a column to the popular feminist *Ms. Magazine*, and received, among other things, a phonecall from a disability rights activist, who challenged her notion of children with disabilities (2000: 6). As a consequence, her book is built on a tension between the feminist roots of amniocentesis in the right-to-choice movement and the eugenic roots of amniocentesis in the racial or genetic hygiene movement.

To explore this tension, Rapp has studied multiple places and people connected to amniocentesis, such as its history, science labs where the tests are processed, and interviewed women of different ethnic origins and class backgrounds that either choose or refuse the procedure, receive 'negative' or 'positive' results, and decide to either abort or keep a foetus with a genetic disability. Exploring these different people and places connects amniocentesis to a variety of other social issues and realities, such as health care, religion, class, race and gender. It also leads her to use multiple methods, from historical research to analysis of discourses, as well as interviewing, participant observation and autobiographic commentary.

In all, the book is a rich multi-sited study, where each chapter examines amniocentesis from a different perspective. Thus, in the first chapter Rapp discusses the history of amniocentesis in science and medicine, and its connections with the women's health movement as well as eugenics. However, Rapp notes that in contemporary United States eugenics is no longer a matter of heinous governmental policies but is a matter of an equally heinous free-market logic, as Rapp explains:

> Threats of eugenic exclusions now involve insurance or its lack, employer discrimination, and struggles around extending coverage of disability legislation to those with genetic susceptibilities. (37)

As this quote illustrates, the first chapter locates amniocentesis within the wider historical, social, political and economic context, paying attention to both general ideologies and practices (feminism, eugenics) as well as the specific present day US context (free-market health care and insurance).

The subsequent chapters mostly evolve around the experiences of different women's experiences with the procedure. Rap recounts, for example, how many white middle-class women that choose to have amniocentesis articulated the tension between the female value of self-sacrifice and their own desire for self-actualization, which they problematized as 'selfishness'. This is illustrated by a woman, who felt that taking care of a disabled child would not allow her to 'get back to work', back to 'my own adult life', concluding the technology gave her a 'possibility' to avoid this, 'even if it's selfish' (138). At the same time, many Latina women saw amniocentesis as a way not to be selfish but selfless, in terms of not bringing into the world a child, who would 'suffer' (143). Furthermore, the mothers of large working-class families saw amniocentesis as a means of avoiding the burden that a disabled child would cause the other children in terms of shouldering them with a life-long obligation for care and investing a lion's share of meagre resources on one child (145).

Many women, who decided against aborting a foetus with genetic disorders had a religious background, but Rapp complicates a simple interpretation of the pro-life stance in terms of simply 'faith'. She points out that spirituality often has very 'material' effects by providing mothers with disabled children social acceptance, support, day-care services and home visits. The story of a 37-year-old single legal secretary, who returned to her Mormon faith after having a positive result from amniocentesis, illustrates the tangible support of spirituality:

> Maybe if I was married, maybe if I had another shot at it. But this was it: take it or leave it. So I took it. I called the Mormons back. … One man, he just came and prayed with me, he still comes. Stevie (her son with Down's syndrome) gets a lot of colds. I can't always make it to the temple. But when we don't make it, he comes over and prays with us. (178)

Together the stories Rapp tells about women of different walks of life, history, healthcare, and science labs (which end up not being populated by white men in white coats but by female immigrant lab technicians) construct a complex and nuanced montage or a mosaic. The different chapters loosely correspond to different sites or phases of amniocentesis (from history to women's contemplations before the amniocentesis, and analysis of labs to living with a disabled child). These sites are contrasted to one another, in the fashion of a montage, illuminating different angles on amniocentesis to the extent that the procedure embodies nearly oppositional meanings and effects in different contexts. Besides, different sites or angles, Rapp also covers various scapes. Even if the focus of the book is on women's lived experience, the thick descriptions of lived lives and ethics tangle the issue of amniocentesis to econoscape (healthcare, insurance, class divisions), sacredscape (religion and its surprising intertwining with econoscape), bodyscape, politocoscape and so on.

Even if Rapp takes a critical stance towards the new social scientific interest in 'writing' (17), her own writing does not stay the same throughout the work. Her reporting of the women's life experiences obeys the classical ethnographic reporting mode, displaying indented verbatim quotes from the women's speech, following Rapp's 'interpretation'. Still, her genre subtly shifts from one chapter and issue to the next. This is illustrated by the difference in the style and 'feel' of the two excerpts from the history chapter and from the Mormon woman's interview. Thus, one can say that Rapp mimes the different areas of life she explores by shifting from a factual and analytical mode of study and writing to a hermeneutic and touching one. Thus, whereas Rapp's analysis of the history of amniocentesis intellectually engaged me, I found myself crying every time I read her account of her own foetus 'XYLO', a shorthand of 'X-or-Y for its unknown sex, and LO for the love we were pouring into it' (318).

As a whole, Rapp's book is exemplary in the sense that it pays fine-grained attention to the specificity of each site she studies, both in terms of the content (different takes on amniocentesis) and the form (gliding from touching descriptions to straightforward historical and economic factual argumentation). As such, the book facilitates a feminist mode of research and politics on reproductive technologies that avoids simplistic judgements and, by paying attention to similarities and differences, works to foster multidimensional agenda based on being open to different views and bringing them into dialogue with one another.

From consensus to dialogues

The Arendtian model

Thinking through the multi-sited research approach, as well as the overall goal of this book to advance qualitative research that would do justice to differences as well as to foster dialogues across both social and methodological differences, I have, in my mind, often come back to the classic social theoretical debate on public discussion or the public sphere. This discussion has its roots in Habermas's landmark work on the 'public sphere' (Habermas, 1989, 1992), in which he argues for a theoretical model of 'rational public dialogue', based on an analysis of the 'real life' public spheres he found in the nineteenth-century Western European bourgeoisie salons and reading rooms (Habermas, 1989). According to Habermas, rational public discussion makes democratic politics possible in two senses. First, it offers equal access to the public discussion, as everyone is allowed to participate in the debate on an equal basis, and the power of an individual's argument is not based on his possessions but on the rationality of its argument. Second, Habermas argues, rational dialogue surpasses the dilemma of respecting plurality and arriving at a consensus, which haunts democratic political decision-making. Thus, he envisions that certain procedural 'rules' for rational discussion, which translate 'private concerns' into 'public matters', work as a benchmark that helps to bring the different opinions together and establish a consensus, which then translates into public policy.

Scholars have both embraced and attacked Habermas's theory for fostering and diluting democratic communication. Scholars have criticized Habermas, on historical grounds, for neglecting that the bourgeoisie public sphere was a highly exclusive one and that, alongside it, there existed working-class (Eley, 1992) and female public spheres, which may have been located in what is termed a 'private sphere' (Ryan, 1992). Furthermore, particularly feminist scholars (Fraser, 1992; Benhabib, 1992a) have pointed out that the prerequisite of 'rational' dialogue over 'public issues' may render the discussion exclusive. They have argued that it corresponds to the mode of communication typical of white, male, middle-class Westerners and marginalizes modes of communications, such as emotions, and areas of life, such as matters deemed 'private', that correspond to the lives and interests of other groups, such as women.

This brings one to methodology in that the traditional, objectivist, positivist science is predicated on a presumption of a rational scholar, who translates other languages or 'material' into a scientific pattern or argument that coheres in 'results'. This attitude, just like the Habermasian discussion, does not take into account that the benchmark, 'rationality' or 'objectivity', that it uses as an arbiter of 'truth' is in and of itself political. For example, there are modes of perceiving and relating to reality, such as sacredness and emotions, which do not pass as 'rational', thereby rendering them invalid from the outset, as illustrated by my discussion of the Finnish forest-activists.

To come up with an alternative notion of public discussion or dialogue more generally, scholarship has turned to the work of Hannah Arendt, who seeks inspiration not from nineteenth-century bourgeoisie salons but from the Ancient Greek polis. According to Arendt (1958), in Ancient Greece the goal of public dialogue was not to engage in rational argumentation but for each participant to assert his uniqueness and to vie for public recognition to this originality through elaborate forms of public oration. Used heuristically, the methodological advantage of this Arendtian sense and feel of public sphere is threefold. First, it acknowledges the 'uniqueness' of the different social voices that vie for recognition in politics and research. Thus, rather than argue for a common benchmark, such as rationality, it highlights the need to bring to the fore the specificity, both in terms of content and form, of different perspectives (whether they represent sites, scapes, or peoples). Second, it draws attention to mode of speaking and representing, viewing public discussion much more in terms of compelling story-telling than rational argumentation. This brings to the fore the fact that different modes of speaking and writing are political, expressing different worldviews or worlds, and trying to muffle them under some benchmark of rationality silences experiences and politics that do not fit under its umbrella. Third, even if Arendt's model has been accused of fostering 'narcissism' (Benhabib, 1992b), it has a strong communal element to it. The Greeks did not engage in public discussion merely to 'show off', but in order to act together and change history. Thus, the Arendtian notion of public sphere articulates in the realm of general theory what multi-sited research aims to articulate in the realm of methodology: The need to find a way, in research and in politics, to do justice to differences and find ways of establishing dialogues between differences in order to facilitate common politics. This need to understand and negotiate the relationship between unity and difference as well as personal and political constitutes the central methodological and political challenge of our times. Both the Arendtian model and multi-sited research provide some ideas on how to begin to respond to these challenges in theory and in practice.

On the personal and the political

To conclude where I started, I will briefly discuss why I ended up imagining my research on anorexia in terms of a multi-sited study, why I found it useful and what it taught me about methodology. The broad purpose of my research on anorexia was initially to critically analyze discourses that had defined the condition as well as to explore how women, who had had the condition, perceived, lived and negotiated these definitions.

After ploughing through an extraordinary amount of early twentieth-century psychiatric articles on anorexia and an equally large amount of media material on anorexia, I decided I had to focus on certain pivotal moments in this material. I chose to further examine the founding psychiatric work of Hilde Bruch on anorexia, because her work has pretty much established the contemporary diagnostic notion of the condition. I also decided to analyze the public image of Karen Carpenter and Princess Diana, not only because they are the most famous celebrities with eating disorders but also because they represent different epochal understandings of the condition. In addition I studied feminist scholarly debates around anorexia and interviewed a group of both American and Finnish women, who had had an eating disorder, about their experience of the condition and the way in which it/they have been defined and treated.

Thus, what led me to study 'sites' was a desire to understand anorexia and discussions around it in a wide political and personal context. Still, examining the different sites, I had to resort to rather different methodological approaches and genres of writing. Making sense of the history of Hilde Bruch's work required standard historical research, whereas analyzing the image of Karen Carpenter obeyed the logic of media or discourse analysis. Trying to under-stand the experiences of other women that had anorexia, and in particular to do justice to the ways in which their experiences were different from my own, or different from what I had expected, I drew on the new ethnographic tradi-tion that aims to comprehend and capture different lived worlds. The same way, when writing about the history of 1920s America and eugenics, and when writing about my own relationship with my father, I had to use different genres of writing in order to convey the phenomenon I was exploring (history, emotions).

Studying the different sites, unravelled a series of contradictions. Studying Bruch led me to her early work on fatness, which focused on fat immigrant children in New York City. This research bravely argued against the eugenic idea that people's personality and behaviour is linked to their intrinsic, racial physique but, also problematically, related the obesity of the immigrant children to the traditional or 'authoritarian' culture (living with extended families, over-powering parenting and importance of food) of their families. Bruch's postwar research on anorexia found its roots in the socially conforming, nearly 'fascist', middle-class, suburban culture, and its frustrated and domesticated mother, who suffocated her children. While Bruch's research attacked a series of prob-lematic social developments and credos (eugenics, middle-class conformism, and domesticated and subordinate femininity), it also singled out weaker social groups (immigrants, women, the lower middle-class or 'mass') and blamed them for not living up to the white, male, middle-class, American ideal of free or autonomous individuality.

In a similar contradictory note, the public image of Karen Carpenter either eulogizes her and her dreamy soft rock or deplores both as the epitome of the pathological nature of the 1970s return to conservative family-values. However, the latter critique of conservatism ends up articulated in rather stale terms, juxtaposing pathological goody girls (Karen Carpenter) to healthy rowdy boys (Vietnam War protesters and so on). Princess Diana, on the contrary, is often celebrated as a survivor of her tumultuous life, changing from the royal virgin bride to an outspoken divorcee and an outcast not only in relation to the royal family but through her affinity with the various groups associated with her life and her charitable activities (people with AIDS, gays, Third World poor, and ethnic minorities). Still, this 'radical', chameleon-like life is usually represented in a fashion that pays little attention to its exclusiveness and privilege. Finally, the feminist debates on eating disorders often end up in a tug-of-war over whether beauty ideals oppress women, or whether claims that women are victimized by beauty ideals play into the ancient sexist tropes that view women as vain and bimbos. Thus, both the social discourses on beauty and the feminist debates around them get stuck in the paradox or double bind where women are, first, damned as ugly, and then damned as 'dopes', if they beautify themselves. Against this tension–riddled social background, it is no wonder that women, who have had anorexia, feel they are caught in a whirlwind of discourses that demands them to be free, self-determining individuals and defines them as hapless, totally subordinate victims.

When I was reading the contradictions embedded in the different sites where anorexia was being articulated, I could not establish any straightforward connections, or much less causalities, between them. On the contrary, the contradictions within and between the sites seemed to slap one another on the face, so that, for example, femininity was alternately evoked as the epitome of subordination or the harbinger of a new 'survivalist' lifestyle. However, this does not mean that there were no connections or resonances. Thus, the American postwar, one-eyed political and social fixation on free individuality and the free world, resonated with the women's description of being caught between a jagged dichotomy between freedom and victimization. It could be said that the feature that ends up connecting the different sites is the judgemental drive to splice the world and people into true, righteous and free and dangerous, misguided and wrong. It is this dichotomous normative logic that ends up undoing the radical critical potential of much of the politics around anorexia, such as when criticism of social conformism and conservatism ends up being argued, using a young, suburban woman as a scarecrow.

Against these simplistic normative dichotomies, what emerges from this multidimensional landscape of anorexia is a call for a less judgemental and more conversational way of relating to our own selves, others (including immigrants and suburban women), and the social world (such as the presumably 'non-free' world). This conversational mode of relating to the world would operate less according to an either/or, and more according to a both/and logic. It would, for instance, be able to capture the human predicament that one is hardly entirely free or completely enslaved, and that acknowledging that individual's life is always conditioned by the social world may enable one to reach a more productive relationship with one's self, the world and its others. One could also say that the plea for dialogues applies not only to discussions on anorexia but to methodological debates as well. Too often methodological schisms are fought in polarized terms, resulting in stalemates over, for example, whether one should study the political economic 'reality' or pay attention to multiple realities. Rather, one could study the common global, social, political and economic reality that bind our fates together and explore how this reality seems radically different when perceived from different angles.

It is sometimes said that a methodological or political approach that tries to accommodate different perspectives or differences leads to relativism where any view is as any good as any other. However, there is nothing relativist about research and politics that would acknowledge that middle-class anorexic women are privileged and that middle-class culture has its oppressive, gendered features and that would also acknowledge the deeply sexist nature of social critique that operates through ridiculing middle-class femininity or effeminacy. In the same way, there is nothing relativist about a research strategy that aims to comprehend global social, economic and political structures of power and to investigate how these structures of power are lived and understood and challenged in potentially different ways by different groups and in different locations. What multiperspectivalism espouses is not relativism but an approach that is capable of acknowledging that there is more than one side to each issue and of bringing these different sides into a conversation with one another to create more inclusive research and politics.

Conclusions

The aim of multi-sited research is to study how any given phenomenon, such as anorexia, takes shape and transforms across multiple locales or sites. Studying different sites or locations has two aims. First, it draws attention to the way in which a social phenomenon cannot be 'typified' but changes when one looks at it from different perspectives, so that anorexia seems and 'is' very different in different contexts. Second, it locates a social phenomenon within a wider social and, possibly global, context, pointing at connections that exist between what one is studying and other social processes or locations.

What Appadurai's idea of scapes adds to this perspective is that it calls attention to the way in which an object of study may be connected to multiple spheres of life, such as economics, media, emotions or embodiment and so on. The notions of sites and scapes are related in that one can imagine scapes not as static layers of reality but as flows, such as flows of people, money or images, that connect different sites to one another. However, what sometimes happens in multi-sited studies is that they give the impression that they are studying 'everything'. In this case, the notion of scapes helps to specify what exactly a given study is examining. It helps to clarify, for example, that if a study claims that a certain cultural discourse parallels economic practices, it points to a resonance between the two spheres of life but is not able to say how the discourse or practice works within the economic realm.

The art of doing multi-sited research is embedded in piecing together the analysis of various sites and scapes. Some scholars have argued that research should aim to explore 'real' connections between sites, in order to foster common politics based on a comprehension of our common world or interests. One of the crucial goals of multi-sited ethnography is, indeed, to highlight links between different people and places with the hope of enabling social, and even global, projects that would begin to change our common world together. However, at the same time the aim of multi-sited research is to underline that we may perceive this common world in radically different ways in different social, historical and personal contexts. Thus, in order to do justice to both differences and unities, piecing together the different perspectives is best imagined in terms of 'montage' or agonistic dialogues. These two concepts refer to research strategies that carefully listen to the specificity of individual perspectives both in terms of content ('take' or opinion) and their form (the way in which they relate to the world, such as factually or emotionally), while aiming to bring them into conversation with one another. This same goal underpins the logic of this book, in that my aim in discussing the different methodological approaches has been to highlight the way in which they approach the reality differently, not for the sake of respecting difference, but in order to bring both into relief and into dialogue different research and social points of view.

Exercise 9

- Write a proposal for studying a social or cultural issue, using the multi-sited and multi-scape ethnography as a heuristic.
- First, identify the most pertinent 'sites' where the phenomenon occurs (these may be geographical, institutional and so on).
- Discuss whether you would need different methods or methodological approaches to investigate the different sites. Would you need to use different genres of writing?
- Does the phenomenon you are studying have obvious dimensions that point towards different 'scapes' (economic, emotional etc.)? Are the different 'scapes' more pertinent in some of the sites than others?

- Discuss whether it would be feasible, or whether you would be qualified, to study all the sites and scapes that might be pertinent to your topic. Write a rationale for choosing a small number of scapes and sites to study and discuss the strengths and limits of your focus.
- Write a preliminary table of contents for a report on your project. How could you structure your report in a way that would communicate the specificity of the different sites and scapes, while also analyzing how the different dimensions are connected with one another. Should the different sites and scapes be discussed in separate sections or layered together? Discuss your theoretical and political rationale for choosing a particular structure and style for your report.

References

Adorno, T., Frankel-Brunswick, E., Levinson, D.J. and Sanford, R.N. (1950) *The authoritarian personality*. New York: Harper & Row.

Adorno, T. and Horkheimer, M. (1979) *Dialectic of enlightenment*. London: Verso.

Ahmed, S. (2000) *Strange encounters*. London: Routledge.

Alasuutari, P. (1992) *Desire and craving: A cultural theory of alcoholism*. Albany, NY: State University of New York Press.

Alasuutari, P. (1995) *Researching culture: Qualitative method and cultural studies*. London: Sage.

Alasuutari, P. (1999) Introduction: Three phases of reception studies. In P. Alasuutari (ed.), *The media audience* (pp. 1–21). London: Sage.

Alcoff, L. and Grey, A. (1993) Survivor discourse: Transgression of recuperation?, *Signs*, 18(2), 260–90.

Alvesson, M. and Sköldberg, K. (2000) *Reflexive methodology: New vistas for qualitative research*. London: Sage.

Ang, I. (1985) *Watching Dallas: Soap opera and the melodramatic imagination*. London: Methuen.

Ang, I. (1996) *Living room wars: Rethinking media audiences for a postmodern world*. London: Routledge.

Ang, I. (2001) *On not speaking Chinese: Living between Asia and the West*. London: Routledge.

Appadurai, A. (1997) *Modernity at large: Cultural dimensions of globalization*. Minneapolis: University of Minnesota Press.

Arendt, H. (1958) *The human condition*. Chicago, IL: University of Chicago Press.

Arendt, H. (1963) *On revolution*. London: Faber & Faber.

Arias, A. (ed.) (2001) *The Rigoberta Menchú controversy*. Minneapolis: University of Minnesota Press.

Aronowitz, S. (1993) Paulo Freire's radical democratic humanism. In P. McLaren and P. Leonard (eds), *Paulo Freire: A critical encounter* (pp. 8–24). London: Routledge.

Atkinson, P. and Silverman, D. (1997) Kundera's *Immortality*: The interview society and the invention of the self, *Qualitative Inquiry*, 3, 304–25.

Atkinson, P., Coffey, A., Delamont, S., Lofland, J. and Lofland, L. (eds) (2001) *Handbook of ethnography*. London: Sage.

Austin, J.L. (1965) *How to do things with words*. New York: Oxford University Press.

Bakhtin, M. (1981) *The dialogic imagination*. Austin: University of Texas Press.

Bakhtin, M. (1986) *Speech genres and other late essays*. Austin: University of Texas Press.

Barthes, R. (1972) *Mythologies*. London: Cape.

Baudrillard, J. (1980) The implosion of meaning in the media and the implosion of the social in the masses. In K. Woodward (ed.), *The myths of information: Ideology and postindustrial society* (pp. 137–48). London: Routledge.

Baudrillard, J. (1983) *Simulations*. New York: Columbia University Press.

Baudrillard, J. (1994) *The illusion of the end*. Cambridge: Polity.

Bellah, R., Madsen, R., Sullivan, W., Swidler, A. and Tipton, S. (1985) *Habits of the heart: Individualism and commitment in American life*. Berkeley: University of California Press.

Beneke, T. (1997) *Proving manhood: Reflections on men and sexism*. Berkeley: University of California Press.

Benhabib, S. (1992a) *Situating the self: Gender, community and postmodernism in contemporary ethics*. New York: Routledge.

Benhabib, S. (1992b) Models of public space: Hannah Arendt, the liberal tradition and Jürgen Habermas. In C. Calhoun (ed.), *Habermas and the public sphere* (pp. 73–98). Cambridge, MA: MIT Press.

Bennett, A. (1999) Rappin' on the Tyne: White hip hop culture in Northeast England – an ethnographic study, *Sociological Review*, 47(1), 1–24.

Bennett, A. (2000) *Popular music and youth culture: Music, identity and place*. London: Palgrave.

Bennett, T. (1995) *The birth of the museum: History, theory, politics*. London: Routledge.

Bennett, T. (1998) *Culture: A reformer's science*. London: Sage.

Bennett, T. and Woollacott, J. (1987) *Bond and beyond: The political career of a popular hero*. London: Macmillan.

Berger, A.A. (2000) *Media and communication research methods: An introduction to qualitative and quantitative approaches*. London: Sage.

Beverley, J. (1999) *Subalternity and representation: Arguments in cultural theory*. Durham, NC: Duke University Press.

Beverley, J. (2000) Testimonio, subalternity, and narrative authority. In N.K. Denzin and Y. Lincoln (eds), *Handbook of qualitative research*, 2nd edn. (pp. 555–66). Thousand Oaks, CA: Sage.

Bhaskar, R. (1979) *The possibility of naturalism*. Brighton: Harvester Press.

Bignell, J. (1997) *Media semiotics: An introduction*. Manchester: Manchester University Press.

Bordo, S. (1993) *The unbearable weight: Feminism, western culture, and the body*. Berkeley: University of California Press.

Bordo, S. (1997) *Twilight zones: Cultural images from Plato to O.J.* Berkeley, CA: University of California Press.

Bordowitz, G. (1994) Dense moments. In R. Sappington and T. Stallings (eds), *Uncontrollable bodies: Testimonies of identity and culture* (pp. 25–44). Seattle, WA: Bay Press.

Borysenko, J. (1997) *A woman's book of life: The biology, psychology, and spirituality of the feminine life cycle*. New York: Riverhead Books.

Botting, F. and Wilson, S. (2001) *The Tarantinian ethics*. London: Sage.

Bourdieu, P. (1984) *Distinction: A social critique of the judgement of taste*. London: Routledge.

Brady, I. (ed.) (1983) Speaking in the name of the real: Freeman and Samoa, *American Anthropologist*, 85(4), 908–48.

Brain, J. (2002) Addicted to dieting? Rethinking anorexia's construction as an image-reading disorder. Paper presented at 'Figuring Addictions/Rethinking Consumption' conference, Lancaster University, April 4–5.

Bray, A. (1996) Anorexic bodies: Reading disorder, *Cultural Studies*, 10(3), 413–29.

Bruch, H. (1957) *The importance of overweight*. New York: W.W. Norton.

Bruch, H. (1961a) The effects of modern psychiatric theories on our society – a psychiatrist's view, *Journal of Existential Psychiatry*, 2, 213–32.

Bruch, H. (1961b) Transformation of oral impulses in eating disorders: A conceptual approach, *Psychiatric Quarterly*, 35, 458–81.

Bruch, H. (1973) *Eating disorders: Obesity, anorexia and the person within*. New York: Basic Books.

Bruch, H. (1978) *The golden cage: The enigma of anorexia nervosa*. Cambridge, MA: Harvard University Press.

Bruch, H. and Touraine, G. (1940) Obesity in childhood: V. The family frame of obese children, *Psychosomatic Medicine*, 11(2), 141–206.

Brumberg, J.J. (1988) *Fasting girls: The history of anorexia nervosa*. Cambridge, MA: Harvard University Press.

Buber, M. (1970) *I and thou*. New York: Charles Scribner's Sons.

Burawoy, M. (ed.) (2001) Special Issue: Global Ethnography, *Ethnography*, 2(2).

Burawoy, M., Blum, J., George, S., Gille, Z., Gowan, T., Haney, L., Klawiter, M., Lopez, S., O'Riain, S. and Thayer, M. (eds) (2000) *Global ethnography: Forces, connections, and imaginations in a postmodern world*. Berkeley: University of California Press.

Butler, J. (1990) *Gender trouble: Feminism and the subversion of identity*. New York: Routledge.

Butler, J. (1993) *Gender matters*. New York: Routledge.

Butler, M. (1998) Negotiating place: The importance of children's realities. In S. Steinberg and J. Kincheloe (eds), *Students as researchers: Creating classrooms that matter* (pp. 94–112). London: Falmer.

Calas, M. and Smircich, L. (1993) Dangerous liaisons: The 'feminine in management' meets globalization, *Business Horizons*, March/April, 71–81.

Campbell, R. and Reeves, J. (1994) *Cracked coverage: Television news, the anti-cocaine crusade, and the Reagan legacy*. Durham, NC: Duke University Press.

Castells, M. (1996) *The rise of the network society*. London: Blackwell.

Castells, M. (1997) *The power of identity*. London: Blackwell.

Castells, M. (1998) *End of millennium*. London: Blackwell.

Chatman, S. (1978) *Story and discourse: Narrative structure in fiction and film*. Ithaca, NY: Cornell University Press.

Chernin, K. (1994[1980]) *The obsession: Reflections of the tyranny of slenderness*. New York: Harper.

Christians, C. (1988) Dialogic communication theory and cultural studies, *Studies in Symbolic Interaction*, 9, 3–31.

Christians, C. (2000) Ethics and politics in qualitative research. In N.K. Denzin and Y. Lincoln (eds), *Handbook of qualitative research*, 2nd edn. (pp. 133–55). London: Sage.

Clifford, J. (1986) On ethnographic allegory. In J. Clifford and G. Marcus (eds), *Writing culture: The politics and poetics of ethnography* (pp. 98–121). Berkeley: University of California Press.

Clifford, J. (1997) *Routes: Travel and translation in the late twentieth century*. Cambridge, MA: Harvard University Press.

Clifford, J. and Marcus, G. (1986) (eds), *Writing culture: The politics and poetics of ethnography*. Berkeley: University of California Press.

Clough, P. (1997) Autotelecommunication and autoethnography: A reading of Carolyn Ellis's *Final Negotiations*, *Sociological Quarterly*, 38(1), 95–110.

Clough, P. (2000) *Autoaffection: Unconscious thought in the age of teletechnology.* Minneapolis: University of Minnesota Press.

Cole, C.L. (1998) 'Cyborgs, Addicts…'. In G. Rail (ed.), *Sport and postmodernism.* Albany, NY: State University of New York Press.

Collin, M. (1998) *Altered states: The story of ecstasy culture and acid house.* London: Serpent's Tail.

Couldry, N. (2000) *Inside culture: Reimagining the method of cultural studies.* London: Sage.

Crary, J. (1992) *Techniques of the observer.* Cambridge, MA: MIT Press.

Davis, K. (1995) *Reshaping the female body.* New York: Routledge.

Davis, K. (1999) My body is my art: Cosmetic surgery as feminist utopia? In J. Price and M. Shildrick (eds), *Feminist theory and the body: A reader* (pp. 454–65). Edinburgh: Edinburgh University Press.

Davis-Floyd, R. (1998) Storying corporate futures: The Shell scenarios. In G. Marcus (ed.), *Corporate futures: The diffusion of the culturally sensitive corporate form.* Chicago, IL: University of Chicago Press.

Dean, M. (1991) *The constitution of poverty: Toward a genealogy of liberal governance.* London: Routledge.

Dean, M. (1994) *Critical and effective histories: Foucault's methods and historical sociology.* London: Routledge.

Deleuze, G. (1988) Foldings, or the inside of thought (subjectivation). In G. Deleuze *Foucault* (pp. 94–123) Minneapolis: University of Minnesota Press.

Deleuze, G. (1992) Postscript on the societies of control, *October*, 59, 3–7.

Deleuze, G. and Guattari, F. (1987) *A thousand plateaus: On capitalism and schizophrenia.* Minneapolis: University of Minnesota Press.

Denzin, N. (1989) *The research act: A theoretical introduction to sociological methods.* 3rd edition. Englewood Cliffs: Prentice-Hall.

Denzin, N. (1992) The many faces of emotionality: Reading persona. In C. Ellis and M. Flaherty (eds), *Investigating subjectivity. Research on lived experience* (pp. 17–30) Newbury Park, CA: Sage.

Denzin, N. (1997a) *Interpretive ethnography: Ethnographic practices for the 21st century.* Thousand Oaks, CA: Sage.

Denzin, N. (1997b) In search of the inner child: Co-dependency and gender in a cyber-space community. In G. Bendelow and S. Williams (eds), *Emotions in social life: Critical themes and contemporary issues.* (pp. 95–119). New York: Routledge.

Denzin, N. (1999) From American sociology to cultural studies, *European Journal of Cultural Studies*, 2(1), 117–36.

Denzin, N.K. and Lincoln, Y. (2000) The seventh moment: Out of the past. In N.K. Denzin and Y. Lincoln (eds), *Handbook of qualitative research*, 2nd edn (pp. 1047–65). Thousand Oaks, CA: Sage.

Derrida, J. (1976) *On grammatology.* (trans. G. Spivak) Baltimore, MD: Johns Hopkins University Press.

Dimitriadis, G. (2001) *Performing identity/performing culture: Hip hop as text, pedagogy and lived practice.* New York: Peter Lang.

Dines, G. and Humes, J. (eds) (1995) *Gender, race and class in media: A text-reader.* London: Sage.

Dirlik, A. (1994) The postcolonial aura: Third world criticism in the age of global capitalism, *Critical Inquiry*, 20: 328–56.

Doane, M.A. (1990) Information, crisis, catastrophe. In P. Mellencamp (ed.), *Logics of television: Essays in cultural criticism* (pp. 222–39). Bloomington: Indiana University Press.

Douglas, J. (1977) Existential sociology. In J. Douglas and J. Johnson (eds), *Existential sociology* (pp. 3–74) Cambridge: Cambridge University Press.

Ebert, T. (1993) Ludic feminism, the body, performance, and labor: Bringing materialism back into feminist cultural studies, *Cultural Critique*, Winter 1992/93, 5–50.

Eco, U. (1979[1965]) Narrative structures in Fleming. In U. Eco *The role of the reader* (pp. 144–74). Bloomington: Indiana University Press.

Edwards, D. (1994) Afghanistan, Ethnography, and the New World Order, *Cultural Anthropology*, 9(3), 345–60.

Eley, G. (1992) Nations, publics and political cultures: Placing Habermas in the nineteenth century. In C. Calhoun (ed.), *Habermas and the public sphere* (pp. 289–339). Cambridge, MA: MIT Press.

Ellis, C. (1991) Emotional sociology, *Studies in Symbolic Interaction*, 9, 3–31.

Ellis, C. and Bochner, A. (2000) Autoethnography, personal narrative, reflexivity: Researcher as subject. In N.K. Denzin and Y. Lincoln (eds), *Handbook of qualitative research*, 2nd edn. (pp. 733–68). Thousand Oaks, CA: Sage.

Ellsworth, E. (1989) Why doesn't this feel empowering? Working through the repressive myths of critical pedagogy, *Harvard Educational Review*, 59(3), 297–324.

Felski, R. (1995) *The gender of modernity*. Cambridge, MA: Harvard University Press.

Ferguson, M. and Golding, P. (eds) (1997) *Cultural studies in question*. London: Sage.

Fiske, J. (1989) *Understanding popular culture*. London: Unwin Hyman.

Fiske, J. (1994a) Audiencing. Cultural practice and cultural studies. In N.K. Denzin and Y.S. Lincoln (eds), *Handbook of Qualitative Research*, 1st edn. Thousand Oaks, CA: Sage.

Fiske, J. (1994b) *Media matters: Everyday culture and political change*. Minneapolis: University of Minnesota Press.

Flick, U. (1998) *An introduction to qualitative research*. London: Sage.

Foucault, M. (1972) *Archaeology of knowledge*. New York: Pantheon.

Foucault, M. (1978) *History of sexuality. Volume 1. An introduction*. New York: Vintage Books.

Foucault, M. (1979a) *Discipline and punish: The birth of the prison*. Harmondsworth: Penguin.

Foucault, M. (1979b) My body, this paper, this fire, *Oxford Literary Review*, 4, 9–28.

Foucault, M. (1984) Nietzche, genealogy, and history. In P. Rabinow (ed.), *The Foucault reader* (pp. 76–100). New York: Pantheon.

Foucault, M. (1985a) *History of sexuality. Volume 2. The use of pleasure*. New York: Vintage Books.

Foucault, M. (1985b) *History of sexuality. Volume 3. The care of the self*. New York: Vintage Books.

Foucault, M. (1988[1965]) *Madness and civilization: A history of insanity in the age of reason*. New York: Vintage.

Frank, A. (1995) *The wounded story-teller: Body, illness and ethics*. Chicago, IL: University of Chicago Press.

Franklin, S., Lury, C. and Stacey, J. (2001) *Global nature and global culture*. London: Sage.

Fraser, M. (1999) Classing queer: Politics in competition, *Theory, Culture & Society*, 16 (2) 107–31.

Fraser, N. (1992) Rethinking the public sphere: A contribution to the critique of actually existing democracy. In C. Calhoun (ed.), *Habermas and the public sphere* (pp. 109–42). Cambridge, MA: MIT Press.

Fraser, N. (1994) Michel Foucault: A Young Conservative? In M. Kelly (ed.), *Critique and Power: Recasting the Foucault/Habermas Debate* (pp. 185–210). Cambridge, MA: MIT Press.

Frazier, S. (1985) Foreword. In R. Sparks *The papers of Hilde Bruch. A manuscript collection in the Harris County Medical Archive.* Houston Academy of Medicine–Texas Medical Center Library, Houston, Texas.

Freeman, D. (1983) *Margaret Mead and Samoa: The making and unmaking of an anthropological myth.* Cambridge, MA: Harvard University Press.

Freire, P. (1970) Pedagogy of the oppressed. New York: Continuum.

Freire, P. and Macedo, D. (1996) A dialogue: Culture, language and race, *Harvard Educational Review*, 65(3), 377–402.

Friedmann, J. (2000) Reading Castells: *Zeitdiagnose* and social theory, *Environment and Planning D: Society and Space*, 18, 111–20.

Fromm-Reichmann, F. (1940) Notes on the mother rôle in the family group, *Bulletin of the Menninger Clinic*, 4(5), 132–48.

Frow, J. and Morris, M. (1992) Introduction. In J. Frow and M. Morris (eds), *Australian cultural studies: A reader* (pp. vii–xxxii) Urbana: University of Illinois Press.

Gardiner, J.K. (2000) *South Park*, blue men, anality and market masculinity, *Men and Masculinities*, 2(3), 251–71.

Gibson, K., Law. L. and McKay, D. (2001) Beyond heroes and victims: Filipina contract migrants, economic activism and class transformations, *International Feminist Journal of Politics*, 3(3), 1–22.

Gibson-Graham, J.K. (1996) *The end of capitalism (as we knew it).* Cambridge, MA: Blackwell.

Gille, Z. (2000) Cognitive cartography in a European wasteland: Multinational capital and Greens vie for village allegiance. In M. Burawoy *et al.* (eds), *Global ethnography: Forces, connections and imaginations in a postmodern world* (pp. 240–67). Berkeley: University of California Press.

Gille, Z. (2001) Critical ethnography in the time of globalization: Toward a new concept of site, *Cultural Studies/Critical Methodologies*, 1(3), 319–34.

Ginsburg, F. (1997) The case of mistaken identity: Problems in representing women on the Right. In R. Hertz, (ed.), *Reflexivity and voice* (pp. 283–99). London: Sage.

Ginsburg, F. (1998[1989]) *Contested lives: The abortion debate in an American community.* Berkeley, CA: University of California Press.

Giroux, H. (1994a) *Living dangerously: Multiculturalism and the politics of difference.* New York: Peter Lang.

Giroux, H. (1994b) Benetton's 'world without borders': Buying social change. In C. Becker (ed.), *The subversive imagination: Artists, society and social responsibility* (pp. 187–207). London: Routledge.

Golding, P. (2000) Forthcoming features: Information and communication technologies and the sociology of the future, *Sociology*, 34(1), 165–84.

Goldman, R. (1992) *Reading ads socially.* London: Routledge.

Gramsci, A. (1971) *Selections from the prison notebooks of Antonio Gramsci*, ed. and trans. by Q. Hoare and J. Nowell Smith. London: Lawrence & Wishart.

Gremillion, H. (2002) In fitness and in health: Crafting bodies in the treatment of anorexia nervosa, *Signs*, 27(2), 381–414.

Grob, G. (1991) *From asylum to community: Mental health policy in modern America.* Princeton, NJ: Princeton University Press.

Grossberg, L. (1997) *Bringing it all back home: Essays on cultural studies.* Durham, NJ: Duke University Press.

Grossberg, L. (1998) The victory of culture. Part I. Against the logic of mediation, *Angelaki*, 3 (3), 3–29.

Gubrium, J. and Holstein, J. (1997) *The new language of qualitative method.* Oxford: Oxford University Press.

Gurevitch, M., Woollacott, J., Bennett, T. and Curran, J. (eds) (1982) *Culture, society and the media.* London: Methuen.

Haaken, J. (1993) From Al-Anon to ACOA: Codependence and the reconstruction of caregiving, *Signs*, 18(2), 321–45.

Habermas, J. (1989) *The structural transformation of the public sphere.* Cambridge, MA: MIT Press.

Habermas, J. (1992) Further reflections on the public sphere. In C. Calhoun (ed.), *Habermas and the public sphere* (pp. 421–61). Cambridge, MA: MIT Press.

Hacking, I. (1995) *Rewriting the soul: Multiple personality and the sciences of memory.* Princeton, NJ: Princeton University Press.

Hall, S. (1980) Cultural studies: Two paradigms, *Media, Culture and Society*, 2(1), 59–72.

Hall, S. (1982) The rediscovery of ideology: Return of the repressed in media studies. In M. Gurevitch *et al.* (eds), *Culture, society and the media.* London: Methuen.

Hall, S. (1988) *The hard road to renewal: Thatcherism and the crisis of the Left.* London: Verso.

Hall, S. (1996[1986]) On postmodernism and articulation. An interview with Stuart Hall (ed. L. Grossberg) In D. Morley and C. Kuan-Hsing (eds), *Stuart Hall: Critical dialogues* (pp. 131–50). London: Routledge.

Hall, S. (1997) The spectacle of the 'Other'. In S. Hall, *Representation: Cultural representations and signifying practices* (pp. 223–90). London: Sage.

Hall, S. and Jefferson, T. (eds) (1976) *Resistance through rituals: Youth sub-cultures in post-war Britain.* London: Hutchinson.

Hall, S., Hobson, D., Lowe, A. and Willis, P. (eds) (1980) *Culture, media language.* London: Hutchinson.

Hammersley, M. and Atkinson, P. (1995) *Ethnography.* London: Routledge.

Haraway, D. (1988) Situated knowledge: The science question in feminism and the privilege of partial perspective, *Feminist Studies*, 14(3), 575–99.

Haraway, D. (1997) *Modest_Witnesses@Second_Millennium. FemaleMan©_Meets_ OncoMouse™: Feminism and technoscience.* London: Routledge.

Harding, S. (1991) *Whose science? Whose knowledge? Thinking from women's lives.* Ithaca, NY: Cornell University Press.

Harding, S. (1993) Introduction: Eurocentric scientific illiteracy – a challenge for the world community. In S. Harding (ed.), *The racial economy of science: Toward a democratic future* (pp. 1–29). Bloomington: Indiana University Press.

Harding, S. (2001) Comment on Walby's 'Against epistemological chasms: The science question in feminism revisited'. Can democratic values and interests ever play a rationally justifiable role in the evaluation of scientific work, *Signs*, 26(2), 511–25.

Harvey, D. (1989) *The condition of postmodernity: An inquiry into the origins of cultural change.* London: Blackwell.

Hatch-Bruch, J. (1996) *Unlocking the golden cage: An intimate biography of Hilde Bruch M.D.* Carlsbad, CA: Gürze Books.

Hebdige, D. (1974) *The meaning of mods.* Birmingham: Centre for Contemporary Cultural Studies.

Hebdige, D. (1976) The meaning of mod. In S. Hall and T. Jefferson (eds), *Resistance through rituals: Youth sub-cultures in post-war Britain* (pp. 87–98). London: Hutchinson.

Hebdige, D. (1988) *Hiding in the light: On images and things.* London: Routledge.

Held, D. (1980) *Introduction to critical theory: From Horkheimer to Habermas.* London: Hutchinson.

Hepworth, J. (1999) *The social construction of anorexia nervosa.* London: Sage.

Hill, M.R. (1993) *Archival strategies and techniques.* Newbury Park, CA: Sage.

Hoggart, R. (1992[1957]) *The uses of literacy: Aspects of working-class life with special reference to publications and entertainments.* London: Penguin.

hooks, b. (1990) *Yearning: Race, gender and cultural politics.* Boston, MA: South End Press.

hooks, b. (1992) *Black looks: Race and representation.* London: Turnaround.

Ince, K. (2000) *Orlan.* Oxford: Berg.

Irvine, L. (1999) *Codependent forevermore: The invention of self in a twelve-step group.* Chicago, IL: University of Chicago Press.

Jackson, M. (1998) *Minima ethnographica: Intersubjectivity and the anthropological project.* Chicago, IL: The University of Chicago Press.

Jameson, F. (1991) *Postmodernity, or the cultural logic of late capitalism.* London: Verso.

Jones, K. (2000) *Living between danger and love: The limits of choice.* New Brunswick, NJ: The University of Chicago Press.

Journal of Contemporary Ethnography (1992) Special issue: *Street Corner Society* revisited. 21(2), 3–132.

Kaplan, C. (1995) A world without boundaries: *The Body Shop's* trans/national geographics, *Social Text*, 43, 45–66.

Kaur, R. and Hutnyk, J. (eds) (1999) *Travel worlds: Journeys in contemporary cultural politics.* London: Zed.

Kellner, D. (1995) *Postmodern media culture.* New York: Routledge.

Kendall, G. and Wickham, G. (1999) *Using Foucault's methods.* London: Sage.

Kiesinger, C. (1998) From interview to story: Writing Abbie's life, *Qualitative Inquiry*, 4(1), 71–95.

Kilbourne, J. (1995[1989]) Beauty and the beast of advertising. In G. Dines and J. Humes (eds), *Gender, race and class in media: A text-reader* (pp. 121–5). London: Sage.

Kincheloe, Joe and McLaren, Peter (1994) Rethinking critical theory and qualitative research. In N.K. Denzin and Y.S. Lincoln (eds), *Handbook of qualitative research*, 1st edn (pp. 138–57). Thousand Oaks, CA: Sage.

Kirby, K. (1996) *Indifferent boundaries: Spatial concepts of human subjectivity.* New York: Guilford Press.

Kvale, S. (1996) *InterViews: An introduction to qualitative research interviewing.* London: Sage.

Laclau, E. and Mouffe, C. (1985) *Hegemony and socialist strategy: Towards a radical democratic politics.* London: Verso.

Lather, P. (1991) *Getting smart: Feminist research and pedagogy with/in the postmodern.* London: Routledge.

Lather, P. (1993) Fertile obsessions: Validity after poststructuralism, *The Sociological Quarterly*, 34(4), 673–93.

Lather, P. (2001) Postbook: Working the ruins of feminist ethnography, *Signs*, 27(1), 199–227.

Lather, P. and Smithies, C. (1997) *Troubling angels: Women living with HIV/AIDS*. Boulder, CO: Westview Press.

Latour, B. (1993) *We have never been modern*. Cambridge, MA: Harvard University Press.

Laughlin, K. (1996) Representing 'Bhopal'. In G. Marcus (ed.), *Connected: Engagements with media* (pp. 221–46). Chicago, IL: University of Chicago Press.

Lavery, P., Hague, A. and Cartwright, M. (1996) *Deny all knowledge: Reading the X-Files*. Syracuse, NY: Syracuse University Press.

Levi-Strauss, C. (1970) *The raw and the cooked*. London: Cape.

Levinas, E. (1985) *Ethics and infinity*. Pittsburg, PA: Duquesne University Press.

Lewis, J. (2002) *Cultural studies: The basics*. London: Sage.

Lincoln, Y. (1995) Emerging criteria for quality in qualitative and interpretive research, *Qualitative Inquiry*, 1, 275–89.

Lincoln, Y. and Guba, E. (1985) *Naturalistic inquiry*. London: Sage.

Lincoln, Y. and Guba, E. (1994) Competing paradigms in qualitative research. In N.K. Denzin and Y.S. Lincoln (eds), *Handbook of qualitative research*, 1st edn (pp. 105–17). Thousand Oaks: Sage.

Lowe, S. (2002) Miskinetic neuropolitocology: The politics of constructing and disciplining of the organism of the brain, *Culture Machine*, 4 (available at: http://culturemachine.tees.ac.uk).

Lury, C. (1996) *Consumer culture*. London: Polity.

Lury, C. (2001) The united colors of diversity. In S. Franklin, C. Lury and J. Stacey, *Global nature, global culture* (pp. 146–87). London: Sage.

MacCabe, C. (1973) Realism and the cinema: Notes on some Brechtian theses, *Screen*, 15(2), 7–27.

Malson, H. (1998) *The thin woman*. London: Routledge.

Maltby, R. (1995) *Hollywood cinema: An introduction*. London: Blackwell.

Marcus, G. (1986) Contemporary problems of ethnography in the modern world system. In J. Clifford and G. Marcus (eds), *Writing culture: The politics and poetics of ethnography* (pp. 165–93). Berkeley: University of California Press.

Marcus, G. (1995) Ethnography in/of the world system: The emergence of multi-sited ethnography, *Annual Review of Anthropology*, 24, 95–117.

Marcus, G. (1998a) *Ethnography through thick and thin*. Princeton, NJ: Princeton University Press.

Marcus, G. (ed.) (1998b) *Corporate futures: The diffusion of the culturally sensitive corporate form*. Chicago, IL: University of Chicago Press.

Martin, E. (1994) *Flexible bodies: The role of immunity in American culture from the days of polio to the age of AIDS*. Boston, MA: Beacon Press.

Martin, E. (1995) *Flexible bodies: Tracking immunity in American culture from the days of polio to the age of AIDS*. Boston, MA: Beacon Press.

Maso, I. (2001) Phenomenology and ethnography. In P. Atkinson *et al.* (eds), *Handbook of ethnography* (pp. 136–44). London: Sage.

Massey, D. (1994) *Space, place and gender*. London: Polity.

Massey, D., Allen, J. and Sarre, P. (eds) (1999) *Human geography today*. London: Polity.

Massumi, B. (1992) *A user's guide to capitalism and schizophrenia*. Minneapolis: University of Minnesota Press.

McConnell, T. (2000) Return journey to the interior, *Times Higher Education Supplement*, 15 December.

McGuigan, J. (1992) *Cultural populism*. London: Routledge.

McGuigan, J. (1997) *Cultural methodologies*. London: Sage.

McRobbie, A. (2000) *Feminism and youth culture*, 2nd edn. London: Macmillan.

Mead, M. (1929) *Coming of age in Samoa: A psychological study of primitive youth for Western civilization*. London: Jonathan Cape.

Melechi, A. (1993) The ecstasy of disappearance. In S. Redhead (ed.), *Rave off: Politics and deviance in contemporary youth culture* (pp. 29–40). Aldershot: Avebury.

Menchú, R. (1984) *I, Rigoberta Menchú, an Indian woman in Guatemala* (ed. E. Burgos-Debray). London: Verso.

Merleau-Ponty, M. (1962) *Phenomenology of perception*. London: Routledge.

Minh-Ha, Trinh (1989) *Woman, native, other: Writing postcoloniality and feminism*. Bloomington: Indiana University Press.

Montague, K. (1994) The aesthetic of hygiene: Aesthetic dress, modernity and the body as sign, *Journal of Design History*, 7(2) 91–112.

Moraga, S. and Anzaldua, G. (eds) (1984) *This bridge called my back: Writings by radical women of color*. San Franscisco: Kitchen Table Books.

Morley, D. and Brunsdon, C. (1999[1980,1987]) *The 'Nationwide' television studies*. London: Routledge.

Morris, M. (1990) Banality in cultural studies. In P. Mellencamp (ed.), *Logics of television: Essays in cultural criticism* (pp. 14–43). Bloomington: Indiana University Press.

Morton, D. (ed.) (1996) *The material queer: A LesBiGay cultural studies reader*. Boulder, CO: Westview Press.

Murdock, G. (1997) Base notes: The conditions of cultural practice. In M. Ferguson and P. Golding (eds), *Cultural studies in question* (pp. 86–101). London: Routledge.

Narayan, K. and George, K. (2001) Personal and folk narrative as cultural representation. In P. Atkinson *et al.* (eds), *Handbook of interview research* (pp. 815–32). London: Sage.

Naylor, I. (2001) Is coke taking over clubland?, *Ministry*, February, pp. 32–8.

Nightingale, V. (1992) What's 'ethnographic' about ethnographic audience research? In J. Frow and M. Morris (eds), *Australian cultural studies: A reader* (pp. 149–61). Urbana: University of Illinois Press.

Ong, A. (1999) *Flexible citizenship: The cultural logics of transnationality*. Durham, NC: Duke University Press.

Pickering, M. (2001) *Stereotyping: The politics of representation*. London: Palgrave.

Polan, D. (2000) *Pulp Fiction*. London: British Film Institute.

Polkinghorne, D. (1995) Narrative configuration in qualitative analysis. In J. Hatch and R. Wisniewski (eds), *Life history and narrative* (pp. 5–23). Washington, DC: Falmer.

Poster, M. (1997) *Cultural history and postmodernity*. New York: Columbia University Press.

Pratt, G. (1999) Geographies of identity and difference: Marking boundaries. In D. Massey, J. Allen and P. Sarre (eds), *Human geography today* (pp. 151–67). Cambridge: Polity.

Pratt, M.L. (2001) *I, Rigoberta Menchú* and the 'Culture Wars'. In A. Arias. (ed.), *The Rigoberta Menchú controversy* (pp. 29–57). Minneapolis: University of Minnesota Press.

Preston, J. and Decker, H. (1974[1975]) American Psychiatric Association (APA) interview, conducted with Hilde Bruch. Series I. Box 2. The papers of Hilde Bruch. A manuscript collection in the Harris County Medical Archive. Houston Academy of Medicine–Texas Medical Center Library, Houston. Texas.

Probyn, E. (1987) The anorexic body. In A. Kroker and M. Kroker (eds), *Body invaders: Panic sex in America* (pp. 201–11). New York: Saint Martin's Press.

Probyn, E. (1993) *Sexing the self: Gendered positions in cultural studies.* New York: Routledge.

Probyn, E. (1996) *Outside belongings.* New York: Routledge.

Propp, V. (1968) *Morphology of the folktale.* Austin: University of Texas Press.

Radway, J. (1984) *Reading the romance: Women, patriarchy, and popular literature.* Chapel Hill: The University of North Carolina Press.

Radway, J. (1988) Reception study: Ethnography and the problems of dispersed audiences and nomadic critics, *Cultural Studies*, 2(3), 359–76.

Rapp, R. (2000) *Testing women, testing the fetus: The social impact of amniocentesis in America.* London: Routledge.

Redhead, S. (ed.) (1993) *Rave off: Politics and deviance in contemporary youth culture.* Aldershot: Avebury.

Reed, L. (2000) Domesticating the personal computer: The mainstreaming of a new technology and cultural management of a widespread technophobia, *Critical Studies in Media Communication*, 17(2), 159.

Richardson, L. (1992) The consequences of poetic representation: Writing the other, rewriting the self. In C. Ellis and G. Flaherty (eds), *Investigating subjectivity: Research on lived experience* (pp. 125–37). Newbury Park, CA: Sage.

Richardson, L. (1997) *Fields of play: Constructing an academic life.* New Brunswick, NJ: Rutgers University Press.

Richardson, L. (2000) Writing: A method of inquiry. In N. Denzin and Y. Lincoln (eds), *Handbook of qualitative research*, 2nd edn (pp. 923–48). London: Sage.

Riesman, D. (1976[1950]) *The lonely crowd: A study of the changing American character.* New Haven, CT: Yale University Press.

Rose, N. (1985) *The psychological complex: Psychology, politics and society in England, 1869–1939.* London: Routledge.

Rose, N. (1996) *Reinventing our selves.* Cambridge: Cambridge University Press.

Rose, N. (1999) *Powers of freedom: Reframing political thought.* Cambridge: Cambridge University Press.

Rose, N. and Miller, P. (1992) Political power beyond the state: Problematics of Government, *British Journal of Sociology*, 43, 173–205.

Rothschild, J. and Ollilainen, M. (1999) Obscuring but not reducing managerial control: Does TQM measure up to democracy standards, *Economic and Industrial Democracy*, 20, 583–623.

Ryan, M. (1992) Gender and public access: Women's politics in nineteenth century America. In C. Calhoun (ed.), *Habermas and the public sphere* (pp. 259–88). Cambridge, MA: MIT Press.

Said, E. (1995[1978]) *Orientalism.* Harmondsworth: Penguin.

Saukko, P. (1998) Poetics of voice and maps of space: Two trends within empirical research in cultural studies, *European Journal of Cultural Studies*, 1(2), 259–75.

Saukko, P. (1999) Fat boys and goody girls: Hilde Bruch's work on eating disorders and the American anxiety about democracy, 1930–1960. In J. Sobal and D. Maurer (eds), *Weighty issues: Constructing fatness and thinness as social problems* (pp. 31–49). New York: Aldine de Gruyter.

Saukko, P. (2000) Between voice and discourse: Quilting interviews on anorexia, *Qualitative Inquiry*, 6(3), 299–317.

Saukko, P. (2002a) Connected? On economy, experience, violence and care, *Cultural Studies/Critical methodologies*, 2(1), 131–47.

Saukko, P. (2002b) Studying the self: From the subjective and the social to personal and political dialogues, *Qualitative Research*, 2(2), 245–64.

Saussure, F. (1960) *Course in general linguistics*. London: Peter Owen.

Savigliano, M. (1995) *Tango: The political economy of passion*. Boulder, CO: Westview Press.

Schwartz, T. (1983) Anthropology: A quaint science, *American Anthropologist*, 85(4), 919–29.

Schwichtenberg, C. (ed.) (1993) *The Madonna connection: Representational politics, subcultural identities and cultural theory*. Boulder, CO: Westview Press.

Seale, C. (1999) *The quality of qualitative research*. London: Sage.

Sernhede, O. (2000) Exoticism and death as a modern taboo: Gangsta rap and the search for intensity. In P. Gilroy *et al.* (eds), *Without guarantees: In honour of Stuart Hall*. (pp. 302–17). London: Verso.

Shelton, A. (1995) Foucault's madonna: The secret life of Carolyn Ellis, *Symbolic Interaction*, 18(1), 83–8.

Shor, I. (1993) Education is politics: Paulo Freire's critical pedagogy. In P. McLaren and P. Leonard (eds), *Paulo Freire: A critical encounter* (pp. 25–35). London: Routledge.

Shore, B. (1983) Paradox regained: Freeman's Margaret Mead and Samoa, *American Anthropologist*, 85(4), 935–44.

Shostak, M. (1983) *Nisa: The life and words of a !Kung woman*. Harmondsworth: Penguin.

Shostak, M. (2000) *The return to Nisa*. Cambridge, MA: Harvard University Press.

Silverman, D. (1992) *Interpreting qualitative data: Methods for analysing talk, text and interaction*. 1st edn. London: Sage.

Silverman, D. (1997) *Discourses of counselling: HIV counselling as social interaction*. London: Sage.

Silverman, D. (2001) *Interpreting qualitative data: Methods for analysing talk, text and interaction*, 2nd edn. London: Sage.

Skeggs, B. (1997) *Formations of class and gender*. London: Sage.

Skolnick, A. (1991) *Embattled paradise: The American family in the age of uncertainty*. New York: Basic Books.

Slade, C. (2001) *The real thing: Doing philosophy with media*. New York: Peter Lang.

Smart, B. (2000) A political economy of new times?: Critical reflections on the network society and the ethos of informational capitalism, *European Journal of Social Theory*, 3(1), 51–66.

Soja, E. (1996) *Thirdspace: Journeys to Los Angeles and other real-and-imagined spaces*. London: Blackwell.

Soja, E. (2000) *Postmetropolis*. London: Blackwell.

Spence, J. (1986) *Putting myself in the picture: A political personal and photographic autobiography*. Seattle, WA: The Real Comet Press.

Spignesi, A. (1980) Interview with Hilde Bruch. Series VII. The papers of Hilde Bruch. A manuscript collection in the Harris County Medical Archive. Houston Academy of Medicine–Texas Medical Center Library, Houston, Texas.

Spivak, G. (1976) Translator's preface. In J. Derrida, *Of grammatology* (pp. ix–lxxxvii). Baltimore, MA: The Johns Hopkins University Press.

Spivak, G. (1993) *Outside in the teaching machine.* London: Routledge.

Stabile, C. (1995) Resistance, recuperation, and reflexivity: The limits of a paradigm, *Critical Studies in Mass Communication,* 12(4), 403–22.

Steedman-Rice, J. (1996) *A disease of one's own: Psychotherapy, addiction, and the emergence of co-dependency.* New Brunswick, NJ: Transaction Publishers.

Stern, J. (1999) Back to the future? Manuel Castells' The Information Age and the prospects for social welfare, *Cultural Studies,* 14(1), 99–116.

Stoll, D. (1999) *Rigoberta Menchú and the story of all poor Guatemalans.* Boulder, CO: Westview Press.

Susman, W. (1989) Did success spoil the United States? Dual representations in post-war America. In L. May (ed.), *Recasting America: Culture and politics in the age of Cold War* (pp. 19–37) Chicago, IL: University of Chicago Press.

Terry, J. (1999) *The American obsession: Science, medicine and the place of homosexuality in modern society.* Chicago: University of Illinois Press.

Thrift, N. (1999) The place of complexity, *Theory, Culture & Society,* 16(3), 31–69.

Thrift, N. (2000) Still life in nearly present time: The object of nature, *Body & Society,* 6(3–4), 34–57.

Tomlinson, J. (1999) *Globalization and culture.* London: Polity.

Treichler, P. (1999) *How to have theory in an epidemic: Cultural chronicles of AIDS.* Durham, NC: Duke University Press.

Tseelon, E. (1995) *The masque of femininity.* London: Sage.

Umiker-Sebeok, J. (2001) The semiotic swarm of cyberspace: Cybergluttony and Internet addiction in the global village. Available at: http://www.slis.indiana.edu/umikerse/papers/cgsec1.html

Volosinov, V. (1973) *Marxism and the philosophy of language.* New York: Seminar Press.

Walby, S. (2001) Against epistemological chasms: The science question in feminism revisited, *Signs,* 26(2), 485–509.

Walkerdine, V. (1993) Beyond developmentalism? *Theory & Psychology,* 3(4), 451–69.

Walkerdine, V. (1998[1989]) *Counting girls out: Girls and mathematics,* new edn. London: Falmer.

Wallis, R. and Malm, K. (1984) *Big sounds from small peoples: The music industry in small countries.* New York: Pendragon.

Watermann, P. (1999) The brave new world of Manuel Castells: What on earth (or in the ether) is going on?, *Development and Change,* 20, 357–80.

Weiner, A. (1983) Ethnographic determinism: Samoa and the Margaret Mead controversy, *American Anthropologist,* 85(4), 909–19.

Whyte, W.F. (1955[1943]) *Street corner society: The social structure of an Italian slum.* Chicago: University of Illinois Press.

Whyte, W.F. (1993) *Street Corner Society* revisited, *Sociological Forum,* 8(2), 285–98.

Willis, P. (1977) *Learning to labour: How working-class kids get working-class jobs.* Westmead: Saxon House.

Wilson, E. (1991) *The sphinx and the city: Urban life, the control of disorder, and women.* Berkeley, CA: University of California Press.

Yasuda, M. (2002) *Modernity, urban space and music industries: Hip hop and reproduction of street music in Paris and Tokyo.* Unpublished PhD thesis. Centre for Mass Communication Research, University of Leicester.

Yúdice, G. (1991) *Testimonio* and postmodernism, *Latin American Perspectives,* 18(3), 15–31.

Zeglin-Perry, (2000) (ed.), *Beauty matters.* Bloomington: Indiana University Press.

Index

Lightning Source UK Ltd.
Milton Keynes UK
UKOW03f0223230713

214188UK00003B/90/P